TAX GUIDE 2003/2004

JANE VASS

P
PROFILE BOOKS

First published in Great Britain in 2003 by
Profile Books Ltd
58A Hatton Garden
London EC1N 8LX
www.profilebooks.co.uk

1 3 5 7 9 10 8 6 4 2

Typeset in Lapidary 333 by MacGuru Ltd
info@macguru.org.uk

Printed and bound in Great Britain by
Clays, Bungay, Suffolk

A CIP catalogue record for this book is available from the British Library.

ISBN 1 86197 489 2

Contents

Acknowledgements

Writing about tax has many challenges and I have been fortunate in having skilled and enthusiastic colleagues. My thanks go to Jonathan Harley, Tony Hazell, Janet Law, Virginia Wallis, Eleanor Whalley and Penny Williams. And I have been grateful to Stephen Brough at Profile Books throughout for his guidance and support.

Special thanks are due to Jane Moore, technical director of the charity TaxAid. She read the book with a keen technical eye, but, just as important, an understanding of the problems that people face when grappling with tax. Since it was founded in 1992, TaxAid has helped more than 10,000 people with their tax problems, as well as promoting public understanding of tax and pressing for a simpler and fairer tax system.

However, all errors remain my own, and I welcome comments, via the publisher.

Jane Vass

NOTE

Everyone's personal circumstances are different and tax rules can change. This book has been carefully researched and checked. If by chance a mistake or omission has occurred I am sorry that neither I, the *Daily Mail*, nor the publisher can take responsibility for any loss or problem you suffer as a result. But if you have any suggestions about how the content of the guide could be improved, please write to me, care of the publisher, Profile Books, 58A Hatton Garden, London EC1N 8LX.

Introduction

Sometimes it feels as though we're working solely for the benefit of the taxman, but when you consider the facts it's hardly surprising. The average person starting work today will contribute more than £200,000 to the Exchequer in income tax and National Insurance by the time they retire. And it doesn't stop there. We're taxed again on any interest we earn from our savings, any dividends paid on shares and any profits from other investments such as property. When we retire our pensions are taxed and when we die our estate can be raided for inheritance tax.

There can be no disputing the fact that the way we are taxed is becoming more complicated and the burdens on the individual are increasing. More than nine million people are expected to fill in their own tax returns and the penalties for filing them late or mistakenly paying too little can be severe. You're expected to keep your own records, chase up documents that aren't sent automatically and, if you're not quick enough in filing your tax return, you even have to calculate your own tax bill.

If you're self-employed, a higher-rate taxpayer, own a second property or receive an income from certain sources the taxman will expect you to wade through the complex self-assessment procedures.

The Inland Revenue are also much more likely to check up on you. Last year they made around 300,000 simple enquiries into just one or two aspects of a return and conducted more than 41,000 thorough examinations. The government doesn't even make it easy for the retired and elderly. If your income is low and you want to reclaim the tax taken from your savings, there's more form-filling to do. And even investing in National Savings & Investments' Pensioner Bonds can trigger a tax return because the income is paid before tax is deducted and the Inland Revenue want to be absolutely certain you don't owe them a single penny.

It's little wonder there's a booming industry for accountants in filling in tax returns. However, with prices typically ranging from £150 to £500, this is not an option some people want to consider.

Despite this, it is important to understand the tax system otherwise we could pay too much by missing out on one of the many forms of relief available. This is why the *Daily Mail* has decided to publish a tax guide. Our aim is simple. We want to give you the advantages enjoyed by the wealthy who can afford expensive accountants.

We're cutting through the technical language and complicated forms to provide help by presenting a guide written in the style we use in *Money Mail* week in, week out.

You'll find all the facts and figures you need as well as specific help with some of the most common situations you're likely to find yourself in.

For instance, the buy-to-let boom means that many people now own a second home. If it's properly handled you can keep any income tax bill to a minimum by setting any rental income against your mortgage interest and the costs of running the property, including repairs and cleaning.

Pensioners can face a particularly stiff task dealing with their tax. While they may initially be given higher allowances before they have to pay tax, these can be clawed back if their taxable income is too high. But it is possible to mitigate the effects of the iniquitous rule by using investments which don't count as taxable income and by couples balancing their income between them.

On the bright side the Inland Revenue is not staffed by ogres. And their staff are now well-trained, friendly and helpful. They want only the tax that is due, not an penny more and not a penny less. If they discover you've paid too much tax, they'll refund it. So as long as you are honest and deliver your tax return on time, you should have nothing to fear.

Tony Hazell
Editor, *Money Mail*
March 2003

How this book can help you

Some people worry unnecessarily about tax. Others could do with paying it a bit more attention. Most of the time, your tax affairs tick along in the background, but every so often they demand your attention – when the deadline for sending in your tax return approaches, or you suddenly realise that your company car has been costing you thousands of pounds in tax each year.

This book is designed as your road map to the tax system. You're unlikely to need every chapter, so each one starts out by telling you whether or not it is likely to be relevant to you.

You can use the book to help you:

- *Make sense of the tax system* – Chapter 1 gives you an introduction to the different types of tax covered in this book, and advises you on trouble-shooting and where to get more help. If tax is deducted from any of your income before you get it, see Chapter 2 for how it is worked out and collected on a day-to-day basis, whether or not you get a tax return. Chapter 3 applies only if you get a tax return: it explains how the system of self-assessment works. Chapter 4 helps you save tax: it covers tax allowances and tax reliefs.
- *Understand your tax affairs* – Chapters 5 to 10 each cover particular situations, e.g. work, investment, property. Chapters 11 and 12 explain capital gains tax and inheritance tax and whether you need to worry about them. Each chapter guides you through what counts as tax-free

income and explains how the tax is worked out, what to tell the Revenue, the records you need to keep and what forms you may need to fill in.

- *Keep your tax bill down* – watch out for the tips throughout the text. Each chapter ends with a summary of tax-planning hints.
- *Fill in your tax return and other tax forms* – each chapter illustrates key sections of tax forms and explains how to fill them in or check them, with worked examples. If you want to know which chapter covers a particular form or a particular question in the self-assessment tax return, use the 'Form finder' in the Fact File at the end of the book.
- *Keep up to date* – Budget 2003 tax changes have been incorporated throughout the book. There is a summary of key changes inside the back cover, and a table of the new tax rates and allowances inside the front cover.
- *Organise your papers* – you have a legal duty to keep records to back up your tax return or tax claim for a minimum length of time. The 'Record-keeping' section in each chapter covers the records you should keep.
- *Find out more* – the Fact File at the end of the book summarises some key facts and figures, gives you a checklist of tax-free income, and has lists of useful leaflets, Inland Revenue helplines and addresses for all the organisations mentioned in the book.

Dealing with your tax is a necessary chore. We hope that this book makes it a bit easier, a bit less mystifying, and helps you keep your tax bill as low as possible.

1

A quick tour of the tax system

First the bad news: you're increasingly likely to have to get to grips with the Inland Revenue and its labyrinthine ways. Its role now extends far beyond income tax, capital gains tax and inheritance tax. National Insurance contributions and even student loan repayments have been added to its responsibilities in recent years.

And the good news? As well as collecting your tax, the Revenue may give you extra money, in the form of a tax credit.

This chapter explains how it all fits together, with introductions to all the various forms of tax covered in the book and which chapter to go to for further information. If you're having problems, or think you need further help, see the section on 'Troubleshooting' on page 7.

How tax is collected

You pay tax on your income or gains made in a 'tax year'. The tax year starts on 6 April and runs until 5 April in the next year. In this book, the 12-month period starting on 6 April 2002 and ending on 5 April 2003 is called the '2002–03 tax year'.

Rates of tax for each tax year used to be set in the budget (traditionally March but delayed until April in 2002 and 2003). These days announcements may be made at any time (such as the pre-budget report in November), to take effect at any point in the future. The Revenue also announce Statements of Practice from time to time, and Extra-statutory

Concessions (when they agree not to collect tax that is legally due).

Watch out for changes

Tax allowances and bands are automatically increased in line with inflation each year, unless a positive decision is made to change them by a different amount. The Chancellor's proposals become law only when the annual Finance Act is passed, which is usually in July. These proposals may be rejected or amended, so do not count on a particular proposal going through.

The tax system aims to collect as much tax as possible from your income before you get it, by requiring:

- employers to deduct tax from your salary under the Pay As You Earn (PAYE) system
- insurance companies and employers' pension schemes to deduct tax from pensions they pay you, usually under PAYE
- financial organisations and companies to deduct tax from savings interest, dividends and so on.

Not all your tax can be collected this way – e.g. if you have profits from a business or letting out property or are a higher-rate taxpayer. If so, or if your affairs are complex, you will probably be sent an annual self-assessment tax return. However, the Revenue try to avoid bringing people within the self-assessment regime unnecessarily. Instead, you may receive a variety of other forms.

The tax system doesn't just collect tax. Changes in recent years have meant that it is increasingly being used to redistribute taxes, through tax credits such as the Working Tax Credit and Child Tax Credit.

The sort of contact you have with the Revenue differs:

- ➨ If any of your tax is paid 'at source', by deducting it from your income before you get it, Chapter 2 will help you sort out your tax affairs.

- If you get a tax return, see Chapter 3.
- Child Tax Credit and Working Tax Credit are covered in Chapter 7.

Income tax

Most of what counts as income is obvious: earnings, pensions, business profits, interest and dividends. However, income tax applies to some items that you might not regard as income, such as the proceeds of life insurance policies, and other types of income are completely tax-free, such as maintenance from an ex-spouse (see the checklist in the Fact File). Even when income is taxable, you can deduct various reliefs, such as your pension contributions.

After deducting tax-free income and reliefs, your income from all sources is added up. The first slice of your total income is not taxable – your personal allowance. This is £4,615 in the 2002–03 and 2003–04 tax years, but you may get extra allowances if you are aged 65 at any point in the tax year, or if you are blind.

- For more information about allowances and reliefs see Chapter 4.

Any remaining income is split into tax bands as shown in Figure 1.1 on page 5. The income in each band is taxed at a particular rate, but the rates vary depending on the types of income. The detailed rules are explained in the following chapters:

- If you are an employee, or a director of a company, see Chapter 5.
- If you are a sole trader, or in a partnership, see Chapter 6.
- If you receive taxable state benefits, or a pension, see Chapter 7.
- If you receive income from letting land or property, see Chapter 8.
- If you receive income from abroad, see Chapter 9.
- If you have savings, investments or life insurance, see Chapter 10.

What are 'schedules'?

You may see employees referred to as 'Schedule E' taxpayers, and the self-employed as 'Schedule D' taxpayers. This is tax shorthand for the different types of income. The rules are slightly different for each schedule. There is also Schedule A (rental income) and Schedule F (share dividends), but Schedules B and C no longer exist.

Capital gains tax

This is a tax on gains you make when you dispose of an asset such as investments, land, property, businesses and valuables. You pay tax on the proceeds of the transaction, after deducting expenses and taper relief (which reduces the taxable gain in line with the length of time you have owned the asset).

In practice, however, most people do not have to grapple with capital gains tax because the first slice of taxable gains made in each tax year is tax-free. The tax-free amount is £7,700 in 2002–03, £7,900 in 2003–04.

Your capital gains are added to your taxable income for the year and taxed as if they were your top slice of income (see Figure 1.1).

➡ For more information about capital gains tax, see Chapter 11.

National Insurance contributions

You have to pay National Insurance contributions on earnings from employment, profits from self-employment and wages you pay employees. The rules for what counts as income for the purpose of National Insurance contributions, and what expenses can be deducted, differ from those for income tax, although the differences are gradually disappearing.

There are several types of contribution:

- If you are an employee, you pay employees' Class 1 contributions on your earnings. (See Inland Revenue leaflet CA01 *National Insurance contributions for employees*.)
- If you are an employer, you pay employers' Class 1 contributions on

Figure 1.1: Income and capital gains tax rates for 2002–03 (2003–04)

The first slice of your income or gains is tax-free. The remaining taxable income fills up your bands in this order:

- Earnings (including pensions and business profits)
- Interest
- Dividends
- Life insurance gains
- Capital gains

Tax rates for 2002–03 (2003–04 rates in brackets) ***Example***

No tax	**Personal and blind person's allowances** Minimum £4,615 (£4,615)	Bill's income in 2002–03 was £35,000, made up of business profits of £30,000, interest of £3,000 and share dividends of £2,000. His business profits of £30,000 use: ■ all his personal allowance (tax-free) ■ all his starting-rate band (tax at 10% is £192) ■ £23,465 of his basic-rate band (taxed at 22% i.e. £5,162) *Tax: £192 + £5,162 = £5,354*
Taxed at 10%	**Starting-rate band** First £1,920 (£1,960)	
Taxed at 20% if income is interest or capital gains, 10% if dividends, otherwise at 22%	**Basic-rate band** Next £27,980 (£28,540)	His £3,000 interest fits in the rest of his basic-rate band, and is taxed at 20%. His bank deducts the tax. *Tax: £600, paid at source* £1,515 of his dividends fits into his basic-rate band, taxable at 10% (£152). The remaining £485 falls in the higher-rate band, taxed at 32.5% (£158). *Tax: £152 + £158 = £310, of which £200 is paid at source*
Taxed at 40%, or 32.5% if dividends	**Higher-rate band** Anything above £29,900 (£30,500)	Bill has capital gains above the annual tax-free amount. His £4,000 of taxable gains all fall in the higher-rate band, taxable at 40%. *Tax: £1,600* *Bill's total tax bill is £5,354 + £600 + £310 + £1,600 = £7,864, but £800 was paid at source. He has £7,064 to pay now.*

your employees' earnings, and Class 1A contributions on any taxable fringe benefits you give your employees (the employee does not pay National Insurance on these).

- If you are self-employed, you pay Class 2 contributions at a flat weekly rate (£2.00 in 2002–03 and 2003–04), as well as Class 4 contributions on a percentage of your profits.
- Your entitlement to some state benefits – most notably state retirement pension – is reduced if you have not paid enough Class 1 or Class 2 contributions. If you want to boost a reduced entitlement, you can choose to pay Class 3 contributions at a flat weekly rate (£6.85 in 2002–03, £6.95 in 2003–04). (See Inland Revenue leaflet CA08 *Voluntary National Insurance contributions*.)

You do not have to pay National Insurance if your income is below the level of the personal allowance (£4,615), or for Class 2 contributions £4,025 in 2002–03 (£4,095 in 2003–04), or if you are over state retirement age. And if you are liable to pay more than one class of contribution (because, say, you are self-employed as well as having a job), there is a maximum amount that you will have to pay. See the Fact File for some useful leaflets.

➧ For details of contributions if you are an employee, see Chapter 2 and Chapter 5.
➧ For details of contributions for self-employed people, see Chapter 6.

Student loan repayments

Repayments on student loans taken out after August 1998 are collected by the Revenue along with your tax. These loans are known as 'income-contingent' because your repayments are related to your level of income.

The Student Loans Company notify the Revenue when you leave university. If you have a job, your employer will be required to deduct the repayment along with your PAYE; otherwise, it will be collected through your tax return. The repayments normally start in the April after you have finished your course, subject to your income exceeding a minimum level.

The loans are repaid at a rate of 9 per cent of your income above £10,000. Any investment income of £2,000 or less is ignored.

➡ For more about student loan repayments if you have a job, see Chapters 2 and 5.

Inheritance tax

This is a tax on the value of what you leave when you die (your estate). Tax may have to be paid during your lifetime if you make a gift to a company or to some types of trust. Other lifetime gifts are called 'Potentially Exempt Transfers', which means that they will be counted as part of your estate only if you die within seven years of making them. However, the first slice of your estate (£250,000 in 2002–03, £255,000 in 2003–04) is tax-free, and some gifts are completely tax-free.

➡ For more about inheritance tax, see Chapter 12.

Troubleshooting

The Inland Revenue are committed to:

- treating your affairs in strict confidence
- asking you to pay only the right amount of tax
- providing clear and simple forms, and accurate and complete information
- handling your affairs promptly and accurately
- keeping your costs to the minimum necessary
- being accessible and taking reasonable steps to meet special needs
- courtesy and professionalism.

In addition, all Revenue offices have targets for customer service and work to various codes of practice. For example, if tax has been deducted from your savings income, but you are not liable for tax, they aim to deal with the claim (and repay the tax) within 20 working days of receiving it. If they fail to meet any of their service commitments, or you are dissatisfied with the service you have received for any other reason, you can complain. You can find details of the Revenue's service standards in the leaflet *CSS1 Customer Service Standards* and on their website (see the Fact File).

Strengthening your case

You will have a better chance of sorting out problems amicably with the Revenue if you can show that you keep accurate and up-to-date records, pay on time, tell your tax office if your circumstances change, and provide correct and complete information when asked.

How to complain

First give the person you are dealing with, or their manager, a chance to put things right. If you have no joy, contact the director with responsibility for the office you are dealing with (listed in Inland Revenue Code of Practice 1 *Putting things right when we make mistakes*).

If you are still dissatisfied, there is an independent Adjudicator whose services are free. You must normally apply to the Adjudicator within six months of receiving a response from the Inland Revenue director who has dealt with your case. For more information, see leaflet A01 *How to complain about the Inland Revenue and the Valuation Office Agency.*

You may also be able to complain to the Parliamentary Commissioner for Administration, known as the 'Ombudsman'. However, note that while the Ombudsman can investigate complaints that the Adjudicator has already considered, the Adjudicator cannot handle complaints that have been investigated by the Ombudsman. Complaints to the Ombudsman must be made through an MP within 12 months of the cause for complaint arising.

While a complaint is under way, you still have to pay any tax you owe.

Keep track of costs

You can claim any reasonable costs you have had to pay as a result of the Revenue's mistake or delay, such as postage, phone calls, travelling expenses, professional fees and interest on overpaid tax. You can claim earnings lost as a direct result of having to sort things out. You may also be entitled to compensation for worry and distress caused by the Revenue's mistakes or delays.

Complaint or appeal?

Do not confuse your right to complain about shoddy treatment with your right to make a formal appeal against a Revenue decision. The appeals procedure is laid down by law, and covers things such as your tax assessment, a penalty or surcharge, a claim for tax relief, your National Insurance contributions, or whether you are employed or self-employed.

Whenever relevant, the Revenue will tell you if you have a right of appeal against a particular decision, and should automatically send you information about how to appeal and an appeal form. Check this information carefully, because you have only 30 days in which to appeal, unless you can show that there are good reasons for any delay. Be prepared to pay any disputed tax in the meantime – you may be able to postpone paying it, but interest will usually be added from the date the tax was due if your appeal is unsuccessful.

If you make an appeal, the Revenue will try to settle it by agreement. Failing this, the case will go before commissioners who will hear it and make a decision. (See Inland Revenue leaflet IR37 *Appeals*.) The decision of the commissioners is normally final, but it can be challenged in the courts on a point of law.

Unexpected tax bills

You should not face an unexpected bill if you keep your tax affairs in order and give the Revenue full details of your income, capital gains and personal circumstances. If the Revenue then tell you that something has gone wrong and you have paid too little tax, they may agree to waive the tax, under extra-statutory concession A19. This concession usually applies only if you were notified of the arrears more than 12 months after the end of the tax year in which you supplied the relevant information.

If you do face a bill that you cannot pay, you may be able to negotiate a 'time to pay' arrangement. But you will still incur interest on the outstanding tax.

Enquiries and investigations

If you have to complete a tax return, the Revenue have one year after the latest date for submitting it within which they can start a formal 'enquiry'. An enquiry does not necessarily mean that the Revenue think something is wrong with your return – some are chosen at random.

You can still be investigated after the one-year period if the Revenue suspect fraud or negligence, or if you have not supplied full and accurate information. In the worst cases the charge will be for being 'knowingly concerned in the fraudulent evasion of income tax', which is punishable by an unlimited fine or up to seven years in prison.

If you are faced with a Revenue investigation, full co-operation is your best bet (and get professional help if your tax affairs are in any way complicated). If the investigation finds that you do owe tax, you may have to pay what is owed, plus interest, plus a penalty, which could be as much as the amount of the tax owed. But the Revenue will reduce the penalty if you are co-operative and depending on the seriousness of the case. See Inland Revenue leaflets IR73 *Investigations*, Code of Practice 11 *Self Assessment. Local office enquiries* and Codes of Practice 8 and 9 covering investigations by the Revenue's Special Compliance Office.

Thinking about coming clean?

If you have broken the rules – e.g. not declaring income paid in cash – you can get advice on how to sort matters out on a no-names basis by ringing the Revenue's confidential helpline on 0845 608 6000.

Getting help

Various governments have tried to prune the tax tree, but overall it does not seem any less complex. When it comes to dealing with specific problems, you may need help.

Help from the Inland Revenue

- *Pros:* Free and trying hard to improve customer care. Your own tax office will have your file and is probably the best place to start.

- *Cons:* Variable standards. You have to do the legwork. No help with tax planning.

If you are an employee or receive a pension, your tax office will be that of your employer or main pension payer; self-employed people are dealt with by the 'Schedule D' section at their local tax office. If you change jobs you will be transferred to a new tax office.

If you become unemployed, you stay with your existing tax office. But if you do not have a job or pension and have claimed tax repayments in the past, your records may find their way to one of the Revenue's offices that specialises in repayments. And if your affairs are complex, you may be dealt with by one of the Revenue's complex personal returns teams.

All this means that, unless you are self-employed, the chances of being geographically close to your own tax office are slim. If you need help about something specific to you, it is always best to contact your own tax office, by phone, as they will have your file. For general queries you can contact any tax office (in the phone book under 'Inland Revenue') and there are also Inland Revenue enquiry centres that can arrange face-to-face meetings. You can always ask the tax office to call you back to save on phone bills and if you are housebound you can arrange for them to visit you at home.

There are a number of specialist helplines, covering, for example, tax credits, National Insurance and non-residents. These are listed in the Fact File. For general information, the Inland Revenue have a wide range of leaflets. These are all on the website, together with the Revenue's own internal guidance manuals.

Keep reference numbers handy

When you contact the Revenue, you will be asked for your reference number. A ten-figure 'unique taxpayer reference' (UTR) will be on the front of your tax return, if you get one. Tax offices can also track your records down if you quote your National Insurance number.

In doubt about the tax treatment?

The Revenue will not help with tax planning. You can ask for information about the Revenue's interpretation of tax law, although there may a charge for this. And if, after a particular transaction, there is genuine uncertainty about the tax treatment – because it was an unusual transaction, say – you can ask for a 'post-transaction ruling'. Rulings about inheritance tax treatment are not available. (See Inland Revenue Code of Practice 10 *Information and advice.*)

Help from a professional

- *Pros:* Independent of the Revenue. Good professionals can do the legwork for you, provide help with tax planning and negotiate with the Revenue if necessary. Advice could pay for itself.
- *Cons:* Cost. Variable standards. The Revenue will still hold you responsible if things go wrong – though you might have a claim against your adviser.

The Revenue considers anyone who does your tax return for you on a professional basis your 'agent'.

Many accountancy and law firms offer tax services. Lists of firms specialising in particular areas are available in libraries or from their professional body (see the Fact File).

Alternatively, you can go to a specialist 'chartered tax adviser', with the 'ATII' or 'FTII' or 'CTA' qualifications awarded by the Chartered Institute of Taxation. A lower-level qualification is run by the Association of Tax Technicians (ATT). ATT members who meet requirements such as having insurance and up-to-date knowledge are described as 'Registered with the Association of Taxation Technicians as a Member in Practice'.

There is also a charity – TaxAid – that offers free advice to people who cannot afford to pay an accountant or tax adviser. Their address is in the Fact File.

Record-keeping

The law requires you to keep records so that you can complete a tax return if you are asked to do so, or to back up a tax claim. If you do not, you could end up paying more tax than necessary, or you may have to pay a penalty to the Revenue.

You must keep records for at least 22 months from the end of the tax year to which they relate, or for five years and ten months after this date if you are self-employed or let property. You also need to keep records longer if you received a late tax return, or if the Revenue are enquiring into your tax return or a tax claim. (See Inland Revenue leaflet SA/BK4 *Self Assessment. A general guide to keeping records.*)

The law does not say which records you must keep, but the Revenue make various suggestions, and examples are given towards the end of each chapter. Note that if you keep your records on computer you must still keep your original paper records unless you microfilm them or use an optical imaging system. All vouchers and certificates of tax deducted from your income must be kept.

Tax-planning hints

1. You can sometimes 'put together' different types of tax to your advantage – for example, avoiding higher rates of income tax on investments by choosing schemes that produce capital growth, rather than income.
2. Watch out for tax changes – you may need to reassess your tax plans every so often.
3. If you have a job and are also self-employed, there are rules to cap the amount of National Insurance contributions you have to pay.
4. You have a legal obligation to keep records to back up your tax return or tax claim. Make a habit of keeping key documents.
5. Make a note of your taxpayer reference or National Insurance number. It will save time if you quote it in correspondence or in phone calls to your tax office.
6. Keep a record of any phone calls to your tax office, including the name of the person you spoke to.

7 If you have to complain because the Revenue have made a mistake or been slow, keep a note of any costs you incur – you may be able to claim them back.
8 The Revenue will sometimes waive tax if you are faced with a late and unexpected tax bill, due to their error – ask whether extra-statutory concession A19 applies to you.
9 The Revenue have been trying to improve their customer service – don't be afraid to ask for help.
10 If you are looking for a professional tax adviser, useful qualifications are those awarded by the Chartered Institute of Taxation or (at a lower level) the Association of Tax Technicians.

2

If your tax is paid at source

Wherever possible, the Inland Revenue collect tax 'at source' – by deducting it from income before it is paid. In many cases, this means that you do not need to fill in a tax return.

There are two main ways of collecting tax at source:

- through the Pay As You Earn (PAYE) system, if you have a regular source of taxable income, such as a job, private pension or employer's pension (no tax is deducted from state pensions, although in many cases they are taxable)
- by requiring financial organisations to deduct tax from some types of savings and investment income.

PAYE applies to income tax, but your employer also has to deduct National Insurance contributions and, possibly, student loan repayments.

This chapter gives you practical information on checking the amount of tax and National Insurance deducted.

➡ For what happens if you get a tax return, see Chapter 3.
➡ For the tax rules relating to income from a job see Chapter 5; for pension income see Chapter 7.
➡ For how tax is deducted from savings and investments, see Chapter 10.

You need to think about tax even if you don't get a tax return

Even if all your income is taxed before you get it, you may be paying too much or too little tax. Keep an eye on what is being deducted, particularly if your circumstances change; it could save you money and avoid problems later.

If you are taxed through PAYE and everything works smoothly, you should still check your PAYE code, which tells your employer (or pension provider) how much tax to deduct.

Tax deducted at source from savings and investment income is usually at 20 per cent (10 per cent on dividends).

- If your income is low, you may be able to claim tax back (but not the 10 per cent deducted at source on dividends). If so, you may have to fill in a form R40 *Claim for repayment* (see page 33).
- Alternatively, you may have more tax to pay. This is collected through PAYE if you have income from a job or pension, in which case you will see an entry on your Coding Notice (explained below). If it is not, you will have to fill in a tax return (see Chapter 3).

Keeping below the tax threshold

No PAYE or National Insurance contributions are payable if your earnings are below the level of the basic personal allowance (£4,615 a year, £89 a week or £385 a month in both 2002–03 and 2003–04).

How your income tax is worked out under PAYE

PAYE is a way of spreading your tax bill over the tax year by deducting tax from every salary or pension payment. Your tax office notifies your employer (or the pension payer) how much of your pay to give you tax-free. It does this by giving you a 'PAYE code'. Using special tables, your employer can then work out how much tax to deduct from the rest of your pay.

PAYE is normally cumulative. It takes into account the amount of pay and tax deducted since the start of the tax year, so that the correct proportion of the annual lower-, basic- and higher-rate tax liability is deducted on each pay day. If your income goes up, more tax will be deducted; if your income goes down, too much tax may have already been deducted and the excess tax will be refunded in your pay packet.

At the end of the tax year

By 31 May following the end of the tax year, your employer must give you a form P60 telling you how much pay you have received, how much tax has been deducted and what your PAYE code is. (If you leave your job, your employer must give you a form P45 with this information.) By 6 July, your employer must also give you a form P11D or P9D with details of your taxable expenses and benefits.

This information is copied to the Revenue, and enables them to check the tax bill of PAYE taxpayers who do not get a tax return:

- *If too much tax has been deducted*, the overpayment will first be set against any other tax you owe. You should be sent a cheque for any remaining overpayment – though if the amount is £10 or less this will not happen automatically.
- *If you have underpaid tax*, this will usually be collected by adjusting your tax code for a future tax year (see Chapter 1 if the underpayment arose due to a Revenue mistake). For example, tax underpaid in 2002–03 will usually be recovered through the 2004–05 PAYE code. You can ask for the amount collected to be limited to the amount of your PAYE bill for the current year (with the rest collected through the next year's code), or less in case of hardship. You may be asked to make a repayment direct to the Revenue if the amount is large.

Checking your PAYE code

Your PAYE code shown on your payslip will look something like this: 461L. This is all your employer sees – not how the code is made up.

In January or February each year, you will be sent a P2 Coding Notice, which explains how your tax office has arrived at your code. The rates of state pensions and benefits, and some of the next year's allowances are often announced in time to be incorporated into your PAYE code for the coming year. The letters in the code allow your employer to make automatic adjustments for some budget changes. If you are affected by other budget changes, or if your own circumstances change, you may be sent a new PAYE code after the start of the tax year.

To work out your PAYE code, your tax office starts with the total allowances (and other reliefs) you are entitled to. But your PAYE code can also be used to collect tax on other income that has nothing to do with your job, such as a state retirement pension or interest received without tax deducted. Your code is calculated by deducting estimates of this sort of income from your tax-free allowances:

- *If your allowances come to more than the deductions*, you will have some allowances left to set against your pay (see Example 2.3 on page 22).
- *If your deductions come to more than your allowances*, any remaining amount is treated as additional pay for the purposes of working out how much tax to deduct. The letter in your code will be K (see Example 2.4 on page 24).

Allowances are shown on the left-hand side of the Coding Notice, and deductions on the right. (See Figure 2.1 for common entries that might appear on your Coding Notice, and Chapter 4 for more information on allowances.) Note that payments to your employer's pension scheme or charitable payroll giving scheme do not appear on your Coding Notice because they are deducted before PAYE is worked out.

The number in your PAYE code is simply the value of all your allowances, minus the amounts taken away, with the final digit knocked off (the PAYE tables round in your favour). The letters in PAYE codes mean the following:

- **L, P, V** or **Y** codes help your employer to adjust your code easily to account for budget changes – they show that you get the following allowances:
  - **L** if you get only the basic personal allowance
  - **P** and **V** if you get the full personal allowance for people aged 65 to

74, plus (in the case of a **V** code) the full married couple's allowance, and are a basic-rate taxpayer
  - **Y** if you get the full personal allowance for people aged 75 and over.
- The **T** code is used for any special cases not covered by the codes above, or if you ask your tax office to use it (e.g. because you do not want your employer to know what allowances you get).
- The **BR** or **DO** codes mean that all your pay from this job or pension should be taxed at the basic rate or higher rate respectively (used for second jobs, for example).
- The **K** code means that the amounts taken away from your allowances come to more than your allowances themselves, so you are regarded as receiving additional pay for the purposes of working out your PAYE deduction. However, not more than 50 per cent of your pay can be taken in tax.

Figure 2.1: Coding Notice entries

Your tax allowances

- Personal allowance
- Married allowance
- Blind person's allowance
- Maintenance payments
- Loan interest (if it qualifies for tax relief)
- Job expenses
- Personal pension relief (higher-rate relief only)
- Charity gifts relief (higher-rate relief on Gift Aid payments)

Deductions

- Allowance restriction
- Pensions and state benefits
- Other pensions
- Jobseeker's allowance
- Incapacity benefit
- Benefits and expenses provided by your employer (e.g. car or car fuel benefit)
- Part-time earnings/tips/ commission
- Other items of untaxed income (e.g. property income, untaxed interest)
- Tax underpaid

Allowances minus deductions gives the number in your PAYE code

Allowance restrictions

The married couple's allowance and maintenance payments give tax relief at only 10 per cent of the full amount, but if the full value of the allowance is given in your tax-free pay, you will get tax relief at your top rate of tax. You will see a 'restriction' in the right-hand column of your Coding Notice to account for this (see Example 2.1). The restriction is deducted from the full allowance, and what's left will give you the correct amount of relief when multiplied by your top rate of tax.

Example 2.1: **Checking your allowance restriction**

George is a basic-rate taxpayer aged 70 and entitled to a full married couple's allowance of £5,565 in 2003–04. On his Coding Notice, he sees 'Married Allowance' of £5,565 in the left-hand-column, and 'Allowance restriction' of £3,030 in the right-hand column. To check the restriction he takes the following steps:

1	Take the full allowance you are entitled to	£5,565.00
2	Multiply this by 10% to find tax relief due	£556.50
3	Multiply the tax relief due (from Step 2) by 100⁄22 if your top rate of tax is 22%, 100⁄10 if it is 10%, 100⁄40 if it is 40%	× 100⁄22 = £2,529.55
4	The allowance restriction is the Step 1 figure minus the Step 3 figure. This will be rounded down to the nearest £10	£3,035.45

The restriction is correct. Without it, the PAYE system would give him tax relief of £5,565 × 22% = £1,224.30. With it, he gets £5,565 – £3,030 = £2,535 × 22% = £557.70.

Children's Tax Credit

Children's Tax Credit may have been shown in your PAYE code for 2002–03, with an allowance restriction calculated in the same way as for married couple's allowance. However, the administration of tax credits has changed, and they are not in your PAYE code for 2003–04 (see Chapter 7). More tax may be deducted from your pay as a result.

Adjustments for tax underpaid

Sometimes PAYE is used to collect tax underpaid in the previous year. If so, you will see something like 'Unpaid tax £300' on your Coding Notice, but a *higher* amount will be taken away from your allowances. This is because the deduction has to be large enough to produce the amount of unpaid tax when multiplied by your top rate of tax.

Example 2.2: **Collecting tax underpaid**

Halina underpaid £300 tax because her company car changed during the tax year. Her top rate of income tax is 40%. On her Coding Notice she sees a deduction of £300 × $^{100}/_{40}$ = £750. This deduction will collect £750 × 40% = £300, which is the tax she owes.

Estimated amounts

PAYE Coding Notices are usually sent out in January or February for the tax year starting in April. So, if your PAYE code includes an allowance for an item on which you get tax relief (such as a pension contribution) or a deduction to account for other taxable income (such as untaxed interest) your tax office has to make an estimate of how much the item is likely to be. The estimate may be based on the previous year's figure, information from your employer, or information in your tax return (for example, regular claims for tax relief on gifts to charity).

Check estimates

Always check any estimated amounts in your PAYE Coding Notice. If the amount has changed substantially, let your tax office know, or you could pay too much or too little tax.

More than one job or pension

If you have more than one source of income within PAYE, you will probably get a separate PAYE code and Coding Notice for each source of income, but your allowances will be given against the main source. If any allowances are left over, you will see the remaining allowances given as 'Balance of allowances' in your code for the second source.

Your tax office may instruct whoever pays your second income to deduct tax at just the basic rate or higher rate, using a BR or DO code, but give you a special 'starting rate allowance' if you have not used all your starting-rate band against your main source of income. If too much of your income is taxed at the lower or basic rates, you could see a deduction called 'starting rate tax adjustment' or 'basic rate tax restriction'.

Checking how much PAYE has been deducted

Because PAYE is worked out on a cumulative basis, you need to use the Revenue tables if you want to check that the right amount has been deducted. These tables, and other guidance, are included in the Revenue's annual Employer's Pack (available on the Inland Revenue website) or contact your local tax office or enquiry centre.

Example 2.3: If allowances are more than deductions

George has recently retired with a pension from his previous employer. His Coding Notice for 2003–04 shows that he is entitled to an age-related personal allowance, restricted to £6,000 because his income exceeds £18,300. George also gets a full married couple's allowance of £5,565 – allowances of £11,565 in total.

The right-hand side of George's Coding Notice shows an allowance restriction of £3,030 (see Example 2.1). The notice also shows that the tax on his state pension of £6,136 will be collected through his PAYE on his employer's pension. Total deductions are £9,166.

George's allowances come to more than his deductions (£11,565 − £9,166 = £2,399) and the letter in his code is T because he gets a reduced age allowance. His PAYE code is therefore 239T, which means that he gets £2,399 ÷ 12 = £199 of his monthly pay tax-free.

Figure 2.2: PAYE Coding Notice (see Example 2.3)

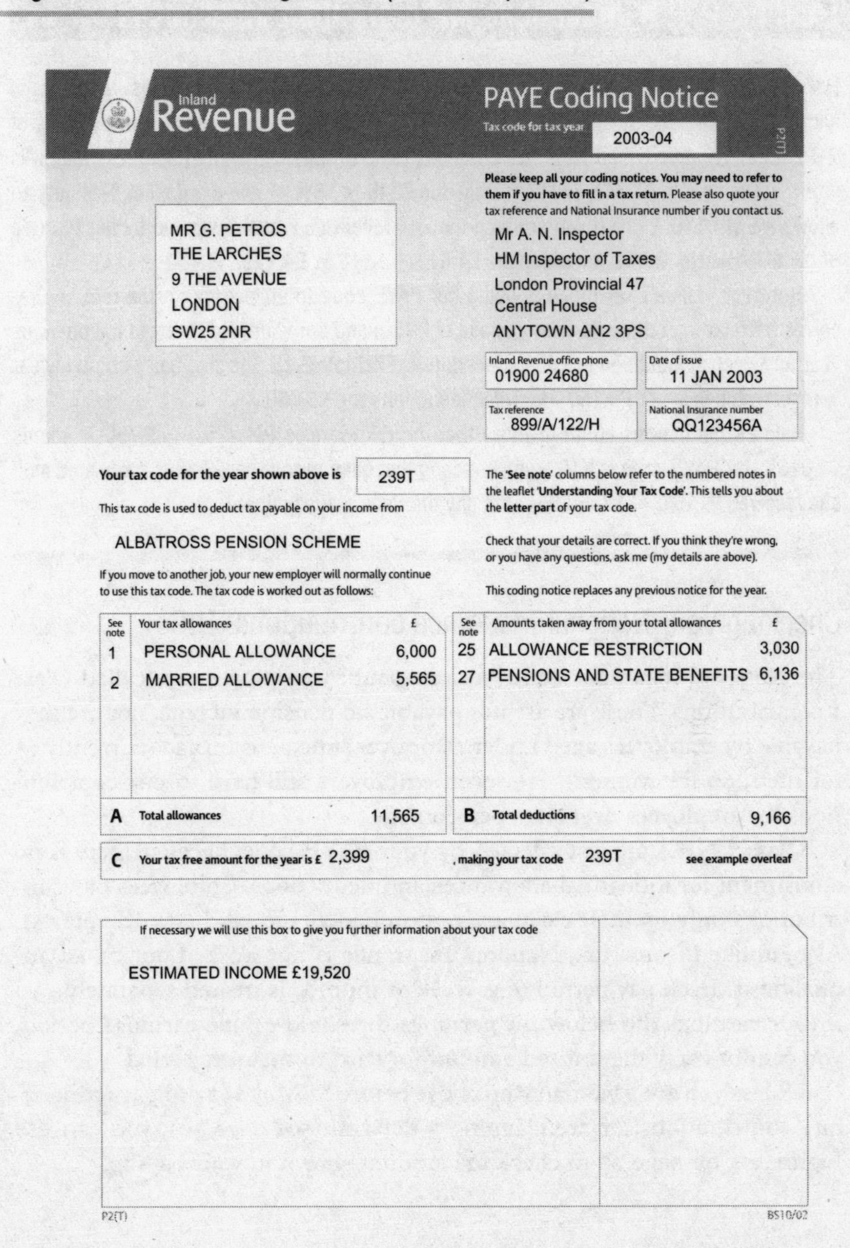

Inland Revenue

PAYE Coding Notice

Tax code for tax year 2003-04

P2(T)

Please keep all your coding notices. You may need to refer to them if you have to fill in a tax return. Please also quote your tax reference and National Insurance number if you contact us.

MR G. PETROS
THE LARCHES
9 THE AVENUE
LONDON
SW25 2NR

Mr A. N. Inspector
HM Inspector of Taxes
London Provincial 47
Central House
ANYTOWN AN2 3PS

Inland Revenue office phone: 01900 24680

Date of issue: 11 JAN 2003

Tax reference: 899/A/122/H

National Insurance number: QQ123456A

Your tax code for the year shown above is 239T

This tax code is used to deduct tax payable on your income from

ALBATROSS PENSION SCHEME

If you move to another job, your new employer will normally continue to use this tax code. The tax code is worked out as follows:

The **'See note'** columns below refer to the numbered notes in the leaflet **'Understanding Your Tax Code'**. This tells you about the **letter part** of your tax code.

Check that your details are correct. If you think they're wrong, or you have any questions, ask me (my details are above).

This coding notice replaces any previous notice for the year.

See note	Your tax allowances	£
1	PERSONAL ALLOWANCE	6,000
2	MARRIED ALLOWANCE	5,565
A	**Total allowances**	11,565

See note	Amounts taken away from your total allowances	£
25	ALLOWANCE RESTRICTION	3,030
27	PENSIONS AND STATE BENEFITS	6,136
B	**Total deductions**	9,166

C **Your tax free amount for the year is £** 2,399 **, making your tax code** 239T **see example overleaf**

If necessary we will use this box to give you further information about your tax code

ESTIMATED INCOME £19,520

P2(T) BS10/02

Example 2.4: If deductions are more than allowances

Halina is aged 45 and a 40% taxpayer. Her Coding Notice for 2003–04 shows her personal allowance of £4,615. She also makes a regular Gift Aid payment to her favourite charity of £192. She has already had 22% basic-rate tax relief on this by handing over less than it is worth to the charity (£246), so she is only due £246 × 18% = £44 extra relief. She gets an allowance of £110 – which will produce the £44 relief due when multiplied by her top rate of tax of 40%. Her total allowances are £4,615 + £110 = £4,725.

However, Halina's tax office is using her PAYE code to collect tax on the rent she receives from letting out her holiday cottage (£1,750) and some unpaid tax from the previous year for which a deduction of £750 appears (see Example 2.2). She also has a company car with a taxable value of £3,250. Her total deductions are £5,750.

Halina's deductions come to more than her allowances (£4,725 − £5,750 = minus £1,025). Her PAYE code is K102 which means that each month her PAYE is calculated as if she received £1,020 ÷ 12 = £85 more pay than she actually does.

Checking your National Insurance contributions (NICs)

The National Insurance contributions paid by employees are called Class 1 contributions. These are are not payable on pension income, nor are they payable by employees aged under 16 or over state pension age (currently 65 for men, 60 for women). However, employers still have to pay contributions for employees over state pension age.

Class 1 NICs are not affected by your PAYE code, because there is no adjustment for individual allowances and deductions. Employees pay contributions only on their earnings, not on benefits in kind (see Chapter 5). Also, unlike income tax, National Insurance is not worked out on an annual basis. Each pay period (e.g. week or month) is treated separately – so if your earnings dip below the earnings threshold in one earnings period, you cannot carry the unused amount forward to the next period.

Unless you are a woman who chose before 11 May 1977 to pay reduced-rate contributions, or are claiming a deferral (see page 30), you can use Figure 2.4 on page 27 to check the amount shown in your payslip.

Figure 2.3: PAYE Coding Notice (see Example 2.4)

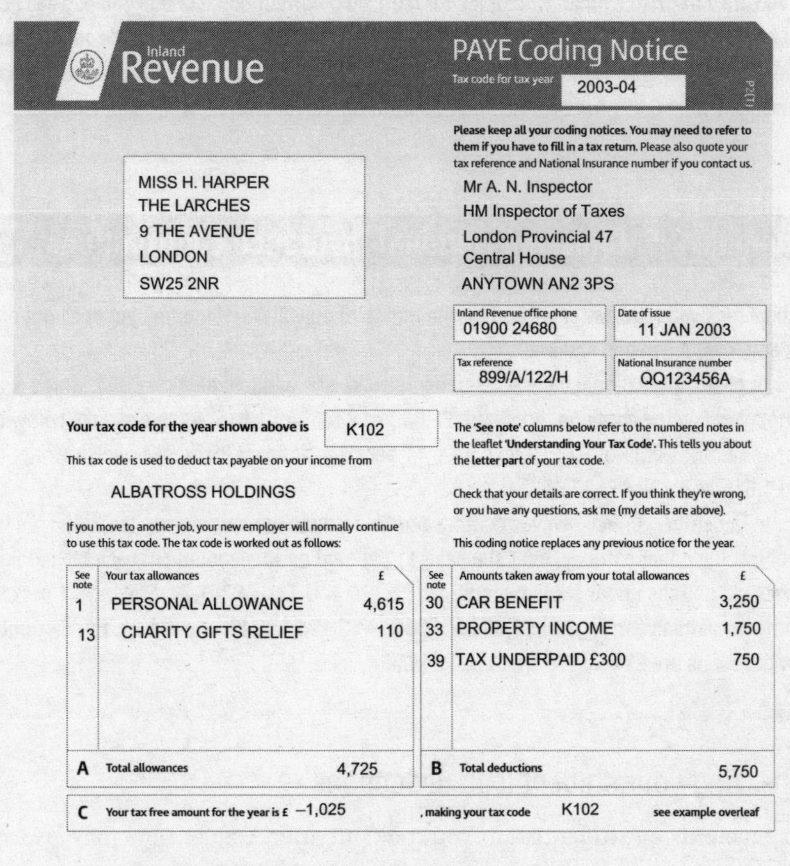

Inland Revenue

PAYE Coding Notice

Tax code for tax year 2003-04

P2(T)

MISS H. HARPER
THE LARCHES
9 THE AVENUE
LONDON
SW25 2NR

Please keep all your coding notices. You may need to refer to them if you have to fill in a tax return. Please also quote your tax reference and National Insurance number if you contact us.

Mr A. N. Inspector
HM Inspector of Taxes
London Provincial 47
Central House
ANYTOWN AN2 3PS

Inland Revenue office phone	Date of issue
01900 24680	11 JAN 2003
Tax reference	**National Insurance number**
899/A/122/H	QQ123456A

Your tax code for the year shown above is K102

This tax code is used to deduct tax payable on your income from

ALBATROSS HOLDINGS

If you move to another job, your new employer will normally continue to use this tax code. The tax code is worked out as follows:

The **'See note'** columns below refer to the numbered notes in the leaflet **'Understanding Your Tax Code'**. This tells you about the **letter part** of your tax code.

Check that your details are correct. If you think they're wrong, or you have any questions, ask me (my details are above).

This coding notice replaces any previous notice for the year.

See note	Your tax allowances	£	See note	Amounts taken away from your total allowances	£
1	PERSONAL ALLOWANCE	4,615	30	CAR BENEFIT	3,250
13	CHARITY GIFTS RELIEF	110	33	PROPERTY INCOME	1,750
			39	TAX UNDERPAID £300	750
A	**Total allowances**	4,725	**B**	**Total deductions**	5,750

C **Your tax free amount for the year is £** –1,025 **, making your tax code** K102 **see example overleaf**

If necessary we will use this box to give you further information about your tax code

P2(T) BS10/02

Married women paying reduced contributions

If you are a married woman who opted for reduced contributions, the rate you pay has gone up from 6 April 2003, from 3.85% to 4.85%. These contributions do not entitle you to a state pension in your own right and you should consider switching to the full rate. (See Inland Revenue leaflet CA13 *National Insurance contributions for women with reduced elections.*)

Example 2.5: **Checking National Insurance contributions**

Amina received total pay of £2,000 for the month of July 2003. Her employer does not offer an employer's pension scheme.

To check the National Insurance on her payslip, she deducts the first £385, which is the amount below the earnings threshold. £2,000 – £385 = £1,615. As this all falls below the upper earnings limit of £2,579, she pays 11 per cent National Insurance, which works out at £1,615 × 0.11 = £177.65.

In December Amina receives commission that brings her earnings up to £3,000. As this is above the upper earnings limit she pays 11 per cent on the amount between the earnings threshold and the upper earnings limit, i.e. £2,194 × 0.11 = £241.34. She pays 1 per cent on her remaining earnings of £3,000 – £385 – £2,194 = £421, i.e. £4.21. Her December contributions are £241.34 + £4.21 = £245.55.

Checking your student loan deductions

Repayments on student loans you took out after August 1998 may also appear on your payslip. The amount of the repayment is related to your level of income, so they are called 'income-contingent' loans.

If you have one of these loans, the Student Loans Company will notify your employer – they will not appear on your PAYE Coding Notice. The same earnings (i.e. excluding fringe benefits) are taken into account as for NICs. You do not have to make repayments on the first £10,000 a year of income (£192 weekly, £833 monthly) in 2002–03 and 2003–04. Investment income is ignored unless it exceeds £2,000. The repayments are 9 per cent of anything above £10,000.

Figure 2.4: Checking the National Insurance on your payslip

Is your pay below the earnings threshold?
(£89 weekly, £385 monthly, £4,615 annually in 2002–03 and 2003–04)

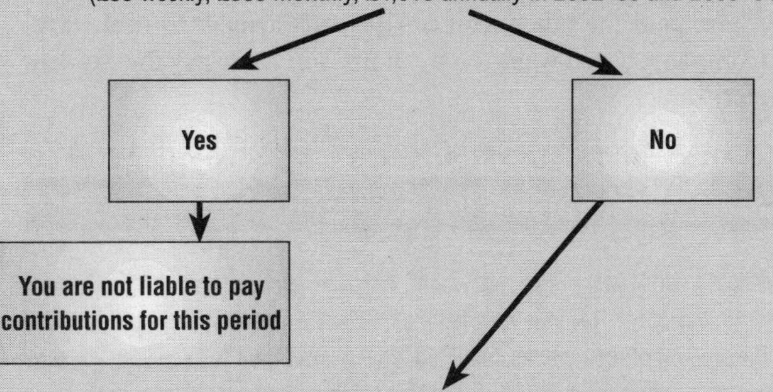

Is your pay above the upper earnings limit?
(£585 weekly, £2,535 monthly in 2002–03, £595 weekly, £2,579 monthly in 2003–04)

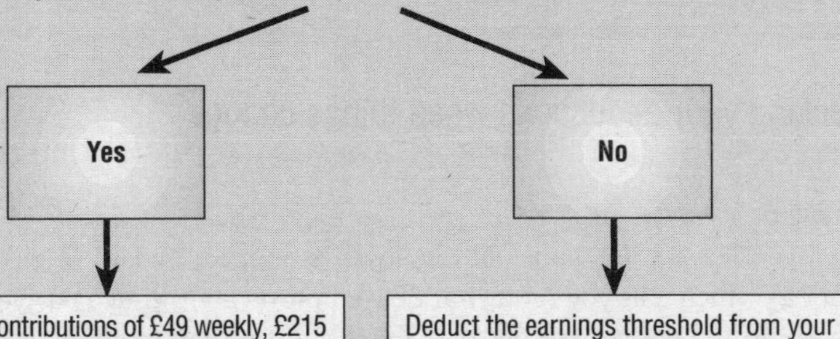

You pay contributions of £49 weekly, £215 monthly in 2002–03, £55 weekly, £241 monthly in 2003–04. If you are a member of an employer's scheme which is contracted-out of the State Earnings Related Pension Scheme (SERPS), the contributions are reduced to £41 weekly, £180 monthly in 2002–03, £47 weekly, £206 in 2003–04. Plus, from 6 April 2003, an extra 1% on any earnings above £595 a week (£2,579 a month).

Deduct the earnings threshold from your pay (£89 weekly, £385 monthly in 2002–03 and 2003–04)
Your contributions are 10% of the remaining pay in 2002–03, 11% in 2003–04. If you are a member of an employer's scheme which is contracted-out of the State Earnings Related Pension Scheme (SERPS), the rate is reduced to 8.4% in 2002–03, 9.4% in 2003–04.

The Inland Revenue's help sheet IR235 *Calculation of student loan repayments* includes a calculator for student loan repayments (available on the Inland Revenue website).

Like National Insurance contributions, student loan repayments are non-cumulative and each pay period is treated separately. If, at the end of the year, you have paid too much, you can get a repayment from the Student Loans Company. If you want to pay more, you must pay the Student Loans Company direct.

Who to contact about student loans

The Revenue collect your student loan repayment, but it is administered by the Student Loans Company. However, the Revenue only tell the Student Loans Company after the end of the tax year the amount of repayments deducted, so it is important to keep your payslips in case you need to query something. The Student Loans Company have a repayment helpline on 0141 204 5605.

Checking your deductions when things change

Starting or leaving a job

When you leave a job, your old employer is obliged, by law, to give you a form P45 which tells you (and your new employer) how much pay you have received in the tax year so far, how much tax you have paid, whether you are liable to pay student loan deductions and what your PAYE code was at leaving. You should give this to your new employer so that the right amount of tax can be deducted straight away.

If you don't have a P45 – either because this is your first job, or for some other reason – your new employer will ask you to fill in a form P46 which is sent off to your tax office (unless you are earning below the PAYE threshold and this is your only or main job). Your tax office will try to trace your records so they can give you your proper code. If they can't, they will send you a form P91 asking for details of your previous jobs. Until a correct code is issued for you, your employer will give you the 'emergency code' (see below). School-leavers may find Inland Revenue leaflet IR33 *Income tax and school leavers* useful.

Avoid the 'emergency' code

If your employer does not know what your PAYE code is, you will be taxed on the 'emergency' code of 461L (in 2002–03 and 2003–04). This gives you only the basic personal allowance for someone aged under 65, and, unless this is your first job, it is applied as if you started work at the beginning of the tax year. This ignores any tax-free pay that might have built up before you started your new job. So it is in your interests to give your new employer your P45 or, if you do not have one, to get your PAYE code sorted out quickly.

Sick pay

Statutory sick pay, and any sick pay from an insurance scheme paid for by your employer, is taxable. Your employer will continue to deduct PAYE and National Insurance, but because your sick pay is likely to be less than your normal pay you may get a refund of some of the tax paid so far. If you receive incapacity benefit for more than 28 weeks, the Department for Work and Pensions (DWP) may also deduct tax (see Chapter 7).

Maternity or paternity leave

Maternity and paternity payments from your employer, including statutory maternity, paternity or adoption pay, are taxable and your employer will continue to deduct PAYE and National Insurance. If you do not have the right to return to work after the birth, your employer will give you a P45 either when the final payment is made, or as soon as you stop work. Any payments made after receiving your P45 will have basic-rate tax deducted, so you may be able to claim a tax refund from your tax office.

When your child is born you may be entitled to the Child Tax Credit. Contact the Revenue's Tax Credit Office to claim it (details are in the Fact File). Chapter 7 gives more information.

A student with a holiday job

If you think your income over the year is likely to be below the basic personal allowance (£4,615 in 2002–03 and 2003–04), your wages can be paid without deduction of tax. Ask your employer for form P38(S). Note that you cannot fill this in if you are on an overseas course, unless special arrangements apply, or if you are working part-time outside normal holiday times. (See Inland Revenue leaflet IR60 *Income tax and students*.)

Form P38(S) does not affect your National Insurance, which will be worked out in the normal way (although no contributions are due on earnings below £89 a week, £385 a month, in 2002–03 and 2003–04).

Getting work through an agency

If a UK agency pays you direct, it will normally be responsible for operating PAYE and deducting NICs. If an employer pays you, it should operate PAYE. There are special rules for entertainers, models and homeworkers. (See Inland Revenue leaflet CA25 *Agencies and people working through agencies*.)

Having a second job

You will get a second PAYE code for the second job – see page 22.

Under the normal Class 1 National Insurance rules, you could end up paying contributions at the full rate (10% in 2002–03, 11% in 2003–04) on each job, even though overall your income is above the limit on which this rate is payable. So there is an annual maximum contribution, worked out as if all your earnings came from one job. If you expect to pay contributions on earnings of at least £595 a week from one job (or combination of jobs) throughout the 2003–04 tax year, you can ask to put off paying contributions on your second job. You can settle up, or get a refund, when it is clear, at the end of the tax year, what you have earned.

If you are employed in one job and self-employed in another, you can also apply to defer your Class 2 or Class 4 contributions. See Inland Revenue leaflet CA72 *National Insurance contributions: deferring payment* which contains a form you can use to apply for deferral.

Becoming unemployed

If you are claiming Jobseeker's Allowance, you should give your P45 to the DWP when you claim the allowance. Jobseeker's Allowance is liable to income tax (up to a maximum), and the DWP operate a modified form of PAYE to collect this.

However, tax is not deducted from Jobseeker's Allowance when it is paid – instead any liability is calculated when the claim ends or at the end of the tax year. The DWP, or sometimes your next employer, will repay any tax overpaid. You will get a P60U at the end of the tax year, or a P45U to hand to your new employer. (See Inland Revenue leaflet IR41 *Income tax and job seekers.*)

If you don't go to another job and don't start claiming Jobseeker's Allowance, you may be entitled to a tax repayment. After a month, ask for a repayment claim form P50 which you should complete and return to your tax office with your P45.

Retiring

If you are retiring on an employer's or private pension you will receive either a P45, or a similar form (P160) or letter notifying you of your pay and tax in the tax year to date.

Your pension will be paid using your existing PAYE code until the end of the tax year or until your tax office reassess your code, but you will not have to pay National Insurance. If you receive a P45, be sure to give it to the pension payer or you will be taxed on the emergency code.

To help your tax office reassess your code, or decide what new code to give you, you might be asked to complete a 'pension enquiry' form (P161). This is a simple form asking what sources of income you have, and how you expect this to change in retirement.

Note that under your new code more tax may be deducted from your pension than you expect. This is because your code will also collect the tax on any state pensions, which are paid out before tax.

Being widowed

When somebody who is being taxed under PAYE dies, their P45 is sent to their tax office. If their widow or widower is entitled to a spouse's pension from an employer's or private pension scheme, the pension scheme will notify the widow or widower's tax office, and will pay the pension with basic-rate tax deducted from the whole amount (i.e. code BR) until a new PAYE code is issued.

You may be sent a 'pension enquiry' form (P161) to help your tax office decide what your new code should be.

What to tell the Inland Revenue

Your tax office will get most of the necessary information from your employer or pension payer. After the end of the tax year, they must tell the Revenue how much they have paid each employee, how much tax they have deducted, and what taxable expenses and fringe benefits they have paid you. Your employer must also tell your tax office during the tax year if you have changed your company car.

However, the Revenue have other sources of information:

- Banks and building societies must tell the Revenue how much interest they have paid in the tax year to each customer with a UK address.
- Businesses can be asked to give details of all payments made to non-employees for services rendered.

You may also need to give the Revenue information. For example, if you do not get a tax return:

- You should notify the Revenue within six months of the end of the tax year in question if you have received taxable income or made capital gains, unless all your income is taxable under PAYE or by deduction of tax at source (e.g. savings interest).
- If you have allowances or deductions in your PAYE code which vary in amount (such as property income or untaxed interest), you may receive a 'targeted review' form (P810) every so often, asking the questions necessary to adjust your code.
- If you want to claim tax relief on work expenses, ask your tax office for expenses claim form P87.
- If you need to claim tax back (because too much tax has been deducted from investments), you can do this on a form R40 *Claim for repayment*. You can get this from your tax office, or contact the

Revenue's Taxback helpline (see the Fact File). If you claim tax back in one year, you are likely to receive a form R40 automatically in future years. Alternatively, you can register to get your interest paid before tax (on form R85, see Chapter 10). There is a similar form R89 if you receive an annuity with tax deducted at basic rate.

- If you want to tell the Revenue about changes in your circumstances which won't be notified by your employer, see below.

Things to tell your tax office

- Change of address.
- Having a child, or being widowed.
- Getting married or divorced or (if claiming tax credits) a change of partner.
- Starting to work for yourself; you must notify the Revenue within three months or risk a £100 penalty.
- New sources of untaxed income, e.g. from letting out a property.
- Savings or investments that produce taxable income paid out without deduction of tax.
- If you are a higher-rate taxpayer and need to claim higher-rate tax relief on regular pension contributions or gifts to a charity; this will be picked up through your tax return, but if the amounts are substantial and you are on PAYE you might want to notify them earlier so that they can be incorporated in your PAYE code as soon as possible.

Filling in form R40 *Claim for repayment*

The R40 is a simple four-page form that collects the information necessary to assess whether you are entitled to a tax repayment. You do not need to send your dividend vouchers, interest certificates or other documents with the form, unless you are unsure that you have completed it correctly.

You do not need to wait until the end of the tax year to make your claim. You can either send it in as soon as you have received all your income for the year, or send in an interim claim, ticking the 'interim claim' box on the front page. Note, though, that repayments of less than £50 are not normally made before the end of the tax year. If you make an interim claim you can use estimates if necessary, but you may need to back these up with the actual figures after the end of the tax year.

Claiming on behalf of someone else

Repayment claims may be signed on behalf of a child or an adult who is incapable of doing so. However, you must have proper legal authority to do this, e.g. as the parent or guardian of a child, the person authorised by the courts to look after the affairs of a mentally incapacitated adult, or the executor or administrator of the estate of someone who has died.

Example 2.6: **Claiming back tax**

Arnold is 74. His main income consists of a state pension of £7,000 a year. However, he also has savings interest of £1,000 a year, which takes his total income to £8,000. This exceeds his personal allowance, but all his taxable income falls in the 10% band.

Because Arnold is liable to pay some tax, he cannot register to have his interest paid gross. However, the tax on his savings income is deducted at 20% (£200), although he is only liable to pay tax at 10% (£100). He gets a form R40 each year to claim back the £100 overpaid tax.

Record-keeping

Make sure you keep your Coding Notices, payslips and P60s and (if you get one) your P45 or P160. Your employer is not allowed to give you copies of a P45 if you lose it, though your tax office should have the information from the employer's regular returns. Also keep a photocopy of any completed forms you send the Revenue, copies of any correspondence, and notes of any phone calls.

➡ For specific documents relating to employment, pensions, state benefits or savings and investments, see Chapters 5, 7 and 10.

➡ For how long to keep your records, see Chapter 1.

Figure 2.5: Claim for repayment (see Example 2.6)

Inland Revenue

Your reference	Tax reference
	12345 67890

Claim for Repayment

LONDON PROVINCIAL 99
POLAR HOUSE
SHACKLETON
TYNE & WEAR
SR1 RQ3

MR A RIDLEY
FIRST COTTAGE
2 SECOND STREET
ANYTOWN
X12 2SZ

If any of these details are wrong please cross them out and enter the correct details

. UK savings income with tax paid

or accounts held jointly enter only your share or the share of the person you are claiming for

Name of payer and account number(s)	Income before tax £	p	Tax deducted £	p	Income after tax £	p
Anywhere Bank – X01234	600	00	120	00	480	00
5% Treasury 2004	400	00	80	00	320	00
Total	1,000	00	200	00	800	00

See Note 2a for other types of taxed income to enter in this section.

2b. UK savings income without paid tax

For accounts held jointly enter only your share or the share of the person you are claiming for. Please remember to include interest from all accounts registered for gross interest

Name of payer and account number(s)	NSB ordinary account?	* R85 completed?	Amount received £	p
		Total		

** See Note 2b for conditions for ticking this box. Note 2b lists other possible types of untaxed interest to enter here.*

3. State Retirement Pension

State retirement pension is taxable. Enter the total for the year not the weekly or monthly amount. **Do not include** attendance allowance or disability living allowance. £ 7000 p 00

If you are a woman aged over 60 or a man over 65 **and you do not** receive state retirement pension tick this box. ☐

4. Earnings, pensions (other than State Pension) and other income on which tax paid

Please indicate clearly if income arises from gains on life annuity contracts

Nam... P45/P60 ... before tax Tax deducted £ p

Tax-planning hints

Checking your PAYE Coding Notice

1 Check that all the allowances and reliefs you are claiming are shown.
2 Check any estimated amounts.
3 Check any allowance restriction is correct (see Example 2.1).
4 If your circumstances have changed, keep the Revenue informed so that your code can be changed if necessary.

Checking up on the Revenue

5 Check that the figures given in your PAYE codes for the taxable value of fringe benefits are consistent with those shown on the form P11D or P9D your employer gives you (see Chapter 5).
6 Check the figures for any state pension or other taxable state benefits in your PAYE code.
7 Any claims for a repayment should be processed within 20 days of reaching the Revenue. If not, chase up your claim.

Checking up on your employer (or pension company)

8 Is your employer (or pension company) using the right PAYE code? The code should appear on your payslip.
9 At the end of the tax year, make sure your P60 (or P45 when you leave) is consistent with your payslips.
10 If you suspect that your employer is failing to deduct PAYE or National Insurance correctly, or to hand it over to the Revenue, contact your tax office.
11 The Revenue are also responsible for enforcing some aspects of the national minimum wage, and have a special helpline (see the Fact File). (See Inland Revenue leaflet COP20 *National Minimum Wage.*)

Minimising National Insurance

12 If you employ a relative in your own business, consider paying a salary below the threshold for deducting National Insurance and PAYE. (You may have problems if you pay less than the national minimum wage.) And it is a good idea to pay enough to reach the lower earnings level (for 2003–04, £77 a week) to protect the employee's rights to state pension and other contributory benefits.

13 Remember that National Insurance is not worked out on a cumulative basis – if your earnings dip below one of the contribution thresholds in one earnings period, you cannot carry the unused amount forward. Try to avoid irregular earnings if this is likely to affect you.

14 Married women paying a reduced contribution should check whether paying the standard amount would make sense. (See page 26.)

15 Check whether you can defer some National Insurance contributions if you have more than one job or are self-employed as well. (See page 30.)

Keeping things simple

16 To ensure that you pay the right amount of tax when you change jobs, give your P45 to any new employer straight away.

17 If you are a student with a holiday job, ask your employer if you are eligible to complete form P38(S) to get your payments made without tax deducted.

18 If you employ someone in your home, such as a nanny, you are still liable to operate PAYE provided they earn more than the earnings threshold, but there is a simplified deduction scheme. Contact the Revenue's helpline for new employers (see the Fact File).

3

If you get a tax return

A self-assessment tax return is not just a form to fill in: it brings you within a system of paying tax, with its own strict timetables, record-keeping requirements and penalties for non-compliance. 'Self-assessment' shifts the responsibility for working out your tax on to you, although all tax returns are checked for accuracy and the Revenue will do the sums for you if you send your return in on time.

Even if you get a tax return, your income may still be taxed largely under PAYE, so you may find it helpful to read Chapter 2 first. However, if you have income that is not taxed under PAYE, you may have to make 'payments on account'. These are twice-yearly payments of your tax, due at the end of each January and July, estimated on the basis of the previous year's income. You will have to manage your financial affairs so that you are able to make these payments.

Does self-assessment affect you?

Around nine million people have to complete a self-assessment tax return each year. You will be one of them if you are a higher-rate taxpayer, a director of a limited company, self-employed or in partnership, or if your tax affairs are complex.

You may also have to submit a tax return if you have untaxed income, e.g. from investments, land and property or from overseas, which comes to more than £2,500 a year. You should tell your tax office by 5 October 2003 if you received income of this sort in the 2002–03 tax year, if arrangements have not been made to collect the tax under PAYE (see Chapter 2), and you have not already been sent a tax return.

Although the Revenue try not to bring people within the self-assessment regime unnecessarily, many pensioners who have hitherto been taxed under PAYE find themselves having to deal with a tax return once they retire. However, if you are claiming back tax, you may be sent a form R40 *Claim for repayment* instead – this is covered in Chapter 2.

Can you stop returns being sent?

If you are sent a return, you must fill it in. Tax offices review taxpayers' records in January or February each year to decide whether to send a return in April. If your circumstances have changed, send back your previous year's return (or notify your tax office) early so that the information is logged before the review takes place.

How the tax is worked out

Submitting your return

The tax return is the key document in working out your tax. As well as your income tax, it covers capital gains tax, Class 4 National Insurance contributions (payable by the self-employed) and student loan repayments.

There are two steps to submitting your return:

- *Enter the necessary information on the return itself.* There is a 'Filling in your tax return' section at the end of this and all later chapters.
- *Work out the amount of tax due.* You can delegate this to the Revenue or do the calculation yourself, for which you can use either the Revenue's tax calculation guide that is sent out with the return, or one of the computer-based returns now available. If you file your tax return using the Internet, the calculation is done automatically.

Note that you do not always get a paper tax return. If you use a computerised return or the Revenue's Filing by Internet service (see below), or your tax adviser has done so on your behalf, you may get a *Notice to Complete a Tax Return* (SA316) instead of a full return the following tax year.

Whether your return is paper-based or electronic, Table 3.1 on page 42 shows the latest dates for sending it in for the 2002–03 tax year. In practice, however, it is often worth getting your return in early:

- The Revenue will work out the tax for you, provided you get your return in by 30 September (or within two months if the return was issued after 31 July). If you send it in later, they will still do it, but not necessarily before you have to pay any tax due, in which case you would have to estimate the amount.
- If you owe tax of less than £2,000 and you are taxed under PAYE, you can ask the Revenue to collect this through your PAYE code over the next tax year, rather than paying it in one go. You should get your return in by 30 September (if you use a paper return) to give the Revenue time to organise this. If you make your return using the Internet, the deadline is 30 December.
- If you leave your return to the last moment, the information on it may not reach the rest of the Revenue's systems in time.

Computerised returns and Filing by Internet

You can complete your return using the Revenue's free internet service and there are computer programs now available that work out the tax for you and submit a substitute tax return through the Revenue's internet service. Filing by Internet doesn't save you any tax, but your return should be processed more quickly and accurately, and if you have made an obvious mistake your return will be rejected automatically. There are full details and a list of Revenue-approved computer-based returns on the Revenue website.

Penalties, surcharges and interest

Penalties are charged if you get your return in late – usually £100, but possibly more. Surcharges are extra tax you have to pay if you fail to pay your tax on time. And interest is charged on any amount paid late, including surcharges and penalties, so you should pay the amount demanded even if you are appealing against it. See Inland Revenue leaflets SA/BK6 *Self Assessment. Penalties for late tax returns* and SA/BK7 *Self Assessment. Surcharges for late payment of tax.*

Acceptable and unacceptable excuses

The Revenue will not accept the following excuses for late returns or late payment of tax:

- pressure of work
- failure by your accountant or tax adviser (you may have a case against them instead)
- lack of information (send provisional figures instead)
- the tax return was too difficult (ask your tax office for help)
- inability to pay
- not receiving a reminder that the return or payment was due.

Excuses that the Revenue may accept (if you have sufficient evidence):

- unforeseeable postal difficulties, such as a postal strike
- loss of your records by fire, flood or theft
- serious illness immediately before the filing date
- serious illness or death of a close relative (you need to show that you had already taken steps to submit the return on time).

You have 30 days in which to appeal against a penalty or surcharge if you think it is incorrect or if you have a reasonable excuse (see above). If, when your return is submitted, it shows that your final tax bill is less than the amount of the penalty, the penalty should be reduced to the amount of the tax.

Table 3.1: Self-assessment timetable for 2002–03 tax year

31 January 2003	If you are liable to make payments on account, your first instalment of tax for 2002–03 is due (estimated on the previous year's income). If you don't pay, interest starts to clock up on the outstanding amount.
April 2003	Tax returns for the 2002–03 tax year are issued.
31 May 2003	Your employer must give you your end-of-year statement (P60) by now. You need this to complete your return.
6 July 2003	Your employer must give you your statement of taxable expenses and benefits (P11D or P9D) by now.
31 July 2003	Second instalment of tax for 2002–03 due (estimated). If you don't pay, interest is charged on the outstanding amount.
30 September 2003	Get your return in by this date if you want the Revenue to work out the tax for you and you are not filing by internet.
5 October 2003	If you do not get a tax return you must tell the Revenue by this date if you had taxable income in 2002–03 on which tax was not collected at source, or capital gains.
31 January 2004 (filing date)	You must return your 2002–03 tax return by this date (or within three months of the date of issue if the return was issued after the end of October), or pay a £100 penalty. There is a further £100 penalty if the return is still outstanding six months later (e.g. on 31 July 2004), but the Revenue can apply to charge a daily penalty of up to £60 instead. You must pay any tax still outstanding for 2002–03 by this date, or pay a surcharge of 5 per cent of the tax outstanding on 28 February, and a further 5 per cent of any tax still owed on 31 July (plus interest).
31 January 2005	Your tax office must tell you by now if they intend to open a formal 'enquiry' into your return. They have longer to do so if you sent your return in late, if further information comes to light, or if you have been negligent or fraudulent. If your return for 2002–03 is still not in, you can be penalised an amount equal to the tax that would have been payable under the return (so you'd have to pay double the tax due).

After your tax office gets your return

The Revenue do not acknowledge receipt unless specifically asked to do so. However, if you have made a very basic mistake, such as failing to sign and date it, your return may be rejected altogether. You will have to correct and resubmit it by the 31 January filing date, unless it is rejected after 17 January, in which case you have 14 days to resubmit it.

Once your tax return has been logged, an initial check is run for obvious mistakes, such as inconsistencies, faulty arithmetic and so on:

- *If the Revenue find a mistake,* they have nine months to correct any obvious mistakes and inform you. If you disagree with a correction, you have the right to reject it.
- *If you find a mistake on your return* you can correct it, if you let your tax office know within 12 months of the filing date (i.e. by 31 January 2005 for the 2002–03 tax year). But this won't protect you from Revenue action if they think you have been fraudulent or negligent. If you have overpaid tax due to a mistake or omission, you can claim relief up to five years after the filing date.

In addition to the Revenue's initial check, your return may be one of around 350,000 selected for further checking. The Revenue call this an 'enquiry'. An enquiry may be instigated because something looks odd, or entirely at random. You aren't told why the Revenue have chosen your return, although the questions they ask might identify particular areas of interest ('aspect' enquiries, unlike full enquiries, look at only part of the information on your return).

You need to keep all the documentation backing up the information in your return in case you are involved in an enquiry (and you have a legal duty to do so in any case, see Chapter 1). The Revenue have a code of practice explaining how enquiries are run, COP11 *Self Assessment. Local office enquiries.* However, you should consider getting professional help in responding to the enquiry. (Tips on choosing a tax adviser are given in Chapter 1.) You can claim their costs as a business expense, unless the enquiry uncovers fraudulent or negligent behaviour on your part.

Don't count your chickens

The Revenue have 12 months from the filing date to notify you if they are going to open an enquiry into your return – that is, by 31 January 2005 for returns for the 2002–03 tax year. So even if your return passed through the initial check without problems, don't assume that everything has been settled, and don't throw away any supporting paperwork.

Agreeing your tax liability

The Revenue will only send their tax calculation (on form SA302) to you if you have asked them to work out your tax, or if they disagree with your calculation.

If you have problems reconciling the calculation with your tax return, contact your tax office without delay. If your query is not resolved by the payment deadline pay the tax bill anyway – you will get a refund if one turns out to be due, whereas if you don't pay you could find yourself faced with interest and possibly a surcharge.

Check the Revenue's calculation notice

Even if you ask the Revenue to work out your tax for you, it is worth checking any calculation they send you on form SA302. Although computers have largely taken over, your information is transferred to the computer manually (unless you file by Internet). Check that all your information has been carried across correctly. The SA302 may also reveal a mistake you have made.

How the tax is paid (or repaid)

The Revenue open a tax account for everyone who is sent a tax return. You will get a statement of your account when there are changes to the items on it, or when a tax payment is due.

- *If the Revenue owe you money,* you will be sent a refund (plus interest) if you have ticked Question 19 on page 8 of the basic tax return, or if you write to your tax office asking for one. Otherwise, the money is credited to your account, plus interest.
- *If you owe the Revenue money,* it will be collected by adjusting your PAYE code, if you have income taxed under PAYE and you owe less than £2,000. If you want this to happen, make sure you do not tick box 23.1 on page 9, and get your tax return in by 30 September, or 30 December if filing by internet. Otherwise, the tax is due for payment on the same day as the latest date for sending back your return – that, is by 31 January 2004 for the 2002–03 tax year.

Payments on account

Unless the bulk of your income tax can be collected at source through PAYE, you have to pay tax in instalments, called 'payments on account'. Note that these apply only to income tax and Class 4 National Insurance contributions – capital gains tax is paid in one lump sum on 31 January following the end of the tax year.

Each payment on account is half of your previous year's income tax bill (excluding tax deducted at source). However, you do not have to make payments on account if more than 80 per cent of your tax bill for the previous tax year was met from tax paid at source, or if the tax *not* deducted at source was less than £500. So you are unlikely to have to make payments on account if you are an employee or pensioner.

Payments on account are made on 31 January during the tax year, and 31 July just after the end of the tax year, with a final 'balancing' payment on 31 January following the end of the tax year (by which time your tax return should be in and your final tax bill calculated). If your return is issued after 31 October, you have three months from the date of issue to make your final payment.

Payments on account – a summary

If you are liable to make payments on account for the 2002–03 tax year:

- The first payment on account was due on 31 January 2003 (half your tax bill for 2001–02 not met at source).
- The second payment on account is due on 31 July 2003 (half your tax bill for 2001–02 not met at source).
- If these two payments come to *less* than your total tax bill for 2002–03, a final, balancing payment will be due on 31 January 2004 (unless it is under £2,000 and can be collected through your PAYE code). If they come to *more* than your tax bill for 2002–03, you will be due a repayment instead, which can be set against your first payment on account for the 2003–04 tax year.

Example 3.1: **Calculating payments on account**

Sam is a self-employed plumber. His tax bill for 2002–03 was £8,000, including his Class 4 National Insurance contributions. He made no taxable capital gains. Sam's payments on account for 2003–04 are £8,000 ÷ 2 = £4,000 each, which he pays in January 2004 and July 2004. However, 2003–04 turns out to be a good year and Sam's tax bill comes to £10,000. He has a further £10,000 − £8,000 = £2,000 to pay by 31 January 2005.

On 31 January 2005 Sam must also make his first payment on account for 2004–05. This is half his tax bill for 2003–04, that is £10,000 ÷ 2 = £5,000. The total tax due on 31 January is therefore £2,000 + £5,000 = £7,000.

Planning your tax payments

The final payment for one year overlaps with the first payment on account for the next. If your income is rising, year on year (or if you pay less tax at source, or expect to pay capital gains tax), you need to be careful to put enough cash aside to meet the January payment.

Reducing your payments on account

If your taxable income is falling, you can claim to reduce each payment on account to half of your anticipated tax bill (ignoring capital gains tax). You can claim either in Question 18 of your tax return, or by completing form SA303 that should come with your statement of account.

Your tax office will not 'approve' your claim – you simply go ahead and pay the reduced amount – but your claim may be rejected if you have not given a valid reason for reducing your payment. Note also that:

- If your tax bill turns out to be more than you anticipate, you will have to pay interest on the difference between the full payment and the amount you actually paid, from the date the payment was due – and at a higher rate than the Revenue pay you if you have overpaid tax.
- If you make a fraudulent or negligent claim, the Revenue can charge you a penalty equal to the extra tax that should have been paid.

Example 3.2: **Claiming to reduce your payments on account**

Sam had an unusually good year in 2003–04 (see Example 3.1) and his tax bill of £10,000 means that he should make payments of account of £10,000 ÷ 2 = £5,000 in January and July 2005. However, he has an accident in September 2004 that he thinks will bring his tax bill for 2004–05 down to about £7,000. In his tax return for the 2003–04 tax year he makes a claim to reduce his payments on account for 2004–05 to £7,000 ÷ 2 = £3,500.

Accounting for interest

If you receive a statement of account that includes interest, you might want to pay a bit extra to cover any further interest clocked up from the date of the statement to the date you pay. Your tax office should be able to give you an idea of how much.

Example 3.3: **Understanding your statement of account**

In June 2003 Steven received the statement shown in Figure 3.1. (Note that for the sake of illustration we've included more items than you're likely to see on your own statement.)

The first section covers Steven's balancing payment (**2**) for the 2001–02 tax year. The 'adjustment' (**4**) is because Steven's tax return was amended to include a Gift Aid payment, on which £150 higher-rate tax relief was due. This also affects his payments on account – £75 is deducted from each (**1**). The £170 credit (**5**), by contrast, is tax relief on a pension contribution, which, because it has been 'carried back' from the next tax year, does not affect his payments on account.

The next section shows that Steven miscalculated his January payment on account (**1**), because some of the £4,000 he paid (**3**) went towards his balancing payment for the previous year (**2**). He paid £286 too little, on which he owes £9.38 in interest (**6**), making a total of £295.38 (**7**) by the time he received this statement. So, by 31 July 2003 he must pay £295.38 plus his £4,127.46 payment on account, £4,422.84 in total. But he will still owe some additional interest if he delays payment until then (see page 47).

What to tell the Inland Revenue

Once you are within the self-assessment system, the Revenue send you the forms they think you need, with notes to help you fill them in. The tax return is 10 pages long, but in 2003 the Revenue are also piloting a four-page version for people with simple affairs. As well as the basic self-assessment tax return there are forms to cover such matters as capital gains, self employment and rental income.

Check that you have all the supplementary forms you need, by looking at Questions 1 to 9 on page 2 of the basic return. You can get whatever forms you need from the Inland Revenue Orderline or the Revenue's website (see the Fact File), or you can use a computerised tax return.

If you have to use provisional figures, make sure you tick box 23.2 on page 9 of the return (see page 56). You must send in final figures as soon as you get them. Tell the Revenue in one of the spaces given for 'additional information' if there are any provisional or estimated figures – for example where you have had to use a valuation of property.

Figure 3.1: Steven's Statement of Account (see Example 3.3)

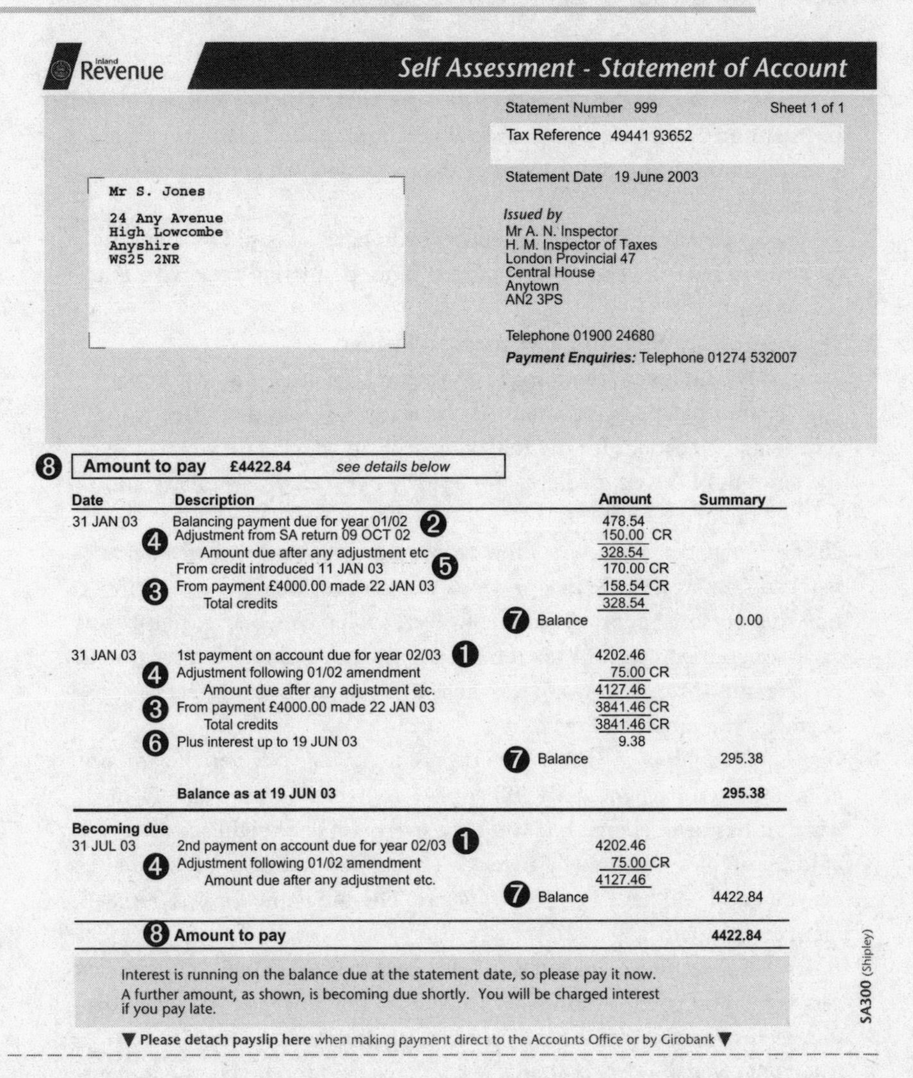

Inland Revenue — **Self Assessment - Statement of Account**

Statement Number 999 Sheet 1 of 1

Tax Reference 49441 93652

Statement Date 19 June 2003

Mr S. Jones
24 Any Avenue
High Lowcombe
Anyshire
WS25 2NR

Issued by
Mr A. N. Inspector
H. M. Inspector of Taxes
London Provincial 47
Central House
Anytown
AN2 3PS

Telephone 01900 24680

Payment Enquiries: Telephone 01274 532007

❽ **Amount to pay £4422.84** *see details below*

Date	Description	Amount	Summary
31 JAN 03	Balancing payment due for year 01/02 ❷	478.54	
	❹ Adjustment from SA return 09 OCT 02	150.00 CR	
	Amount due after any adjustment etc	328.54	
	From credit introduced 11 JAN 03 ❺	170.00 CR	
	❸ From payment £4000.00 made 22 JAN 03	158.54 CR	
	Total credits	328.54	
	❼ Balance		0.00
31 JAN 03	1st payment on account due for year 02/03 ❶	4202.46	
	❹ Adjustment following 01/02 amendment	75.00 CR	
	Amount due after any adjustment etc.	4127.46	
	❸ From payment £4000.00 made 22 JAN 03	3841.46 CR	
	Total credits	3841.46 CR	
	❻ Plus interest up to 19 JUN 03	9.38	
	❼ Balance		295.38
	Balance as at 19 JUN 03		**295.38**
Becoming due			
31 JUL 03	2nd payment on account due for year 02/03 ❶	4202.46	
	❹ Adjustment following 01/02 amendment	75.00 CR	
	Amount due after any adjustment etc.	4127.46	
	❼ Balance		4422.84
	❽ **Amount to pay**		**4422.84**

Interest is running on the balance due at the statement date, so please pay it now.
A further amount, as shown, is becoming due shortly. You will be charged interest if you pay late.

▼ **Please detach payslip here** when making payment direct to the Accounts Office or by Girobank ▼

SA300 (Shipley)

Understanding your statement of account

Statements of account can be tricky to interpret (see Figure 3.1).

1 *Payments on account/Net claims to reduce payment.* The full amount of each payment on account is shown even if you have made a claim to reduce your payments – but the amount of the reduction will appear under each payment.
2 *Balancing payment.* This appears only if you have a tax bill outstanding at 31 January after the end of the tax year (after deducting your payments on account).
3 *Payments made.* What you have paid, and when.
4 *Adjustment.* An amendment made to your return after it is sent in may change your balancing payment (if one is due). It may also affect your payments on account for the following year, in which case you will see the amount of the adjustment split equally between your January and July payments on account.
5 *Credits introduced.* There are a few types of tax-allowable payment that you can treat as if made in a previous tax year, for example a contribution to a personal pension plan. However, such payments are not treated as an amendment to your tax return, nor do they reduce your payments on account. Instead, they are shown as a 'credit' and set against the next payment you are due to make.
6 *Interest/net supplement.* If you have been late paying your tax, the amount of interest you have incurred will appear, together with the date from which it has been charged. If you have overpaid, you might see an amount of 'Net supplement' instead. This is Revenue-speak for the interest you get if you have overpaid your tax. The full name for it is 'repayment supplement'.
7 *Balance/balance unallocated.* If you have paid more than necessary, the excess is held on your account and set against any other tax you owe. Anything left over is shown as your 'balance unallocated'.
8 *Amount to pay/You have overpaid.* If you have paid too much, the money usually stays in your account, to be set against any future tax, unless you ask for it to be paid to you. You can claim a repayment either by ticking Question 19 on the tax return or by writing separately.

Calculating your own tax

Unless you have asked the Revenue to work out your tax, you will have to tell them how much you think you owe. This includes income tax, capital gains tax, Class 4 National Insurance (the type payable on business profits – you do not need to calculate any other type of National Insurance), and student loan repayments.

The Revenue send a tax calculation guide with tax returns to help you do this, but this will not help people with capital gains and some types of income (listed on the front page of the guide). A comprehensive tax calculation guide is available through the Inland Revenue's Orderline and its website.

Tips for calculating your own tax

- It can be a complicated process, so work on a rough copy first and check it before completing the real thing.
- Forget the pennies – you are allowed to round to the nearest £ in your favour. This means rounding income down and deductions up.
- Use the Revenue's help sheets. Many of these contain work sheets to help with particular calculations – e.g. IR330 *Pension payments* shows you how to work out and keep track of your pension contributions.
- Make sure you take into account amounts already paid or included in your PAYE code, and so on. When taking information from your statements on account be careful to use figures for the right tax year (excluding balancing payments for an earlier tax year).
- Give yourself plenty of time. Avoid a last-minute panic in late January.
- Consider using a computerised return or filing by internet to get the calculation done automatically.

Filling in your tax return

Start by filling in page 2 of the basic tax return. This is a checklist of the kinds of income you have, and which supplementary pages you need. Other parts of the return deal with the following:

- Questions 10 and 12 cover savings and investments – see Chapter 10.
- Question 11 deals with pensions and benefits – see Chapter 7.
- Question 13 covers any other income that doesn't fit in elsewhere, such as odd bits of freelance income.
- Questions 14, 15 and 16 cover tax reliefs and allowances you can claim – see Chapter 4, and Chapter 7 for pension contributions.
- Questions 17 to 24 cover other information needed – see below.

Question 17 – Student loan repayments

Tick the 'Yes' box in this question only if you are liable to make *income-contingent* student loan repayments, where the rate of repayment depends on your income. This applies only if you took out a student loan after August 1998. (See Chapters 1 and 2 for more on these loans.)

If you have one of these loans, remember to:

- Enter repayments deducted from your salary on your employment supplementary pages, if you are an employee (see Chapter 5).
- Work out the overall amount of repayments due, if you are calculating your own tax. Use Inland Revenue Help Sheet IR235 *Calculation of student loan repayments on an income-contingent student loan.*

Question 18 – Do you want to calculate your tax?

Tick the 'Yes' box in this question if you want to calculate your own tax and student loan repayment, or if you are filing by internet. You do not have to tick 'yes' if you have sent in your return too late to get the Revenue to do the calculation for you (i.e. after 30 September), but you will need to work out how much to pay if the Revenue do not tell you by 31 January. The other boxes in this question need to be completed only if you tick 'Yes'.

The Revenue's tax calculation guide will help you work out the tax to enter in boxes 18.2A, 18.3 and 18.7, so go through the guide before completing this question.

Boxes 18.1 and 18.2 Unpaid tax included in your tax code

If you are taxed under PAYE, any tax outstanding from one tax year may be collected by adjusting your tax code for a future year. Amounts to go in box 18.1 will be shown as 'Unpaid tax' on the Coding Notice (P2) you should have received from the Revenue early in 2002. Amounts to go in box 18.2 will appear as an 'estimated underpayment' in your 2003 Coding Notice. (Inland Revenue help sheet IR208 *Payslips and Coding Notices* tells you what to look for.)

Boxes 18.4 and 18.5 Tax owed or overpaid for earlier years

You will have something to enter here if you want income or expenditure for the 2002–03 tax year treated as if earned or incurred in 2001–02, thus affecting your 2001–02 tax bill. This applies if you are carrying back contributions to a personal or stakeholder pension (see Chapter 7), if you are carrying back business losses or receipts (see Chapter 6) or if you are a farmer, writer or artist claiming to average your income over several years (see Inland Revenue help sheets IR224 and IR234). Enter the difference that the amount carried back has made to your tax bill for 2001–02, in box 18.4 if you it means you owe extra tax, in box 18.5 if it is a tax saving.

Boxes 18.6 and 18.7 Claiming to reduce a payment on account

Tick box 18.6 if you are claiming to reduce your payments on account due in January and July 2004. Write the reasons for your claim in the 'Additional information' box on page 9 (e.g. your income has fallen), and write the reduced amount of your first payment in box 18.7.

Box 18.8 2003–04 tax you are reclaiming now

You may have something to enter here if you make a pension payment or trading loss after 5 April 2003, but you want to claim tax relief for it in your 2002–03 tax return. You need to work out the difference this makes to your tax for the 2002–03 tax year and enter the saving here. In some circumstances, you can also treat a loss you make on some types of shares in the same way, in which case you should have an entry at box 8.13B of the Capital Gains pages (see page 266).

Example 3.4: **Completing boxes 18.5 and 18.8**

George regularly 'carries back' part of his personal pension contributions, so that they are treated as if paid in the previous year. This allows him to contribute the maximum once he knows his business profits for the year just past.

- In December 2002 (after sending in his 2001–02 tax return) George decides to carry back £1,560 of his 2002 contributions to 2001–02. This is worth £2,000 after adding basic-rate tax relief of £440.
- In November 2003 George decides to carry back £3,000 of his 2003 contributions to 2002–03. This is worth £3,846 after adding basic-rate tax relief of £846.

George can claim carry-back relief for both payments in his 2002–03 tax return, because it does not have to be sent in until 31 January 2004.

First, he needs to work out what difference the payments would make to his tax bills for the previous years. His top rate of tax in both years was 40%, but he has already had 22% basic-rate relief. He is due a further 40% − 22% = 18% on both payments.

- For his 2002 payment, he is due a further £2,000 × 18% = £360. George enters £360 in box 18.5.
- For his 2003 payment, he is due a further £3,846 × 18% = £692. This goes in his 2002–03 tax return as well, but in box 18.8.

The extra relief for both payments will appear on his statement of account. See Figure 3.2 for what George enters in these boxes.

Question 19 – Do you want to claim a repayment if you have paid too much tax?

Tick this box if you want any repayment to be made now. It can be sent to you, or your nominee (such as a tax adviser), or credited to a bank or building society account. But note that the Revenue do not normally send repayments of less than £10, unless you ask them to. If you don't tick this box, any tax overpaid will be set against a future tax bill. From 2004, you will be able to waive a repayment in favour of charity.

Figure 3.2: Completing Question 18 (see Example 3.4)

OTHER INFORMATION *for the year ended 5 April 2003, continued*

Q18 Do you want to calculate your tax and, if appropriate, any Student Loan Repayment? YES ✓

Use your Tax Calculation Guide then fill in boxes 18.1 to 18.8 as appropriate.

• Unpaid tax for earlier years **included in your tax code for 2002-03**	18.1	£
• Tax due for 2002-03 included in your tax code for a later year	18.2	£
• Student Loan Repayment due	18.2A	£
• Total tax, Class 4 NIC and Student Loan Repayment due for 2002-03 **before** you made any payments on account *(put the amount in brackets if an overpayment)*	18.3	£ 13,682
• Tax due for earlier years	18.4	£
• Tax overpaid for earlier years	18.5	£ 360
• Tick box 18.6 if you are claiming to reduce your 2003-04 payments on account. Make sure you enter the **reduced** amount of your first payment in box 18.7. Then, in the 'Additional information' box, box 23.5 on page 9, say why you are making a claim	18.6	
• Your first payment on account for 2003-04 *(include the pence)*	18.7	£ 6,841
• Any 2003-04 tax you are reclaiming now	18.8	£ 692

Question 20 – Have you already had any 2002–03 tax refunded or set off?

You may have received a tax refund part way through the tax year, for example if you are a non-taxpayer and reclaimed tax deducted from a savings account, or if you became unemployed and had a tax refund from the DWP. Enter any such refunds here, including amounts that have not actually been paid to you, but set against tax you owe. However, only include tax which has been refunded directly by your tax office or the DWP – tax refunds from other sources (such as your employer) will be taken into account in your P60 or other end-of-year statement.

Questions 21 and 22 – Personal details

This information keeps your tax record up to date.

Question 23 – Additional information

Box 23.1 – Tick if you do not want tax collected through your tax code

If you pay tax under PAYE, you submit your tax return by 30 September (30 December if you file by internet) and you owe less than £2,000, your tax office will collect it by adjusting your PAYE code, unless you tick here to say that you would prefer to pay it in a lump sum.

Box 23.2 – Tick if this tax return contains provisional figures

The Revenue accepts provisional amounts only if you have taken 'all reasonable steps' to get the final figures (see page 41 for excuses that are not accepted). You need to write at the bottom of the page why the figures are provisional, the box numbers for the figures affected, and the date by which you expect to supply them. If the Revenue do not accept your reasons, they may decide to open an enquiry into your return and you may be penalised if they believe you have been negligent or fraudulent.

Box 23.3 – Tick if you are claiming relief now for 2003–04 losses

This applies if you want to carry back business losses (see Chapter 6) or losses entered in box 8.13B of the capital gains tax pages (see page 266).

Box 23.4 – Tick if you are claiming to have post-cessation etc. receipts taxed as income of an earlier year

This may apply if you have closed a business. If you want income received after closure to be taxed as if received on the date you closed down, tick this box and write in the details in box 23.5.

Question 24 – Declaration and signatures

You must sign and date the return, or it will be rejected. If you are signing someone else's return – because, say, they have died and you are their executor, or they are incapable of signing because of age, or mental or physical incapacity, and you have been legally appointed to act for them, you must also enter the capacity in which you are signing in box 24.2.

Common mistakes on tax returns

- Failing to sign and date your tax return
- Ticking one of the 'Yes' boxes in Questions 1 to 9, suggesting that you need supplementary pages, but failing to send in the correct pages
- Giving information on separate bits of paper, rather than in the tax return
- Entering notes such as 'see accounts' in boxes, rather than giving figures
- Failing to sign box 19.12 if you want a repayment to be sent to a nominee
- Failing to give a reason why you are claiming to reduce your payments on account, if box 18.6 is ticked

Record-keeping

You must keep adequate records to support your tax return. Chapter 1 explains the general rules and other chapters of this book list relevant documents to keep. Also keep your statements of account, a photocopy of everything you send the Revenue and notes of any phone calls. If you forget to keep a copy of your completed tax return, though, your tax office should be able to give you one.

Sorting out your records

The hard part of completing your tax return is collecting the necessary information. It helps to gather it together as it comes in, in a separate file for each tax year.

Tax-planning hints

1 If your circumstances have changed, send back your previous year's return (or notify your tax office) early so that the information is logged before your tax office decides whether to send you a tax return.
2 Don't leave submitting your return until the last minute, particularly if

you also have to make a tax payment. It gets very confusing if the Revenue don't have time to update your records before they issue your next statement of account.

3 The Revenue only accept very good excuses for being late with your return or your tax. Get proof of posting if you are sending in a paper return. If you are very close to the deadline, consider filing by Internet.
4 Information on your tax return is transferred to the Revenue's computers manually. Check everything the Revenue send you about your calculation.
5 If your tax office issues a formal decision or charges a penalty you disagree with, remember that you usually have only 30 days in which to appeal.
6 The Revenue have until 31 January 2005 to notify you if they are going to open an enquiry into your return for the 2002–03 tax year. Hang on to your records until at least that date, or until 31 January 2009 if you are self-employed or have letting income.
7 If the Revenue do open an enquiry into your return, you can claim any professional costs (e.g. your accountant's) as a business expense.
8 If you pay tax through PAYE, you can ask for tax you owe up to £2,000 to be collected by adjusting your PAYE code. To do this, send your tax return in by 30 September (or 30 December if filing by Internet).
9 If you have to make payments on account, and your income is rising, be careful to put enough cash aside to meet the January payment.
10 If you receive a statement on account that includes interest, pay a little bit extra to cover any interest clocked up between receiving the statement and making the payment.

4

Allowances and reliefs

Allowances and reliefs both save you tax. In recent years the distinction between the two has become less clear, as successive governments have phased out some allowances in favour of new forms of relief.

The most recent are Child Tax Credit and Working Tax Credit. These are state benefits administered by the Revenue that don't appear on the tax return, so they are covered in Chapter 7. However, the precursor of Child Tax Credit – Children's Tax Credit – does appear on your 2002–03 tax return and is dealt with in this chapter.

This chapter covers the main allowances and reliefs. Other forms of tax relief are covered in chapters dealing with specific areas of tax (such as pensions). Use Table 4.1 to see what allowances, credits and reliefs you might be able to claim and where to find out more.

Deadlines for relief

You must claim a relief within six years of 31 January in the tax year to which it relates (or later if you did not get the relief because of a mistake by the Revenue). So as long as you claim by 31 January 2004, you can claim reliefs to which you were entitled for tax years back to 1997–98. This includes allowances that have since been abolished, such as additional personal allowance (for single parents), widow's bereavement allowance and married couple's allowance if born after 5 April 1935.

Does this affect you?

Table 4.1: Allowances, credits and reliefs

Who can claim?	*Which relief?*
Anybody (except some non-residents)	Personal allowance (see this chapter)
People who were born before 6 April 1935 (or whose spouse or ex-spouse was)	Married couple's allowance and relief for maintenance or alimony payments (see this chapter)
People looking after a child under 16 or up to 18 in full-time education	Child Tax Credit (see Chapter 7)
Blind people	Blind person's allowance (see this chapter)
Contributors to a pension scheme	Relief for pension contributions (see Chapter 7)
Contributors to some (rare) types of life insurance	See page 73
Employees	Relief for some expenses (see Chapter 5)
Investors in Venture Capital Trusts, Enterprise Investment Schemes and Community Investment Schemes	Income tax relief for money invested (see this chapter and Chapter 10)
People giving to charity (whether cash, investments or land)	Gift Aid and covenants to charity (see this chapter)
People with some types of loan	Business loans (see this chapter and Chapter 6)
	Loans to buy property to rent out (see Chapter 8)
People with overseas income	Foreign tax credit relief (see Chapter 9)
Sole traders, partners	Relief for some business expenditure (see Chapter 6)
	Reliefs for business losses (see Chapter 6)
Working people with low to moderate incomes	Working Tax Credit (see Chapter 7)

How tax relief is worked out

Some allowances and reliefs are more valuable than others. The factors that affect the value of a relief are:

- *The types of income or gains from which you can deduct a relief.* Expenses can be deducted only from the income to which they relate (e.g. property expenses from property income), although if business expenses create a loss, you can claim to set the loss against your other income for the year. Allowances and some reliefs can be set against your income as a whole.
- *The rate at which the allowance or relief is given.* The most valuable (e.g. personal and blind person's allowances, pension contributions, Gift Aid donations and loan interest) are deducted from your overall income at the start of the tax calculation. This reduces your taxable income and therefore any higher-rate tax liability. So a basic-rate taxpayer in 2002–03 saves £22 for each £100 of the allowance/relief, and a higher-rate taxpayer benefits by £40 per £100. Other allowances and reliefs are given only against lower tax rates, not the higher rates – e.g. 10 per cent relief for married couple's allowance and Children's Tax Credit.
- *When non-taxpayers can benefit.* You get basic-rate tax relief on personal and stakeholder pension contributions even if you have no taxable income. But other allowances and reliefs are available only if you have enough taxable income against which to set them.
- *When you can transfer unused allowance to someone else.* You can only do this with blind person's allowance, married couple's allowance and Children's Tax Credit. (See page 80 for how to transfer allowances.)

Personal allowance

Everybody gets a basic personal allowance, except some non-residents (see Chapter 9). This makes the first slice of your income free of income tax. For the 2002–03 and 2003–04 tax years the minimum personal allowance is £4,615, but you may get more if you are aged 65 or over.

If you are aged at least 65 at any point in the tax year you are eligible for an increased personal allowance – the maximum amounts are shown in Table 4.2. A further increase applies for tax years in which you are at least 75. However, the extra age-related amount is gradually withdrawn, once your total income rises above a certain level known as the 'income limit'. It is withdrawn at the rate of £1 for every £2 of income above the income limit, until you reach the minimum personal allowance.

What is 'income'?

When you are working out whether you are above the income limit for age-related allowances, you can deduct the following from your income:

- tax-free income
- pension contributions
- charitable donations and loan interest that qualify for tax relief
- relief for business losses.

Example 4.1: **Calculating age-related allowance**

Harry is 80, so the maximum personal allowance he could claim in 2002–03 was £6,370. However, Harry's income was £20,000, which is above the income limit of £17,900 (in 2003–03), so his personal allowance was reduced. To find the reduced allowance, he checks to see whether he can deduct anything from his income. He can claim tax relief on charitable donations of £156 (£200 after adding back basic-rate relief), so his total income was £20,000 – £200 = £19,800.

His income was still above the income limit, by £19,800 – £17,900 = £1,900. His allowance was reduced by half of this: £1,900 ÷ 2 = £950. So his personal allowance for 2002–03 was £6,370 – £950 = £5,420.

Table 4.2: Personal allowances

For people aged 65 and over, the maximum allowance is reduced by £1 for every £2 of income above £17,900 in 2002–03 (£18,300 in 2003–04). This table shows the amount of allowance at the income limit, and the income level at which it falls to the minimum. See Example 4.1 for how to work out your allowance if your income is between these figures.

		2002–03 tax year	*2003–04 tax year*
64 and under		£4,615	£4,615
65 to 74	Maximum	£6,100 if income is below £17,900	£6,610 if income is below £18,300
	Minimum	*£4,615 if income is £20,870 or more*	*£4,615 if income is £22,290 or more*
75 or over	Maximum	£6,370 if income is below £17,900	£6,720 if income is below £18,300
	Minimum	*£4,615 if income is £21,410 or more*	*£4,615 if income is £22,510 or more*

Making the most of your personal allowance

If your taxable income is below your personal allowance, part of your allowance is wasted – you cannot transfer it to anybody else. However, you may be able to make better use of your allowances in your family by transferring income from higher-income family members to those with lower income, e.g. by putting investments in the name of a non-working spouse. There are three things to note:

- Transferring income to your children does not work if the child is under 18. Although children have their own allowances from birth, any income arising from gifts from a parent counts as the parent's if it amounts to more than £100 a year. This does not apply to gifts from a grandparent or other relative.
- The transfer has to be a genuine gift, with no strings attached.
- The transfer may be liable to capital gains tax, if you are not married to the recipient.

Saving age-related allowances

These are some ways of hanging on to your age-related allowance if you are aged 65 or more and your income pushes you above the income limit (£18,300 in 2003–04):

- Investing in tax-free investments (see Chapter 10), or those which produce capital rather than income.
- If you are close to the income limit, but expect your income to drop, try to put off receiving further income until it does – for example, by deferring your state pension (see DWP booklet NP46, from social security offices).
- Donations to charity through Gift Aid or pension contributions reduce your taxable income and so can increase your age-related allowances.
- Beware of making a taxable gain on insurance bonds (see Chapter 10). Even though basic-rate tax on the payout is settled by the insurance company, the gain counts as income for age-related allowances.
- If you are married, consider splitting income-producing assets between you.

Blind person's allowance

This is worth £1,480 in the 2002–03 tax year (£1,510 in 2003–04) and you can claim it if you are so blind that you cannot perform any work for which eyesight is essential. You automatically qualify if you are registered as blind (but not partially sighted) with the local authority. You must register in order to claim unless your local authority does not keep a register. You can claim for the year before you were registered, provided that you had evidence of blindness, such as an ophthalmologist's certificate.

The tax relief is worked out in the same way as personal allowance – an extra £1,480 of your income (£1,510 in 2003–04) is tax-free. If your income is too low for you to use up all your allowances, you can transfer any unused allowance to your husband or wife (see page 80). To do this, either tick box 16.27 or 16.28 on your tax return, or ask your tax office for form 575. If you are unlikely to use your allowance in future tax years and your spouse could benefit from it, your tax office may adjust your spouse's PAYE code to allow for the expected transfer.

Married couple's allowance

You can now claim this relief only if either you or your spouse was born before 6 April 1935. You must be living with your spouse, or, if not, neither of you must intend to make the separation permanent.

Unlike the personal allowance, you get relief at only 10 per cent of the full allowance, knocked off your tax bill at the end of the calculation.

The amount of the married couple's allowance depends on age and income – the age of the oldest spouse, and the total income of the husband. The maximum amounts are shown in Table 4.3 on page 66.

Once the husband's total income rises above the income limit (£17,900 in 2002–03, £18,300 in 2003–04), his age-related personal allowance is reduced. Then, when his personal allowance has been reduced to the minimum level (or if he is under 65 and gets only the minimum allowance anyway), the married couple's allowance is reduced, by £1 for every £2 of excess income remaining, until it reaches the minimum of £2,110 in 2002–03 (£2,150 in 2003–04). This is why, in Table 4.3, the age of the husband is relevant. Example 4.2 on page 67 shows how the married couple's allowance is worked out.

Note, though, that you get the full allowance for a tax year only if you were married before 6 May in that year. In the year of marriage, you get one-twelfth of the full allowance for each full tax month of marriage (a tax month runs from the 6th of one month to the 5th of the next). And you cannot claim both the married couple's allowance and Child Tax Credit in any one tax year – you have to choose one or the other.

The married couple's allowance is normally given to the husband, but the wife can claim half or all of the minimum allowance (i.e. £2,110 in 2002–03, £2,150 in 2003–04) provided that she does so before the start of the tax year. But whoever claims it, if it turns out that his or her income was too low to make full use of it, the unused part can be transferred to the other spouse after the end of the tax year.

Allowances if you are widowed or divorced

On death, any married couple's or blind person's (but not personal) allowance still unused is transferred to the surviving partner.

On divorce, the partner claiming the married couple's allowance continues to get it for the remainder of the tax year, plus – if either partner was

Table 4.3: Married couple's allowance if born before 6 April 1935
(See Example 4.2 for how to work out allowance if husband's income is between the amounts shown.)

2002–03 tax year		*Husband aged under 65*	*Husband aged 65 to 74*	*Husband aged 75 or over*
Older spouse aged 67 to 74	Maximum	£5,465 if husband's income is below £17,900	£5,465 if husband's income is below £20,870	–
	Minimum	*£2,110 if husband's income is £24,610 or more*	*£2,110 if husband's income is £27,580 or more*	*n/a*
Older spouse aged 75 or over	Maximum	£5,535 if husband's income is below £17,900	£5,535 if husband's income is below £20,870	£5,535 if husband's income is below £21,410
	Minimum	*£2,110 if husband's income is £24,750 or more*	*£2,110 if husband's income is £27,720 or more*	*£2,110 if husband's income is £28,260 or more*
2003–04 tax year				
Older spouse aged 68 to 74	Maximum	£5,565 if husband's income is below £18,300	£5,565 if husband's income is below £22,290	–
	Minimum	*£2,150 if husband's income is £25,130 or more*	*£2,150 if husband's income is £29,120 or more*	*n/a*
Older spouse aged 75 or over	Maximum	£5,635 if husband's income is below £18,300	£5,635 if husband's income is below £22,290	£5,635 if husband's income is below £22,510
	Minimum	*£2,150 if husband's income is £25,270 or more*	*£2,150 if husband's income is £29,260 or more*	*£2,150 if husband's income is £29,480 or more*

born before 6 April 1935 – tax relief on any maintenance paid under a legally binding agreement (see page 70).

From the start of the next tax year after being divorced or widowed, you are taxed as a single person. If you remarry in the same tax year as being divorced or widowed, and you were already getting married couple's allowance, you can continue to get it at the current rate for the remainder of the tax year. Alternatively, you can put in a new claim based on your new spouse's age, but you will only get one-twelfth of the allowance for each month of the new marriage.

Example 4.2: **Calculating married couple's allowance**

Janet and John are both 70. They use Table 4.3 to check the married couple's allowance they can claim for 2002–03. This shows that the allowance would be £5,465 if John's total income was below £20,870, and £2,110 if his income exceeded £27,580. However, John's total income was £25,000.

1	John works out the total amount by which his personal and married couple's allowances will be reduced, by taking the amount of his income above the income limit and halving it.	Total income £25,000 Income limit −£17,900 £7,100 ÷ 2 Reduction £3,550
2	John now finds the maximum personal allowance for someone of his age, and applies the reduction. Because the personal allowance cannot be reduced below a set minimum, only £1,485 of the reduction will take his allowance to the minimum of £4,615.	Personal allowance: Maximum £6,100 Reduction −£1,485 Minimum £4,615
3	Finally, he deducts any remaining reduction (£3,550 − £1,485 = £2,065) from the married couple's allowance. The result is still above the minimum of £2,110, so he can claim £3,400.	Married allowance: Maximum £5,465 Reduction −£2,065 £3,400

Children's Tax Credit

Children's Tax Credit was replaced by Child Tax Credit from 6 April 2003, but do not be misled by the similarity of the names. The old tax credit works in a similar way to the married couple's allowance, and reduces your overall tax bill. The new tax credit (covered in Chapter 7) is effectively a state benefit and does not change your income tax liability.

You can still claim Children's Tax Credit for the 2002–03 tax year if you have not already done so, by completing Question 16 of the tax return or contacting your tax office. Children's Tax Credit started in 2001–02, so contact your tax office if you have not already claimed for that year.

In 2002–03, Children's Tax Credit was £5,290, or £10,490 if your child was born during the year. However, you get tax relief at only 10 per cent of the full amount, taken off your tax bill at the end of the calculation, so it is worth £529 (£1,049 if you had a baby). You lose credit by £2 for every £3 of income liable to higher-rate tax, so you are unlikely to receive any if your income was above £42,450 (£50,250 if you had a baby).

You can claim for 2002–03 if at least one child born after 6 April 1986 was living with you at some point between 6 April 2002 and 5 April 2003. You can get only one credit per family, however many children you have. If you are living with someone, you get only one credit between you.

The person with the higher income normally gets the relief, and must make the claim if a higher-rate taxpayer. Otherwise, you can share the claim. If it turns out that you didn't have enough income to use your share, you can transfer the unused amount to your partner.

Example 4.3: **Losing Children's Tax Credit**

Eleanor is a single parent with a 10-year-old son. She claimed Children's Tax Credit for 2002–03, but £3,600 of her income was liable to higher-rate tax. The full allowance in 2002–03 was £5,290, but she lost £2 for every £3 of income liable to higher-rate tax. She lost £3,600 × 2 ÷ 3 = £2,400, leaving tax credit of £5,290 – £2,400 = £2,890. She received tax relief of 10% of this amount, i.e. £289, deducted from her tax bill.

Tax reliefs

Relief for loan interest

You cannot claim tax relief on a loan to buy your home. However, you can claim relief at your top rate of tax on the following:

- *Loans to buy shares in (or to fund) a 'close' company.* You must either own more than 5 per cent of the shares, or own at least some shares and work in the business most of the time as a director or with significant responsibilities. A close company is one controlled either by its directors or by fewer than six shareholders (or other key 'participators').
- *Loans to buy shares in an employee-controlled company for which you work most of your time.*
- *Loans to buy shares in a co-operative.*
- *Loans to buy into (or fund) a trading or professional partnership.*
- *Loans to buy equipment or machinery you need for your work as an employee.* Note, though, that you cannot claim relief on a loan to buy a car or motorbike you use for your work (see Chapter 5). If the equipment is used partly privately, you can claim relief only on the business part of the interest.
- *Loans to buy equipment or machinery to be used by a partnership of which you are a member* (unless the partnership has already claimed the loan interest as a business expense, see Chapter 6).

Note that you cannot claim relief for interest on credit card debts or bank overdrafts (unless it is a business expense that can be claimed against profits). And you can claim relief only on the interest itself, not any capital repayments. (See Inland Revenue help sheet IR340 *Interest eligible for relief on qualifying loans.*)

Any tax relief of this sort will be given through your self-assessment return, or by adjusting your PAYE code. The lender should give you a 'certificate of interest' paid, which you should keep to back up your claim.

You can, of course, also claim relief for interest on loans for business purposes (including loans to buy a property you rent out). However, you get the relief by deducting the interest from your business profits (see Chapter 6 or Chapter 8).

Relief for maintenance or alimony

Provided that either you or your ex-spouse was born before 6 April 1935, you can get tax relief on the alimony or maintenance you pay, up to £2,110 in 2002–03 (£2,150 in 2003–04). The maximum is the same however many ex-spouses you support. The rate of relief is 10 per cent, so the maximum tax saving in 2003–04 is £2,150 × 10% = £215.

You must make the payments under a legally binding agreement, such as a written agreement, a court order or a Child Support Agency assessment – voluntary payments do not count. Legally binding agreements made in most European countries (listed in the notes to the tax return) also count. But be careful about the wording: to claim relief the payments must be for the maintenance of your ex-spouse or any children aged under 21. Payments directly to a child do not qualify, but you can claim for payments to an ex-spouse under a Child Support Agency assessment.

Note that tax relief stops on the date an ex-spouse remarries.

Relief for some investments

Tax relief usually applies only to investment income or gains, but these forms of investment give you tax relief on the money you invest:

- Approved pension schemes (such as most occupational pension schemes, personal pensions and stakeholder pensions – see Chapter 7)
- Venture Capital Trusts (VCTs)
- Enterprise Investment Schemes (EIS)
- Community Investment schemes

Both VCTs and EIS are designed to encourage investment in unquoted companies. They are covered in more detail in Chapter 10. You get tax relief at 20 per cent on the amount you invest (within limits).

Note that for EIS shares, but not VCTs, you can ask to have up to half of your payment for shares issued between 6 April and 5 October in one year treated as if issued in the previous tax year. (See Inland Revenue help sheet IR341 *Enterprise Investment Scheme – income tax relief.*)

Community Investment schemes were launched in early 2003 as a way of encouraging investment in accredited schemes such as social banks. Investors can claim a community investment tax credit of 5 per cent of the amount invested for up to five years, i.e. 25 per cent in total.

Relief for gifts to charity

Making tax-free gifts to charity has become simpler in recent years. There are now three main routes:

- payroll giving, for donations deducted regularly from your pay
- Gift Aid, for most other donations
- gifts of investments and land.

Before 6 April 2000, you could get tax relief on donations paid under a deed of covenant. Payments under a covenant taken out before then now fall within Gift Aid. Payments under later deeds of covenant do not qualify – but Gift Aid is easier and more flexible. Gifts to charity also qualify for capital gains tax and inheritance tax relief (Chapters 11 and 12). A useful guide is Inland Revenue leaflet IR65 *Giving to charity by individuals.*

Payroll giving

This route is open to employees or pensioners of an employer who runs a payroll giving scheme. You ask your employer to deduct a set amount from your pay packet, which is then passed on to one or more charities through an approved agency. You get tax relief at your highest rate of tax.

Gift Aid

This route suits any cash donations to charity, regular or one-off. You can also give to amateur sports clubs by this route, if they are registered with the Revenue.

The charity or club can reclaim basic-rate tax from the Revenue. With the basic rate of tax set at 22 per cent, the charity can recover 22/78 of your gift. So, for every £10 you give, the charity benefits by £12.82.

If you are a higher-rate taxpayer, you benefit further – you can claim higher-rate relief either through your tax return or by asking your tax office to change your PAYE code. The higher-rate relief works out at 18 per cent of the value of the gift to the charity – the 40 per cent higher rate of tax, minus the 22 per cent relief the charity has reclaimed. So, for every £10 you give, you get tax relief of £12.82 × 18% = £2.31. And, for gifts made after 5 April 2003, you can claim on your tax return to have the payments treated as if made in the previous tax year, providing that you claim by the following 31 January. This is helpful if your top rate of tax is less than in the previous year, and means that you get your tax relief more quickly.

There are no limits on donations, but you must make a 'Gift Aid' declaration – usually, the charity provides a form. Declarations do not have to made for every gift; they can be worded to cover a number of gifts to a particular charity.

Non-taxpayers beware

If you pay little or no tax do not give money via Gift Aid. The Revenue will claw back the basic-rate tax claimed by the charity from you – unless you have paid an amount of tax that is at least as much as the amount the charity will claim. 'Tax' for this purpose is income tax, capital gains tax and tax credits on dividends. If you have made a Gift Aid declaration, you can cancel it by notifying the charity – you do not have to stop donating, but the charity will no longer be able to reclaim the tax.

Example 4.4: **Gift Aid and your tax rate**

Andrew decides to donate to his favourite charity by monthly direct debit, and makes a Gift Aid declaration. He pays £15 a month, £180 a year, and the charity reclaims tax of the amount paid, divided by the basic rate of tax, that is £180 × 22 ÷ 78 = £50. He also claims higher-rate tax relief at 18% of the gift plus the tax: £180 + £50 × 18% = £41. If Andrew doesn't pay at least £50 in tax during the tax year, the Revenue will adjust his tax bill to recover the £50 the charity has already received.

Gifts of investments and land

If you give shares, unit trusts or land (freehold or leasehold) to a charity, or sell them to a charity at a discount, you are likely to qualify for Gift Aid relief. (See Inland Revenue leaflet IR178 *Giving shares and securities to charity* and help sheet IR342 *Charitable giving*.)

Relief for business expenses

Business expenses are usually deducted from the profits of the business. But in a few cases (covered on page 76) you can deduct them from other income. You also can claim to set *losses* against your total income, rather than carrying them forward to set against future profits of the business (see Chapter 6).

Relief on insurance premiums

Tax relief on life insurance premiums was abolished in 1984. However, you can still get relief at your highest rate of tax on:

- Life insurance bought through a personal or stakeholder pension plan or retirement annuity contract (see Chapter 7).
- Compulsory life insurance bought through your employer's pension scheme – either through PAYE or your tax return.
- Half of any part of a trade union subscription that provides pension, life insurance or funeral cover.
- Half of premiums of under £25 a month to some (now unusual) friendly society insurance policies.

What to tell the Inland Revenue

Your personal allowance is given automatically through either your annual tax assessment or your PAYE code. All other reliefs can be claimed on your tax return or, if you do not get one, by contacting your tax office.

If you are approaching 65 you should make sure the Revenue know so that you receive the higher age-related personal and married allowances.

There is space to give your age in Question 22 of the tax return. If you don't get a tax return, you may be asked to complete a form P161.

Filling in your tax return

Allowances, credits and reliefs that are deducted from your total income are claimed on pages 5, 6 and 7 of the basic tax return. These are covered in this chapter. Other tax reliefs are claimed on the supplementary pages dealing with that income – e.g. the Self-employment pages for business expenses. (See relevant chapters.)

Mistakes to avoid

Some questions in the 'Reliefs' section of the tax return ask you to enter the amount paid, others ask for the amount paid up to a maximum and one asks for half the amount paid. Check that you are giving the figures requested.

Question 15 – Do you want to claim any of the following reliefs?

Box 15.1 Interest on qualifying loans

Not many loans now qualify for relief, but if you have one (see page 69), enter in box 15.1 the amount of interest that you paid in the 2002–03 tax year. If you haven't already got the information, ask your lender for a 'certificate of interest paid'. Remember that you claim relief only on the interest paid – not on the cost of paying off the loan itself.

Boxes 15.2, 15.2A Maintenance or alimony payments

This applies only if you or your ex-spouse was born before 6 April 1935, and the payments are made under a legally binding order or agreement. If so, enter the total maintenance paid in 2002–03 up to a maximum of £2,110. If your ex-spouse has remarried, enter only payments up to the date of marriage.

If you are able to claim the relief because your ex-spouse was born before 6 April 1935 but you were born after that date, enter your ex-spouse's date of birth in box 15.2A. In the 'Additional information' (box 23.5) at the end of the tax return you must give the dates of the court order or other agreement under which you are making the payments.

Boxes 15.3 to 15.7 Subscriptions for Venture Capital Trust shares, the Enterprise Investment Scheme and Community Investment Tax relief

Enter in box 15.3 the amount you invested in VCT shares in 2002–03, up to a maximum of £100,000.

Enter in box 15.4 the amount of any EIS investment in 2002–03, up to a maximum of £150,000. Quite a bit of 'Additional information' also needs to be given in box 23.5 (see the guide sent with the tax return). You also need to complete and return the claim form included in the form EIS3 or EIS5 that you should have received from the scheme.

You can claim to have up to half of EIS shares issued before 6 October (with a maximum cost of £25,000) treated as if taxed in the previous year. Remember to adjust the figure you enter in box 15.4:

- by deducting any amounts you are claiming to 'carry back' to 2001–02
- by adding any amounts you are carrying back from 2003–04.

Community Investment schemes have only recently been launched, but if you have invested in one and received the necessary certificate, enter the amount in boxes 15.5 and 15.7 (ignore box 15.6 – it will not be relevant until the 2004 return).

Example 4.5: **Claiming reliefs**

Andrew has tax relief to claim in Question 15 of his tax return (see Figure 4.1). He pays maintenance to his ex-wife under a court order, and as she is 68 he can claim tax relief. He pays her £4,000 a year, but he enters £2,110, as this is the maximum he can claim.

Figure 4.1: Question 15 (see Example 4.5)

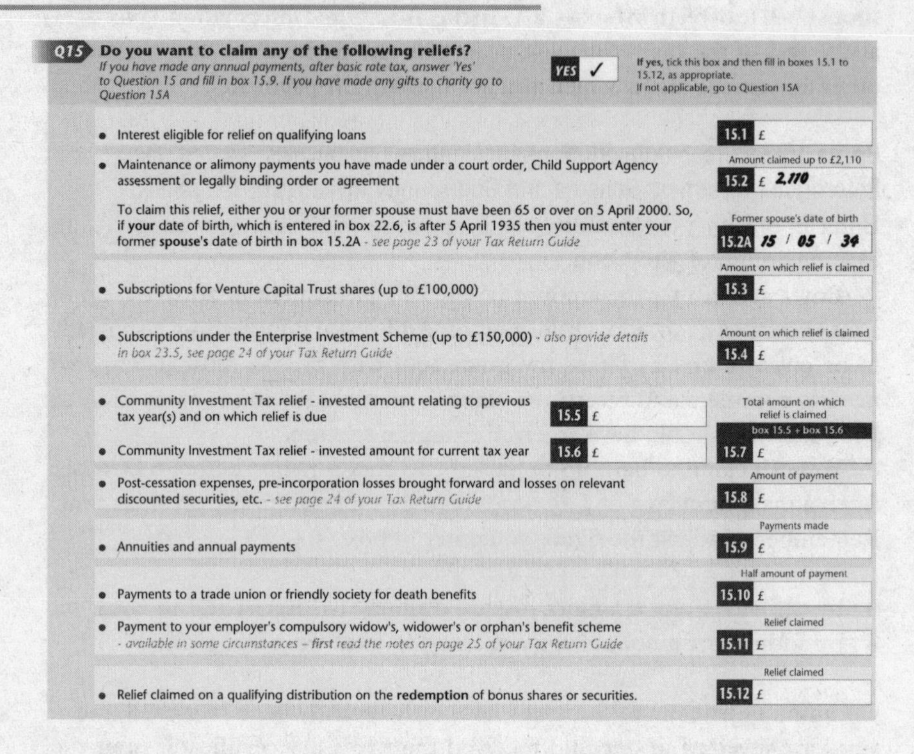

Q15 Do you want to claim any of the following reliefs?
If you have made any annual payments, after basic rate tax, answer 'Yes' to Question 15 and fill in box 15.9. If you have made any gifts to charity go to Question 15A

YES ✓

If yes, tick this box and then fill in boxes 15.1 to 15.12, as appropriate.
If not applicable, go to Question 15A

• Interest eligible for relief on qualifying loans		15.1 £
• Maintenance or alimony payments you have made under a court order, Child Support Agency assessment or legally binding order or agreement		Amount claimed up to £2,110 15.2 £ 2,110
To claim this relief, either you or your former spouse must have been 65 or over on 5 April 2000. So, if **your** date of birth, which is entered in box 22.6, is after 5 April 1935 then you must enter your former **spouse's** date of birth in box 15.2A - *see page 23 of your Tax Return Guide*		Former spouse's date of birth 15.2A 15 / 05 / 34
• Subscriptions for Venture Capital Trust shares (up to £100,000)		Amount on which relief is claimed 15.3 £
• Subscriptions under the Enterprise Investment Scheme (up to £150,000) - *also provide details in box 23.5, see page 24 of your Tax Return Guide*		Amount on which relief is claimed 15.4 £
• Community Investment Tax relief - invested amount relating to previous tax year(s) and on which relief is due	15.5 £	Total amount on which relief is claimed
• Community Investment Tax relief - invested amount for current tax year	15.6 £	box 15.5 + box 15.6 15.7 £
• Post-cessation expenses, pre-incorporation losses brought forward and losses on relevant discounted securities, etc. - *see page 24 of your Tax Return Guide*		Amount of payment 15.8 £
• Annuities and annual payments		Payments made 15.9 £
• Payments to a trade union or friendly society for death benefits		Half amount of payment 15.10 £
• Payment to your employer's compulsory widow's, widower's or orphan's benefit scheme - *available in some circumstances – first read the notes on page 25 of your Tax Return Guide*		Relief claimed 15.11 £
• Relief claimed on a qualifying distribution on the **redemption** of bonus shares or securities.		Relief claimed 15.12 £

Box 15.8 Post-cessation expenses etc.; Box 15.9 Annuities and annual payments

These two boxes cover tax relief arising from a business or job which is set against your income as a whole.

- You can claim post-cessation expenses for up to seven years after you stop trading, for example the costs of collecting debts of your former business. And if you are transferring your business to a limited company, you may be able to claim some pre-incorporation losses. Enter the total amount in box 15.8. Check the conditions in the Revenue's tax return guide before claiming. Do not enter any other business losses here – even if you are claiming to set them against non-business income, the claim is made on the Self-employment or

Partnership pages.

- If you were an employee, costs and liabilities arising from problems with your work can be claimed in box 15.8 (unless you have already claimed in the Employment supplementary pages).
- Payments made under some annuities or covenants for business purposes (e.g. to buy out a retiring partner) can be claimed. Enter the amount you actually paid that qualifies for tax relief in box 15.9.

You can also use box 15.8 to claim tax relief if you made a loss on some types of discounted security (see Chapter 10).

Box 15.10 Payments to a trade union or friendly society for death benefit

Enter half of your payments to a trade union or friendly society that qualify for relief. Check first that your policy qualifies.

Box 15.11 Payments to your employer's compulsory benefit scheme

Only enter here any payments where tax relief has not been given through PAYE. Enter the amount paid, up to a maximum of £100.

Box 15.12 Relief on the redemption of bonus shares or securities

This box applies only if you have entered in box 10.17 on page 3 an amount received when you redeemed bonus shares and securities, and you are a higher-rate taxpayer. If so, see the Inland Revenue's tax return guide.

Question 15A – Do you want to claim relief on gifts to charity?

Enter in box 15A.1 the total amount you actually handed over to charities under the Gift Aid scheme (ignoring any basic-rate tax reclaimed by the charity), or under a deed of covenant made before 6 April 2000.

Then, work out how much of the payments already entered in box 15A.1 were one-off gifts rather than regular donations, and enter the amount of one-off gifts in box 15A.2. Your tax office will adjust your PAYE code if necessary, to give you any higher-rate tax relief on the regular donations at source.

Finally, if you are claiming to have any donations made after 5 April 2003 treated as if paid in 2002–03, enter the amount in box 15A.3.

Boxes 15A.4, 15A.5 Gifts of qualifying investments or land to charities

If you have given shares, unit trusts or land (real property) to charity, enter in boxes 15A.4 and 15A.5 the amount of relief that you are claiming. This is (broadly) the market value at the date of the gift, plus some costs minus anything you (or your family or business associate) receive in return. If you are giving land, you will need a certificate from the charity. (See Inland Revenue leaflet IR178 *Giving shares and securities to charity.*)

Figure 4.2: Question 15A (see Example 4.6)

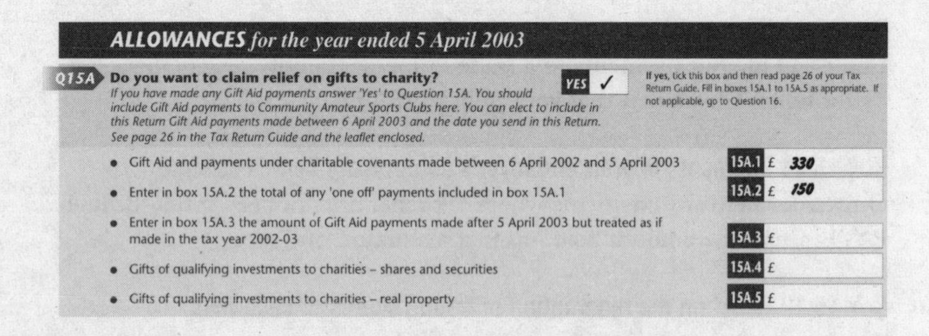

ALLOWANCES *for the year ended 5 April 2003*

Q15A **Do you want to claim relief on gifts to charity?** YES ✓

If you have made any Gift Aid payments answer 'Yes' to Question 15A. You should include Gift Aid payments to Community Amateur Sports Clubs here. You can elect to include in this Return Gift Aid payments made between 6 April 2003 and the date you send in this Return. See page 26 in the Tax Return Guide and the leaflet enclosed.

If yes, tick this box and then read page 26 of your Tax Return Guide. Fill in boxes 15A.1 to 15A.5 as appropriate. If not applicable, go to Question 16.

		£
• Gift Aid and payments under charitable covenants made between 6 April 2002 and 5 April 2003	15A.1	330
• Enter in box 15A.2 the total of any 'one off' payments included in box 15A.1	15A.2	150
• Enter in box 15A.3 the amount of Gift Aid payments made after 5 April 2003 but treated as if made in the tax year 2002-03	15A.3	
• Gifts of qualifying investments to charities – shares and securities	15A.4	
• Gifts of qualifying investments to charities – real property	15A.5	

Example 4.6: **Charitable donations**

Andrew made regular Gift Aid donations of £180 in 2002–03 (see Example 4.4), plus a £150 lump sum donation. He enters in box 15A.1 the total amount donated (£330), not including the basic-rate tax relief, and in box 15A.2 he enters the £150 one-off donation.

Question 16 – Do you want to claim blind person's allowance, married couple's allowance or the Children's Tax Credit?

You do not need to claim personal allowance – this is given automatically.

Boxes 16.1, 16.2 Blind person's allowance

Enter the name of the authority with which you are registered as blind in box 16.2, or 'Scotland claim' or 'Northern Ireland claim' (where there are no registers) as appropriate. If 2002–03 was the first year in which you were registered as blind, enter the date of registration.

Boxes 16.3 to 16.13 Married couple's allowance

This applies only if either you or your spouse was born before 6 April 1935. Married men should always complete this section if they or their wives meet the age condition, but wives complete it only if they are claiming all or half of the minimum amount.

To establish that you have met the age condition:

- enter your date of birth in box 16.3 (if it is before 6 April 1935)
- enter your spouse's date of birth in box 16.4, if you are claiming on the basis of your spouse's age
- if you are a man who separated and remarried during 2003–04, and your previous wife was born before 6 April 1935, enter her date of birth in box 16.9.

The Revenue will use whichever date of birth saves you most tax.

Enter your current spouse's full name, in box 16.5 (if you are a man) or box 16.12 (if you are a woman). If you got married between 6 April 2002 and 5 April 2003, enter the date of marriage in box 16.6 (men) or box 16.13 (women) so that your tax office can work out how much of the full allowance to give you (one-twelfth for each tax month of marriage).

Finally, if you allocated half or all of the allowance to the wife, tick box 16.7 or 16.8 (men) or 16.10 or 16.11 (women) as appropriate. Remember, though, that this will apply only if you changed the allocation before the start of the tax year (before 6 April 2002).

Boxes 16.14 to 16.26 Children's Tax Credit

You get only one credit per family, so it usually makes sense to claim for your youngest child – enter his or her date of birth in box 16.14. The child must also be your own or one you look after at your own expense, so tick 16.15 to confirm this.

Which other boxes you complete depends on your circumstances:

- *If you were a lone parent throughout the tax year.* If your child lived with you throughout the tax year, tick box 16.16. If your child lived part of the year with someone else, complete box 16.17. You and your child's other carer get only £5,290 (or £10,490 if you had a baby in 2002–03) between you: enter your share, and write the other claimant's name, address and the name of the child, under 'Additional information' (box 23.5). If you cannot agree how to share, contact your tax office. The commissioners who make decisions on tax matters will have to decide.
- *If you were married or living with someone as husband and wife throughout the whole year.* You get only one credit between you. The person with the highest income normally gets the relief, and must make the claim if a higher-rate taxpayer. If neither partner is a higher-rate taxpayer, you can choose (by ticking box 16.23 or 16.24) whether the higher-income partner gets all the allowance, or whether to split it. You will be able to tick box 16.25 only if you elected before 6 April 2003 for the whole credit to go the partner with the lower income.
- *If your circumstances changed during the year* (e.g. you married, started living with someone or separated). The tax year is split into 'before' and 'after' sections and your claim is divided between you on a time basis. If your child lived part of the time with someone else, your share of the divided claim may have to be split further. Enter the value of your claim in box 16.26.

If your circumstances changed or you are splitting a claim with someone else, read Inland Revenue help sheet IR343 *Claiming Children's Tax Credit when your circumstances change.*

Boxes 16.27 to 16.33 Transfer of surplus allowances

You can transfer blind person's allowance, married couple's allowance and Children's Tax Credit to your husband or wife if your income is too low to make use of it. You can also transfer Children's Tax Credit (but not blind person's allowance) to your partner if you are unmarried.

To transfer allowances, tick boxes 16.27 to 16.30 as relevant (and ask your partner to tick the equivalent boxes on his or her form). You cannot lose out by ticking these boxes – your tax office will transfer allowances only if it is in your interests. In 'Additional information' (box 23.5) you will

Figure 4.3: Boxes 16.1 to 16.3 (see Example 4.7)

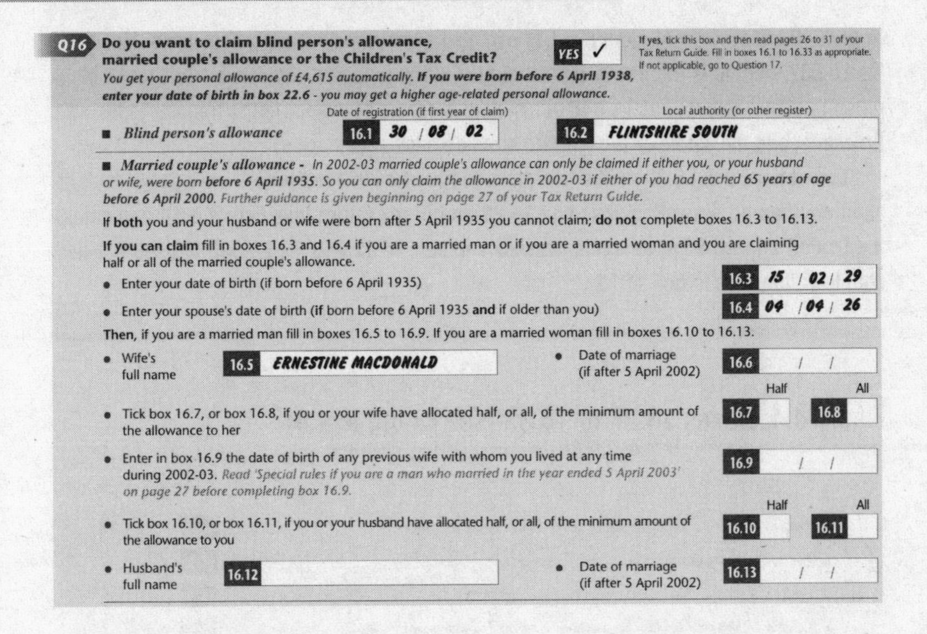

Q16 Do you want to claim blind person's allowance, married couple's allowance or the Children's Tax Credit? YES ✓

If yes, tick this box and then read pages 26 to 31 of your Tax Return Guide. Fill in boxes 16.1 to 16.33 as appropriate. If not applicable, go to Question 17.

You get your personal allowance of £4,615 automatically. ***If you were born before 6 April 1938, enter your date of birth in box 22.6*** *- you may get a higher age-related personal allowance.*

■ *Blind person's allowance* — Date of registration (if first year of claim) 16.1 30 / 08 / 02 — Local authority (or other register) 16.2 FLINTSHIRE SOUTH

■ ***Married couple's allowance -*** *In 2002-03 married couple's allowance can only be claimed if either you, or your husband or wife, were born* ***before 6 April 1935****. So you can only claim the allowance in 2002-03 if either of you had reached* ***65 years of age before 6 April 2000****. Further guidance is given beginning on page 27 of your Tax Return Guide.*

If **both** you and your husband or wife were born after 5 April 1935 you cannot claim; **do not** complete boxes 16.3 to 16.13.

If you can claim fill in boxes 16.3 and 16.4 if you are a married man or if you are a married woman and you are claiming half or all of the married couple's allowance.

- Enter your date of birth (if born before 6 April 1935) 16.3 15 / 02 / 29
- Enter your spouse's date of birth (if born before 6 April 1935 **and** if older than you) 16.4 04 / 04 / 26

Then, if you are a married man fill in boxes 16.5 to 16.9. If you are a married woman fill in boxes 16.10 to 16.13.

- Wife's full name 16.5 ERNESTINE MACDONALD
- Date of marriage (if after 5 April 2002) 16.6 / /
- Tick box 16.7, or box 16.8, if you or your wife have allocated half, or all, of the minimum amount of the allowance to her — Half 16.7 — All 16.8
- Enter in box 16.9 the date of birth of any previous wife with whom you lived at any time during 2002-03. *Read 'Special rules if you are a man who married in the year ended 5 April 2003' on page 27 before completing box 16.9.* 16.9 / /
- Tick box 16.10, or box 16.11, if you or your husband have allocated half, or all, of the minimum amount of the allowance to you — Half 16.10 — All 16.11
- Husband's full name 16.12
- Date of marriage (if after 5 April 2002) 16.13 / /

need to give your spouse's name, address, tax reference or National Insurance number and tax office.

If your partner is transferring allowances to you, and you are working out your own tax, the unused amount to be transferred should be entered in box 16.31, 16.32 or 16.33 as appropriate. If you don't know the unused amount, contact your tax office or get your return in by 30 September 2003 or file by internet.

Example 4.7: **Claiming allowances**

Ernest, aged 74 on 5 April 2003, is married to Ernestine, aged 76. They can claim the married couple's allowance because they were both born before 6 April 1935, but they get the higher age-related allowance for those over 75 (£5,535 in 2002–03) because Ernestine is 76. So in Ernest's tax return (see Figure 4.3), he enters her date of birth as well as her name.

Example 4.8: Transferring allowances

In 2002–03 Ernest (from Example 4.7) can also claim blind person's allowance. However, his £6,532 income is too low to use all of his £6,100 personal allowance and £1,480 blind person's allowance. He has £1,048 of his blind person's allowance left to transfer to his wife Ernestine, and the whole of the married couple's allowance.

Ernest ticks box 16.27 on his tax return to transfer his allowances – he doesn't have to enter any figures. Ernestine ticks box 16.28 on her tax return (see Figure 4.4), and enters the £1,048 unused blind person's allowance in box 16.31 and the £5,535 unused married couple's allowance in box 16.32.

Figure 4.4: Boxes 16.27 to 16.33 (see Example 4.8)

■ ***Transfer of surplus allowances*** - *see page 31 of your Tax Return Guide before you fill in boxes 16.27 to 16.33.*

• Tick box 16.27 if you want your spouse to have your unused allowances	16.27	
• Tick box 16.28 if you want to have your spouse's unused allowances	16.28	✓
• Tick box 16.29 if you want to have your partner's unused CTC	16.29	
• Tick box 16.30 if your surplus CTC should be transferred to your partner	16.30	

Please give details in the 'Additional information' box, box 23.5, on page 9 - *see page 31 of your Tax Return Guide for what is needed.*

If you want to calculate your tax, enter the amount of the surplus allowance you can have.

• Blind person's surplus allowance	16.31	£ 1,048
• Married couple's surplus allowance	16.32	£ 5,535
• Surplus CTC	16.33	£

Record-keeping

Key records you should keep are listed below.

Allowances

- Birth certificate, or other proof of age, if claiming age-related allowances.
- Marriage certificate if claiming married couple's allowance.
- If sharing a claim for Children's Tax Credit, notes of the days your child spent with you.

- For blind person's allowance, notification that you are registered blind and/or an ophthalmologist's certificate.

Reliefs

- Certificate of interest paid on a loan which qualifies for relief.
- If claiming tax relief on maintenance payments, court orders or other legally binding agreements, and proof of amounts actually paid.
- Certificates issued by Venture Capital Trusts.
- Forms EIS3 or EIS5 if you bought Enterprise Investment Scheme shares.
- Copies of Gift Aid declarations, charitable deeds of covenant and records of amounts actually paid. Valuations of shares or other property gifted to charity and related expenses.
- Details of any other payments on which you are claiming relief.

Tax-planning hints

1. If you've forgotten to claim a relief or allowance, you have five years and ten months from the end of the tax year in question to claim.
2. If you cannot use all your personal allowance in one year, it may make sense to transfer income to another family member (see page 63).
3. Transfer any unused blind person's and married couple's allowance to your husband or wife, and Children's Tax Credit to your partner (married or unmarried).
4. If you are losing age-related allowance because you are above the income limit, see page 64 for ways of minimising the loss.
5. Do not give money to charity via Gift Aid if you pay little or no tax. The Revenue will claw back from you the basic-rate tax claimed by the charity.

5

Income from a job

If you are an employee, your employer deducts tax from your income before paying you (see Chapter 2) and you usually have to complete a tax return only if you are a higher-rate taxpayer, a director or your tax is complex. However, there are still ways of saving tax as an employee and tax traps to avoid. Understanding how your tax is calculated enables you to keep an eye on your employer and on the Revenue.

Does this affect you?

In most cases it is clear whether or not you are an employee, but for tax purposes an 'employee' also includes:

- *Directors*, including people who are directors of a company they own. There are many special rules for 'controlling' directors.
- *Casual employees* (although whether or not your employer actually has to deduct PAYE depends on your income – see Chapter 2).
- *Part-time workers*. If you have more than one job, you can be an employee for one, self-employed for the other – it is the nature of the work and your contract with the employer that count.
- *Agency staff* (in most cases – see Chapter 2).

There is often a grey area between being employed and being self-employed (see Chapter 6).

A director or partner of your own firm?

If you are a director of a service company that you control, you may have extra tax to pay, if the Revenue think that you are effectively an employee of a client for whom you are working (see page 90). The same may apply to some partners in a partnership.

Tax-free income

You can start from the assumption that all your rewards for working are taxable – pay, expenses payments and fringe benefits. However, you can claim tax relief on some 'allowable' expenses payments (see page 107) and there are lists of tax-free pay and perks below.

Tax-free income usually comes with conditions. Your employer should ensure that what is offered meets the necessary conditions. See Inland Revenue help sheet IR207 *Non-taxable payments or benefits for employees,* or ask your employer or tax office if you can see the Inland Revenue tome 480 *Expenses and benefits. A tax guide.*

Tax-free pay

- Your (and your employer's) contributions to an approved pension scheme (you still have to pay employee's National Insurance contributions). (See Chapter 7 for more on pensions.)
- Donations to a payroll giving scheme (often called 'Give As You Earn').
- The first £30,000 of some payments when leaving a job (see page 104).
- Working Tax Credit, paid through your pay packet.
- Minor or irregular payments on which your employer pays the tax under a 'PAYE settlement agreement' with your tax office.

Tax-free expenses

- Approved mileage allowance payments (see page 109).
- Expenses for which your employer has agreed a *dispensation* with your tax office (see page 107).
- From 6 April 2003, payments of up to £2 a week from your employer for extra household costs if you regularly work from home. Higher payments can be tax-free if you have supporting evidence.

Tax-free perks

- Free or subsidised meals at a staff restaurant, if available to all employees, and the first 15 pence a day of luncheon vouchers.
- Loans of computers, provided that the taxable value is not more than £500 a year, and directors are not favoured. (The annual taxable value is 20 per cent of the value of the equipment when first provided.)
- Loans of money, in some circumstances (see page 101).
- Some living accommodation (see page 100).
- Most relocation costs paid by your employer, up to a maximum of £8,000 for the relocation as a whole, if you are moving for your job. (See Inland Revenue leaflet IR134 *Income tax and relocation packages*.)
- A phone line at home, if your employer is the subscriber, you have a clear business need for it and any private calls are kept to a minimum.
- Mobile phones (including line rental and calls paid directly by your employer). Payment for using your own mobile phone is taxable.
- Medical check-ups (but not treatment) for you and your family.
- Treatment (or medical insurance) if you fall ill while working abroad.
- Workplace nurseries or playschemes.
- Work-related training, including (in some cases) retraining costs met by your employer on leaving your job.
- Counselling – e.g. welfare counselling or redundancy counselling.
- Long service (20 years) gifts and suggestion scheme awards.
- Entertainment and non-cash gifts, worth under £150 (increasing to £250 in 2003), from someone *other* than your employer.
- Annual staff parties costing less than £75 per head per year (increasing to £150 per head in 2003).
- Special staff sports facilities.

Tax-free travel perks

- Parking provided at or near your work.
- Travel or overnight expenses if public transport is disrupted by strikes.
- Taxis home if you work after 9 at night and public transport has either shut down or it would be unreasonable to expect you to use it.
- The travel expenses of your husband or wife if they have to accompany you on a foreign trip because of your health.
- Personal expenses such as newspapers and laundry if away overnight for work, below a total of £5 a night in the UK, £10 a night overseas (if they come to more, the whole lot is taxable).
- Subsidised works buses from home to your place of work.
- A free bicycle used mainly for travel to work and free meals provided on official 'cycle to work' days.
- Help for travel from home to work if you are disabled.
- Travel expenses of some directors, including unpaid directors of some clubs.

Tax-free share perks

If your employer has given you free shares in the company, or the right to buy shares on special terms, this counts as a tax-free perk *provided* that it is done through one of the schemes below. (If your share scheme is not tax-free, see page 103.)

Your employer will tell you what sort of scheme you are in and what the rules are. Dividends received from the shares and capital gains when you eventually sell them are taxable in the normal way (see Chapters 10 and 11) unless otherwise stated.

- *Approved profit-sharing schemes* give you free shares, which are kept in a trust on your behalf. They are tax-free provided that they are kept in the trust for at least three years. New schemes are not possible, but you may still have shares in one. (See Inland Revenue leaflet IR95.)
- *Approved share incentive plans* (also known as All Employee Share Ownership Plans, ESOPs or Employee Share Plans). Your employer can give you free shares, or you can buy them. They are free of income tax and National Insurance provided that you keep them in the plan

for at least five years (in most cases). There is no capital gains tax on free shares if you keep your shares in the plan until you sell them. (See Inland Revenue leaflet IR2002.)

- *Enterprise management incentives.* You have an 'option' to buy shares at a particular price at some point within ten years. The option is free of income tax and National Insurance provided that the price at which you can buy the shares is not below their market value at the time the option is granted, and provided that, if there is a 'disqualifying event' such as you leaving the company, you buy the shares within 40 days of the event. (See Inland Revenue leaflet IR2006.)
- *Approved savings-related share option schemes.* You have an 'option' to buy shares at a fixed price at a particular time. You can buy the shares only with amounts you have saved under a special Save As You Earn (SAYE) savings scheme, which pays a tax-free bonus at the end of the savings period. The option is usually free of income tax and National Insurance. (See Inland Revenue leaflet IR97.)
- *Approved discretionary share option schemes* (including executive share option schemes and company share option plans) give you an 'option' to buy shares at a fixed price at a particular time. The option is free of income tax and National Insurance provided that (in most cases) you buy shares no earlier than three years, or later than ten years, after receiving the option. (See Inland Revenue leaflet IR101.)

How the tax is worked out

This is how your taxable pay is worked out for income tax purposes (the rules for National Insurance contributions differ slightly, see page 110).

- *Step 1: deduct any tax-free income* (listed at the start of this chapter).
- *Step 2: add up taxable pay* (listed on opposite page).
- *Step 3: add extra taxable pay, for some directors and partners.* The Revenue call this a 'deemed Schedule E payment' but it applies only if you are affected by the 'IR35' rules (see page 90).
- *Step 4: add the taxable value of fringe benefits.* If you get a perk which is

not tax-free, there are special rules for working out the amount on which you are taxed (see page 92).

- *Step 5: add any taxable amounts from share schemes* (see page 103).
- *Step 6: add any taxable lump sums.* This includes some payments when your job changes or ends (see page 104).
- *Step 7: deduct expenses on which you can claim tax relief.* The Revenue call these 'allowable expenses' (see page 107).

The result gives you your taxable pay from employment. You pay tax on this at 10 per cent, if it is in the lower-rate band, 22 per cent if it is in the basic-rate band and 40 per cent if it is in the higher-rate band. (Chapter 1 explains tax bands.)

Documents that make life easier

Your employer should send you two helpful forms after the end of the tax year: the P60 by 31 May, and a P11D (or P9D) by 6 July. The P60 tells you the taxable amount of pay you received, and the P11D or P9D tells you the taxable value of any perks and expenses.

Taxable cash payments

- Payments such as salary, wages, fees, bonuses, commission and overtime – you are taxed on these when you receive them or become entitled to them, whichever is earlier.
- If you are a director, amounts credited to your account in the company's books (taxable from the date they are credited).
- Expenses payments, whether these are reimbursing you for amounts you have laid out, flat-rate expense allowances, or tickets etc. bought for you (don't worry – any expenses for which you can claim tax relief are taken away at Step 7.). The only expenses you can exclude at this stage are the tax-free ones (see the start of this chapter).
- 'Honoraria' from any posts that count as employment rather than self-employment (this can be a grey area – see Chapter 6).
- 'Golden hellos'.

- Sick pay, maternity pay or paternity pay (including any statutory amounts). However, if you contribute to the cost of a sick-pay scheme, any benefits arising from your own contributions are tax-free.
- Loans that have been written off by the lender.
- Taxable amounts from a profit-sharing scheme.
- Payments from someone other than your employer, which you received because of your job, for example tips and sales incentives. You can exclude goodwill entertainment and gifts (other than cash) costing less than £150 a year (rising to £250 in 2003).
- One-off payments to compensate you for agreeing to changes in your terms and conditions of employment.
- In most cases, income from working abroad, if you are resident in the UK for tax purposes – but there may be special rules (see Chapter 9).

Extra taxable pay, for some directors and partners

Some people in service industries work through a company or partnership, rather than as a sole trader. A key reason for setting up in this way is that you can choose to pay yourself in the form of salary or dividends (with a company), or alter the profit-sharing agreement (with a partnership), in order to benefit from differing tax and National Insurance rules.

You can still do this – but if you are providing services and the Revenue think you are effectively an employee of a client, you may be caught by the 'IR35' rules (named after the press release in which they were announced). Guidelines for deciding whether you are self-employed are in Chapter 6. From 10 April 2003, these rules are extended to domestic workers, e.g. nannies, who set themselves up as companies.

The IR35 rules mean that instead of paying tax on the pay or dividends you receive, you will be taxed on the total payment received by the company or partnership for your services, *minus* an allowance of 5 per cent of the contract value (to cover the costs of running a company).

The Revenue call the result a 'deemed Schedule E' payment and add it to your taxable income. Your company or partnership must pay any extra PAYE and National Insurance due on this by 19 April after the end of the tax year in question. (See Inland Revenue leaflet IR2003 *Supplying services. How to calculate the deemed payment.*)

Are you affected?

The rules may affect you if you provide services to a client through:

- *either* a company in which you (or your family) control more than 5 per cent of the ordinary share capital, or are entitled to more than 5 per cent of the dividends
- *or* a partnership in which you (or your family) are entitled to at least 60 per cent of the profits, or where most of the partnership's income comes from a single client.

Even if neither of these applies, you may be caught if you are entitled to receive an income from any payments made to the company or partnership for your services.

If you think you may be affected, see leaflet IR175 *Supplying services through a limited company or partnership.* There is also a Revenue helpline and a special area on the Revenue website (see the Fact File). You can ask the Revenue to give an 'opinion' on whether you are affected, but they will do this only for existing contracts.

Contracts – part, but not all, of the IR35 solution

You cannot sidestep the tests for being self-employed by stating in a contract that you are not an employee – it is the nature of the work that counts. On the other hand, it is sensible to ensure that your contract helps rather than hinders. Take professional advice.

Example 5.1: **What IR35 means**

Hannibal is the only employee of his own company. In 2002–03 he worked on an engineering contract, for which his client paid him £50,000. Hannibal took a salary of only £25,000. If he is caught by the IR35 rules, he is taxed roughly as if he received the whole £50,000 minus a 5% allowance, that is £47,500, and minus the tax and National Insurance he has already paid on £25,000. But he has to work out the extra tax in time to pay it by 19 April 2003 – which can be difficult.

Fringe benefits

Some perks are taxable whatever your income. The tax is collected by adjusting your PAYE code (see Chapter 2). However, other perks may be tax-free (see the start of this chapter), or favourably taxed, if you are lower-paid. Note that any perks provided to your family count as yours.

Are you 'lower-paid'?

Fringe benefits are tax-free for lower-paid employees, except for living accommodation, free or cheap goods, vouchers, credit cards and tokens (see rule 6 opposite).

You are lower-paid if your total gross pay is under £8,500 a year, including any expenses and taxable perks (valued as if you earned £8,500 or more), but minus pension contributions and payroll-giving donations. If you are in a job for only part of the year, the annual equivalent of your pay is used – so if you earn £5,000 for six months, the annual equivalent is £10,000. And if you have more than one job in a year, the £8,500 limit applies to each job separately.

Directors count as lower-paid only if they earn less than £8,500 and:

- they (and others associated with them) control 5 per cent or less of the shares in the company *and*
- *either* they are full-time working directors, *or* the company is a charity or non-profit-making.

How fringe benefits are valued – eight general rules

When it comes to working out the taxable value of your perks, there are special rules for some types. Otherwise, there is a set of general rules that apply in all other circumstances. There is a quick guide to the most common taxable perks in Table 5.1 on page 95, which will tell you where to find more detail. Your employer should give you a form P11D or P9D after the end of the tax year, telling you the taxable value of your perks. Tax-free perks are listed at the beginning of this chapter.

Rule 1: Cheap or free use of something. Tax-free if you are lower-paid, otherwise you pay tax on 20 per cent of the market value of the item (such as a television or motorbike) at the time when it was first provided as a perk, or on the rent or hire charge paid by your employer if greater, plus any running costs or other expenses met by your employer as a result. (See Inland Revenue help sheet IR210 *Assets provided for private use.*)

Rule 2: Gifts of things previously used as a perk. For example, being given a television you have previously borrowed. You are taxed on the market value of the asset at the time of the gift, or (if higher) the initial market value minus any amounts on which tax has already been paid under the rule above (see Example 5.2 on page 94). (See Inland Revenue help sheet IR213 *Payments in kind – assets transferred.*) Cars, vans and living accommodation are always taxed on the market value at the time of the gift.

Rule 3: Cheap or free services. Tax-free if you are lower-paid, otherwise you are taxed on the extra cost to your employer of providing the services (e.g. hairdressing at work). 'Extra' means that if the services are those your employer provides in their business you only have to pay any further cost incurred by your employer, which in practice may be nil (e.g. free travel for rail company employees).

Rule 4: Cheap or free goods. If you are lower-paid, you are taxed on the second-hand value of the goods. If you are not lower-paid, you are taxed on either the second-hand value or, if higher, the extra cost to your employer. 'Extra' here means that if, say, you are given goods your employer makes, you are taxed on the wholesale rather than the retail price.

Rule 5: Credit cards, tokens and vouchers. Spending on these is taxed as cash, unless the item is tax-free (see the list at the beginning of this chapter), or counts as an allowable business expense. You can exclude payments for a company car or van – you are taxed on these separately. Note, too, that for non-cash vouchers you are taxed on the cost to your employer, not the face value, and you are not taxed on any interest or subscription fee on a company credit card. (See Inland Revenue help sheet IR201 *Vouchers, credit cards and tokens.*)

Rule 6: If you pay for something. You can deduct from the taxable value of a perk anything you pay for it.

Rule 7: Restricted use. The taxable value is reduced if you have the benefit for only part of a tax year, or if it is shared with another employee.

Rule 8: If you use a perk partly privately, partly for work. You can claim a deduction from the taxable value for the work use of a perk.

Example 5.2: **How the general rules fit together**

Ian's employer lends him a flat-screen television. Each year, Ian is taxed on 20% of the television's market value at the time he first got it. This was £2,000, so the annual taxable amount is £400 (rule 1).

Eighteen months later, the company gives Ian the television for a token payment of £500. As he had it for only half of the second year, he is taxed only on half of the annual value: £200 (rule 7). The gift itself is taxed at either the current market value (£1,200) or, if higher, the initial market value minus any amounts on which Ian has already been taxed, i.e. £2,000 – £400 – £200 = £1,400 (rule 2). He is taxed on £1,400 minus the £500 he is paying, i.e. £900 (rule 6).

National Insurance contributions on perks

Employees do not generally have to pay National Insurance on fringe benefits, except in the case of:

- fuel for private use in your company car, unless supplied from a company fuel pump, or bought on a company credit card or garage account and the garage is told that the fuel is being bought on behalf of the employer
- other things you buy on a company credit card for your own use, unless the supplier is told that you are buying them on behalf of the employer
- things that are easily convertible into cash, such as shares (unless provided through an approved scheme), fine wine or gold bullion.

Table 5.1: A quick guide to taxable fringe benefits

	Taxable value	*Taxable value if lower-paid*
Chauffeur	Cost to employer (rule 3)	Tax-free
Company cars	Taxed on up to 35% of car's price – see page 96	Tax-free
Company car fuel	Taxed on a set scale – see page 99	Tax-free
Company motorbike	20% of value, or rent if higher (rule 1)	Tax-free
Company vans	£500, or £350 if four or more years old	Tax-free
Free or cheap goods	See rule 3	Second-hand value
Free or cheap services	Cost to employer (rule 3)	Tax-free
Gifts of things previously borrowed	See rule 2	Second-hand value
Living accommodation, unless tax-free (see page 100)	Basic charge of rental/rateable value	Taxable
Loans of goods	20% of value, or rent if higher (rule 1)	Tax-free
Loans of money	Taxed on interest saved, but only if total loans are over £5,000	Tax-free
Mileage allowances	Covered under 'Expenses', see page 108	See previous column
Private medical or dental insurance for UK treatment	Cost to employer (rule 3)	Tax-free
Relocation expenses	The first £8,000 is tax-free (see page 86) – anything else is taxed in the same way as other perks of the same kind	See previous column
Educational assistance for your children	Rule 3 applies, unless help is 'fortuitous'	Tax-free
Vouchers, tokens and credit cards	Taxed on most spending on these	Taxable

Company cars and free fuel

The taxable value of your company car is a percentage of its list price (even if it is second-hand or leased), with reductions if you have the car for only part of the year or pay something for it. The percentage on which you are taxed is a maximum of 35 per cent, reduced if your car's carbon dioxide (CO_2) emissions are low (see Table 5.2 on page 98).

If you get free fuel for private use, its taxable value is shown in Table 5.3. Note that the taxable value is not reduced if you reimburse your employer for some of your private fuel – you can avoid it only if you repay the full cost of all fuel used for private journeys. The charge is reduced if you have free fuel for only part of the year – but from April 2003 the reduction is lost if you receive free fuel again in the tax year. (For more information, see Inland Revenue help sheet IR203 *Car benefits and car fuel benefits*.)

The price of a car – the whole price

You cannot reduce a car's taxable value by excluding the cost of valuable accessories if they were fitted before you got the car (except for disability equipment). Accessories fitted afterwards will also be added to the taxable value if they are worth more than £100 per accessory or set of accessories (e.g. alloy wheels).

Working out the taxable value of a company car

1 *Find its 'price'.* This is usually its list price when registered, including delivery charges, taxes, VAT and accessories, but not road tax or the car registration fee. You can deduct anything up to £5,000 you paid towards the cost of the car – and the maximum 'price' is £80,000. The price of a classic car (at least 15 years old, worth at least £15,000 and worth more now than when first registered) is its market value.
2 *Find the approved CO_2 emissions figure.* Use this to find the relevant percentage in Table 5.2 on page 98. CO_2 emissions appear on your car registration document, if registered after 1 March 2001; if not, try the manufacturer, or the Society of Motor Manufacturers and Traders' website (see the Fact File).

3 *Multiply the car's price by the percentage charge.* This gives its annual taxable value.
4 *Adjust if the car was unavailable for part of the year.* Multiply the annual taxable value by the number of days it was available, and divide the result by 365 (366 in a leap year). Gaps of under 30 days are ignored.
5 *Deduct anything you paid towards your private use of the car.* The result is your car's taxable value.
6 *Find the taxable value of any free fuel.* See Table 5.3 on page 99. If the car was unavailable for part of the year, multiply the charge by the same percentage used in step 4 above.

Example 5.3: **How much tax on your company car?**

Graeme's company car has a price of £18,000, and a CO_2 emissions figure of 240. Table 5.2 shows that he is taxed on 30% of the price in 2002–03, 32% in 2003–04. The taxable value of his car if he has it for the whole of 2003–04 is £18,000 × 32% = £5,760.

Graeme changes his car in July 2003 for one with CO_2 emissions of 190 and a list price of £20,000 – an annual taxable value of £20,000 × 22% = £4,400. He has had his first car for 122 out of the 366 days in 2003–04 (a leap year), his second car for 244 days. The annual taxable values are adjusted as follows:

£5,760 × 122⁄366 = £1,920
£4,400 × 244⁄366 = £2,933
Total for 2003–04 = £4,853

Example 5.4: **How much tax on car fuel?**

A new system is introduced from April 2003. If Graeme's car has an engine capacity of 1,998cc, its taxable value in 2002–03 is £2,850. From April 2003, the taxable value will be worked out using the same percentage as charged on the car itself (32%) but using a set 'price' for the fuel of £14,400. So, over a full year, Graeme would pay tax on £14,400 × 32% = £4,608 on his old car if he had it for the whole of 2003–04, and £14,400 × 22% = £3,168 on his new car.

Table 5.2: Percentage of car's price on which you will be taxed

CO_2 emissions	*Petrol car*			*Diesel car*		
*g/km**	*2002–03*	*2003–04*	*2004–05*	*2002–03*	*2003–04*	*2004–05*
	%	%	%	%	%	%
145–149	15	15	15	18	18	18
150–154	15	15	16	18	18	19
155–159	15	15	17	18	18	20
160–164	15	16	18	18	19	21
165–169	15	17	19	18	20	22
170–174	16	18	20	19	21	23
175–179	17	19	21	20	22	24
180–184	18	20	22	21	23	25
185–189	19	21	23	22	24	26
190–194	20	22	24	23	25	27
195–199	21	23	25	24	26	28
200–204	22	24	26	25	27	29
205–209	23	25	27	26	28	30
210–214	24	26	28	27	29	31
215–219	25	27	29	28	30	32
220–224	26	28	30	29	31	33
225–229	27	29	31	30	32	34
230–234	28	30	32	31	33	35
235–239	29	31	33	32	34	35
240–244	30	32	34	33	35	35
245–249	31	33	35	34	35	35
250–254	32	32	35	35	35	35
255–259	33	35	35	35	35	35
260–264	34	35	35	35	35	35
265 or more	35	35	35	35	35	35

*Grams per kilometre. If there is no approved CO_2 emissions figure, the percentage is: 15% of price if the engine size is under 1,401 cc; 25% for engines of 1,401–2,000cc; 35% for all other engines (or 15%, 22%, 32% if first registered before 1 January 1998). There are discounts for electric or gas-powered cars (see leaflet IR172 *Income tax and company cars*). And diesel cars approved to Euro IV limits are treated as petrol cars.

Table 5.3: The taxable value of free fuel

Engine capacity	2002–03 Petrol £	2002–03 Diesel £	2003–04
Up to 1,400cc	2,240	2,850	A new system applies. You pay tax at the relevant percentage in Table 5.2, but on a set figure of £14,400.
1,401cc–2,000cc	2,850	2,850	
2,001cc or more, or no cylinder capacity	4,200	4,200	

Free fuel – is it worth it?

You will cover the cost of the tax only if you spend more on fuel for private use than the amount of tax you will be charged. If you don't do much private mileage, consider paying for all your private fuel yourself, and negotiating a pay rise instead.

Alternatives to a company car

A company motorbike or van might be a cheaper alternative. Pool cars – used by more than one person, and not usually left overnight at your home – are completely tax-free, as are bicycles used mainly for travel from home to work or between workplaces.

Company vans

A company van you use for private travel is a taxable benefit, unless you are lower-paid (see page 92). There is no income tax on any free fuel, but you may have to pay National Insurance contributions. Note, though, that the taxation of company vans is under review.

The taxable value is £500, or £350 if the van is four or more years old, counted from when it was first registered to the end of the tax year in question. You can deduct anything you paid for its use. The taxable value is also reduced if the van was not available for the whole of the tax year.

If a van or vans are shared by different employees the taxable values of the vans are added together and then divided between the employees who share them. When this produces a taxable value per employee of more than £500, the taxable value is limited to £500.

You can opt to be taxed on a flat £5 per day you use the van – worthwhile if you have only occasional use.

Example 5.5: **Sharing a van**

If Del and Rodney, as directors of their own company, share their new van they simply split the £500 taxable value between them – £250 each. Things get a bit more complicated if Del lets Rodney share it for just part of the year:

1. First, the £500 is split in line with the 84 days the van is shared: £500 × 84⁄365 = £115.
2. Del and Rodney share the taxable value relating to the period of shared use – i.e. £115 ÷ 2 = £57.50. This is the total taxable amount for Rodney.
3. Del is taxed on the rest of the taxable value, i.e. £500 – £57.50 = £442.50.

Free or cheap accommodation

Free or cheap housing is tax-free if it is necessary for you to live there to do your job properly, or it is customary for people doing your type of job (e.g. caretakers) and helps you do your work better. (See Inland Revenue help sheet IR202 *Living accommodation*.) This does not apply to company directors, unless they are 'lower-paid' and they are full-time working directors or they work for a charity or a not-for-profit company. But housing is tax-free for all employees if there is a security threat and they are living there as part of special security measures.

Otherwise you are taxed on any accommodation provided by your employer, however much or little you earn. You are taxed on a basic amount, plus an extra amount if the property cost over £75,000, minus anything you pay for the accommodation. Figure 5.1 shows how this works. If part

Figure 5.1: Tax on free or cheap living accommodation

You are taxed on whichever of the following is higher:

- the yearly rent, if the property is rented
- *or* the gross rateable value of the property (or an estimate agreed with your tax office if there is no rateable value); the rateable value is multiplied by $^{100}/_{27}$ if the property is in Scotland to account for differences in rating revaluations
- *minus* any rent you pay

plus (if the property cost over £75,000)

- the cost (or market value, if whoever provides the property has owned it for at least six years before you moved in)
- *minus* £75,000
- *multiplied by* the 'official' rate of interest, set from time to time by the Revenue

plus (unless you are 'lower-paid')

- any expenses of the property paid by your employer, such as heating (tax-free for the lower-paid if the supplier's contract is with your employer)
- loans of furniture – see page 92. If the accommodation is tax-free (needed for your job, say), the maximum taxable amount is 10% of your taxable pay.

of the property is used for business, or it was available to you for only part of the year, you can also deduct a proportion to account for this.

Note that if you could choose higher pay instead of free accommodation, you are taxed on the extra pay if this is more than the taxable value of the accommodation.

Free or cheap loans

A free or cheap loan is tax-free if:

- your employer is in the loan or credit business, and you get your loan on the same terms and conditions as members of the public

- *or* you could claim full tax relief on the loan (see page 69), with no deduction for personal use
- *or* the total amount you owe throughout the tax year in question comes to £5,000 or less, excluding loans on which you can claim full tax relief. This exemption would normally cover season-ticket loans. If you go over the £5,000, the whole lot is taxable, not just the amount over £5,000.

The taxable amount, if any, is the difference between the interest you actually paid in the tax year (if any), and the interest you would have paid at the 'official' rate of interest set by the Revenue.

The taxable amount is usually worked out using the average of the official rate for the year, and the average loan outstanding. Revenue offices can tell you the current and average rates of interest. However, if the average figures would give an unrealistic answer (because you paid off most of the loan at the start of the year, say) either you or the Revenue can opt to use the real figures worked out on a daily basis.

For full details, see Inland Revenue leaflet IR145 *Low interest loans provided by employers.* A working sheet to help you calculate the taxable amount is included in the employers' section of the Revenue's website.

Example 5.6: **the value of a cheap loan**

Alberta works for a bank and gets a mortgage on preferential terms. She wants to know roughly how much this will cost her in tax in the coming year. She assumes an average 'official' interest rate of 5%, and an average actual rate of 3.5%.

She finds the average loan outstanding by adding the amount outstanding at the beginning of the tax year (£31,000) to the amount outstanding at the end of the tax year (£29,500) and dividing by two. This gives an average loan of £31,000 + £29,500 = £60,500 ÷ 2 = £30,250. She works out the taxable amount like this:

Interest due at official rate (5%)	£1,513
Minus interest due at average actual rate (3.5%)	£1,059
Taxable amount	£454

Share schemes

Various governments have tried to encourage employee share ownership. As a result, there are now five broad categories of 'approved' scheme, covered on page 87. Benefits from approved schemes are taxable only if you breach the conditions in some way (e.g. by withdrawing benefits early).

Because of the restrictions laid down for approval, employers may prefer to give their directors and employees 'unapproved' shares or share options (an 'option' is the right to buy shares at a set price at some point in the future). This is how unapproved share schemes are taxed.

Free or cheap shares

The normal rule, if you receive free or cheap shares from an unapproved share scheme, is that you are liable for income tax on the difference between what the shares are worth and the price you paid for them. (See Inland Revenue leaflet IR16 *Share acquisitions by directors and employees* and help sheet IR219 *Shares acquired from your employment*.)

To prevent employers reducing the taxable value of the shares by artificial schemes, you may also have a further tax bill (a 'post-acquisition charge') on benefits such as perks not available to other shareholders. A charge may also apply if schemes are constructed with restrictions or conversion options which can be used to increase their value later. These rules were tightened further in the 2003 Budget.

There is also special treatment for shares that were issued partly-paid or paid for in instalments, or that for some other reason are not counted as pay from your job. These may be taxed as if you had received an interest-free loan to buy them. (See Inland Revenue help sheet IR216 *Shares as benefits* and page 101.)

Share options

You might have to pay income tax on an option to buy shares:

- When you are granted the option (unless the share scheme is approved). The grant of an option in an unapproved scheme is taxable if the price at which you can buy the shares is less than the market price of the shares at the date the option is granted *and* you can use the option to buy shares more than ten years after receiving it.

- When you use the option to buy shares ('exercise' it).
- If you receive anything in return for cancelling the option – that is, agreeing not to exercise the option, or transferring it to someone else. You are taxed on the amount you receive, whether the scheme is approved or unapproved.

With all taxable options, you are taxed on the difference between the market value of the shares and what you would pay for them using the option. You can deduct anything you paid for the option itself.

How the tax is collected

Generally, if the shares involved are 'readily convertible' (i.e. quoted on a recognised stock exchange or otherwise easy to sell), your employer should deduct income tax and National Insurance from any taxable amount you have received. Exceptions are in Inland Revenue help sheet IR218 *Shares acquired: operation of PAYE.* If no tax has been deducted, or you are not sure that the right amount has been deducted, you must complete the Share Schemes supplementary pages of the tax return.

Sheltering your shares

If you are likely to make a taxable capital gain when you sell your shares, check whether you can transfer them into an Individual Savings Account (ISA). In some cases, transfers are free of capital gains tax, and shares in the ISA are tax-free when you eventually sell them. You may also be able to transfer shares into a personal pension fund.

Taxable lump sums when you leave a job

These payments fall into three categories: always tax-free, always taxable and sometimes taxable. (See Inland Revenue help sheet IR204 *Lump sums and compensation payments.*)

Negotiate before you leave

Lump sums are a difficult area, and much depends on the circumstances. Before leaving do your best to make sure that the deal is set up to produce the smallest tax bill for you. If the sum involved is large, or if you are a director, get professional advice.

Always tax-free

- Payments from an approved pension scheme, statutory pension scheme (e.g. the NHS scheme) or foreign government schemes.
- Special contributions made by your employer into an approved pension plan, if they are within the normal limits for contributions (see Chapter 7).
- If you are in the armed forces, a terminal grant, gratuity or other lump sum paid under Royal Warrant, Queen's Order, or Order in Council.
- Statutory redundancy payments.

Always taxable

- Any payment under your terms of employment – e.g. holiday pay, bonuses or outstanding salary paid out in a lump sum – except those specifically referred to as redundancy pay or benefits.
- Pay in lieu of notice (but this may be in the 'sometimes taxable' category if you were not entitled to this in your contract, and there was no custom of your employer making such payments). The Revenue regard payment during 'gardening leave', where notice is given but not worked, as taxable earnings.
- A non-contractual payment that your employer is accustomed to make or that you could reasonably have expected to receive.
- Compensation for changes in the terms and conditions of your job.
- Payment in return for agreeing to restrict your behaviour, e.g. not poaching your ex-employer's staff.

These payments will have tax and National Insurance deducted through PAYE like your ordinary pay.

Sometimes taxable

Other payments and benefits, including non-statutory redundancy pay, compensation for loss of your job and genuine ex gratia payments, are potentially taxable, but you can deduct:

- Payments if your job ends because of your death, injury or disability.
- Some or all payments if your job involved 'foreign service' (help sheet IR204 will help you work this out).
- The first £30,000 in total of any 'sometimes taxable' payments. Note that statutory redundancy pay, while tax-free itself, must be included when working out how much of the payment is over £30,000.

Any taxable amount is treated separately from your earnings, and taxed after your investment income. This works to your advantage because it means that a one-off lump sum does not push your investment income (which is favourably taxed in the lower- and basic-rate bands) into a higher tax-bracket. (See Chapter 1 for more on tax bands.)

Contributions made by your employer to an unapproved pension scheme for you when you leave are taxable unless your employer paid them because of an accident at work. Lump sums paid to you from such a scheme are also taxable unless you paid the contributions, or your employer paid them but you paid tax on them at the time, or (in some cases) they come from an overseas scheme. Include any taxable amounts in the Employment pages; if you have left the job and are not filling in the Employment pages, put them in Question 13 in the main return.

Example 5.7: **Leaving a job**

Alphonso is made redundant, with redundancy pay of £40,000 and pay in lieu of notice. He is taxed on the pay in lieu of notice because this was in his contract. The first £30,000 of his redundancy pay is tax-free, and the remaining £10,000 is taxable at his highest rate of tax.

Tax reliefs you can claim

Expenses

You can deduct from your employment income some payments you have to make in order to do your work. However, any expenses you claim must meet quite stringent tests in order to be 'allowable' (see below). Check also the list of tax-free income at the beginning of this chapter – some expenses are tax-free to start with, so they are not included in your taxable pay and you do not need to claim a deduction. The same applies to expenses covered by a 'dispensation' between your employer and your tax office (an arrangement to ignore particular allowable expenses).

Travel expenses

If you have to travel for work, whether or not you are reimbursed, you can claim tax relief on travel expenses, such as fares, and the cost of 'subsistence', e.g. accommodation and meals arising from business travel.

There are two types of journey for which you can claim relief (in both cases, the travel must be 'necessary', not just for personal convenience):

- Travel 'on the job', e.g. between two workplaces, or between appointments if you work at your clients' premises.
- Travel to or from a place that you go in order to do your job – but not ordinary commuting, or private travel to a place you do not have to attend for work purposes.

It is usually quite clear when the first type of journey applies, but the second can be tricky. It is easiest to start by ruling out ordinary commuting, which is defined as any travel between a permanent workplace and home, or any place that is not a workplace. 'Permanent' can apply to an area, if you have no single permanent workplace and your work is defined by reference to a particular area that you visit regularly – as area representative for Cornwall, say.

You *can* claim tax relief for travel between your home and a temporary workplace – somewhere you go to for a limited time or for a temporary purpose. But you cannot claim tax relief if you carry out, or expect to carry out, a significant part of your duties there over a period of 24 months, or as long as your job lasts if less than 24 months. The Revenue interpret 'significant' as more than 40 per cent of your working time

The Inland Revenue tome 490 *Employee travel. A tax and NICs guide for employers* has many examples of how these rules apply.

More generous rules for foreign travel

If you travel abroad for your work – and providing your employer pays the expenses or reimburses you – you can claim the cost of all journeys from anywhere in the UK and for a spouse and children who accompany you, if your work keeps you abroad for 60 days or more. See Chapter 9 for the rules if you do all your work abroad.

Example 5.8: **Is it business travel?**

Annie, Betty and Charlie are all full-time engineers based at head office in Reading. They are all sent to work on a contract in Norwich:

- Annie is sent to work full-time on a particular phase of the work expected to last about 14 months. Norwich counts as a temporary workplace, and she can claim tax relief on the cost of getting there, hotel bills and meals.
- Betty spends only three days a week in Norwich, but as this is more than 40% of her working week and her work there is expected to last for three years, Norwich is not a temporary workplace and she cannot claim tax relief.
- Charlie is also expected to be in Norwich for three years, but he spends only one day a week there. This is not a significant part of his duties so he can claim relief.

Using your own car, van or bike for work

Whichever way your employer reimburses you – flat-rate allowance, mileage allowance, or not at all – you are entitled to the same amount of tax relief, worked out using Revenue-approved mileage rates. These 'approved mileage allowance payments' (AMAP) are shown in Table 5.4.

- If your employer pays you more than the approved rates, any excess is taxable pay and will be shown on your P11D.
- If your employer pays you the approved rates the amount will not appear on your P11D, but you cannot claim any tax relief.
- If your employer pays you less than the approved rates, you can claim tax relief on the difference between the approved rates and what you received (see Example 5.9 on page 110). You need to keep a tally of business mileage – there is a log sheet in Inland Revenue leaflet IR124 *Using your own vehicle for work*.
- Your employer can also pay you an allowance of up to 5p per mile, tax-free, if you carry other employees on business travel, but you cannot claim tax relief if you are paid less than 5p a mile.

The AMAP rates are designed to take account of the capital cost of buying a car. You cannot claim any additional tax relief to cover the cost of buying or renting the car, or for depreciation.

Note that if you have a company car but no free fuel, and your employer reimburses you for the cost of your business mileage, this is tax-free and will not appear on your P11D.

Table 5.4: Approved mileage rates for 2002–03 and 2003–04

	First 10,000 business miles — in tax year —	*Each mile over 10,000 miles — in tax year —*
Cars and vans	40p	25p
Motorcycles	24p	24p
Bicycles	20p	20p

Example 5.9: **Tax relief if you use your own car**

Annie works as an educational adviser. In 2002–03, she drove 12,000 business miles in her own car. Her employer paid her 35p a mile. This is less than the approved rates, so nothing is shown on the form P11D provided by her employer, and she does not have to enter the amounts received on her tax return. Annie works out that she has received £300 less than the approved rates, so she can claim tax relief on this amount.

Using approved rates	
First 10,000 miles at 40p a mile	£4,000
Next 2,000 miles at 25p a mile	£500
Total approved mileage payments	£4,500
Using employer's rates	
12,000 miles at 35p a mile	£4,200
Difference	£300

Other expenses

In order to qualify for tax relief on non-travel expenses, you must have incurred them 'wholly, exclusively and necessarily in the performance of the duties of the employment'. It is for the courts to interpret this, but Table 5.5 lists the main expenses that you might be able to claim.

National Insurance contributions (NICs)

You have to pay NICs on your 'earnings', unless you are over state pension age. Your earnings for National Insurance purposes are different from your taxable pay for income tax purposes, although the rules are gradually being aligned. Here are the main differences:

- You do not have to pay NICs on most fringe benefits (see page 94), but your employer does.
- Contributions you make to a pension scheme or payroll-giving scheme are included in your pay when working out your NICs. You

Table 5.5: Non-travel expenses you might be able to claim

Books	If needed to do your job, not just to keep up to date. May have to claim capital allowances instead if costly and expected life of over two years.
Business entertaining	You can claim only if you work for: ■ a non-trading organisation *or* ■ a trading organisation which has not itself claimed tax relief on the payments (look for a tick in section O of your form P11D), and which has reimbursed you or provided a special entertaining allowance.
Capital allowances for cost of buying equipment and machinery necessary for your work, e.g. office equipment	Percentage of the cost of things such as office equipment, but not cars, motorbikes or bikes. If you make a profit when you sell things on which you have claimed an allowance, there is a taxable 'balancing charge'. (See Inland Revenue help sheet IR206 *Capital allowances for employees and office holders.*)
Employee liabilities and indemnities	Cost of meeting claims for your errors or omissions as an employee, or insurance to cover such costs.
Guide dog if blind	Cost of keeping and replacing a dog.
Home phone	May be a tax-free perk, see page 86. If not, you can claim work-related share of call charges if a phone is necessary (e.g. for a health worker on call or if you are required to work at home). You cannot claim line rental costs, so get your employer to pay direct.
Loan interest	Only if you can also claim capital allowances on the item you are buying, and the loan is repaid within three years.
Professional fees and subscriptions	Payments that are relevant to your work, or a condition of working (e.g. as a solicitor). Ask your professional body or tax office which fees qualify.
Special security measures	If they are necessary because of your job.
Cost of maintaining or replacing tools, special clothing (but not ordinary clothing worn at work)	Fixed expense deductions have been agreed for workers in some industries, e.g. £115 for carpenters. You can claim more if you spend more. Check with your union or tax office.
Working at home	Provided the work you do at home is part of your central duties, and you are contractually required to work there, you can claim a share of running costs, e.g. heating and lighting bills. But from 6 April 2003 payments by your employer to cover such costs are tax-free.

get income tax relief on these payments, but no relief from your NICs.

The contributions payable are shown in Table 5.6, and Chapter 2 explains how they are collected and how to check the deductions. Note that employees used to pay contributions only on what they earned between an earnings threshold and the upper earnings limit. However, from April 2003, an extra contribution of 1 per cent is payable by employees on earnings above the upper limit.

Saving tax on pension contributions

You pay National Insurance on your own contributions to a pension, but not on your employer's contributions. You may save money by giving up some of your salary in return for a higher employer's pension contribution. This won't work if you pay and your employer reimburses you – if your employer is paying into a personal pension for you, the pension application form should state that these are your employer's contributions.

What to tell the Inland Revenue

Your employer should give your tax office all the information it needs. But it is worth telling your tax office if your circumstances change (see Chapter 2). You also need to contact your tax office if you want to claim tax relief on work expenses and do not get a tax return – ask for Expenses Claim form P87.

If you get a tax return and receive any income or benefit from employment, tick Question 1 in the main tax return and fill in the Employment supplementary pages *unless:*

- all your employment income is from overseas and you are claiming that you were not resident in the UK (see Chapter 9)
- *or* you are a director who received no payment in any form, or held a position, such as honorary secretary, and received only expenses.

Table 5.6: Class 1 National Insurance contributions 2002–03 (2003–04)

Earnings	*Employee*	*Employer*
First £89 (£89) weekly, £385 (£385) monthly, £4,615 (£4,615) annually	**Nil**	**Nil**
Earnings threshold		
Next £496 (£506) weekly, £2,150 (£2,194) monthly, £25,805 (£26,325) annually	**10% (11%)** or **8.4% (9.4%)** if a member of an occupational pension scheme 'contracted out' of the State Earnings Related Pension Scheme (SERPS). Some married women may pay less, see page 26	**11.8% (12.8%)** reduced if employer offers a 'contracted-out' pension scheme
Upper earnings limit		
Anything above £585 (£595) weekly, £2,535 (£2,579) monthly, £30,420 (£30,940) annually	**Nil (1%)**	**11.8% (12.8%)**

Even in the two cases described above, you need to tick Question 1 and write an explanation in 'Additional information' at the end of the return.

You will also have to tick Question 2 in the main return and fill in the Share Schemes supplementary pages if:

- you have received taxable benefits from an unapproved employee share scheme in 2002–03, or breached the conditions of an approved share scheme (see pages 87 and 103) *and*
- your employer has not already deducted the full amount of tax due under PAYE. If tax has been deducted under PAYE, remember to enter it on the Employment supplementary pages.

Filling in the Employment supplementary pages

If you had more than one job during the tax year, you will need to fill in one copy of these pages for each employer. Usually, you can just carry information across from the P60 your employer gives you after the tax year (or P45 if you left a job), and from your P11D *Expenses and benefits* form, or the equivalent form P9D if you are 'lower-paid'. (See Inland Revenue help sheet IR208 *Payslips and Coding Notices* for where to find the information.)

If you had two jobs, or are unemployed at the end of the tax year, note that your P60 may include figures for both jobs and any taxable Jobseeker's Allowance. If so, you will need to separate the figures to put them on separate pages, using your payslips, P45 or other records.

Boxes 1.1 to 1.7 Details of employer

This will allow your tax office to check and update your file. Note that you have to tick box 1.6 if you are a director, and box 1.7 if a director of a 'close' company (one controlled either by its directors or by less than six shareholders or other key 'participators'). This is because special rules often apply to directors, for example when taxing fringe benefits.

Boxes 1.8 to 1.11 Money

You should include in boxes 1.8 to 1.10:

- all the taxable income listed on page 89, excluding expenses payments (these go in box 1.23); don't include pension contributions and payroll-giving donations (your P60 will already have excluded these)
- any extra taxable pay, if you are a director or partner affected by the IR35 rules (see page 90)
- any taxable income from share schemes that has already been taxed under PAYE (this should be included in the figure on your P60).

Box 1.11 is for any tax deductions shown on your P60 (or P45). It is not always clear what your employer has included in the P60 figure, say if you have received a taxed lump sum on leaving a job or paid tax on share perks, so you may need to ask your employer what has been included.

Enter non-UK tax either on page 2 or claim a separate relief for it in the Foreign supplementary pages (see Chapter 9).

Boxes 1.12 to 1.23 Benefits and expenses

Enter here any taxable benefits and expenses you have received. You should be able to take all the figures straight from your P11D or P9D. See page 92 onwards for how these figures are arrived at, but note that:

- you need to enter a figure in box 1.15 (mileage allowance) only if your employer pays you *more* than the Inland Revenue approved mileage rates shown in Table 5.4
- the 'balancing charges' referred to in box 1.23 apply only if you have disposed of (e.g. sold) something on which you previously claimed capital allowances.

Common mistakes

- Failure to complete a separate supplementary page for each job.
- Entering your pay in box 1.8 but not entering any tax deducted in box 1.11.
- Entering your gross pay in box 1.8, before deducting pension contributions and payroll giving.
- Entering tax deductions more than once – e.g. tax on a lump sum should go in either box 1.11 or box 1.30, not both.

Boxes 1.24 to 1.30 Lump sums

If you received a redundancy payment in 2002–03, the first £30,000 is tax-free. Put the tax-free amount in box 1.24 and anything else in box 1.29.

However, it is not always clear whether a payment counts as 'redundancy', and amounts such as pay in lieu of notice are always taxable (for an overview, see page 104). If you are unsure, or receive any payments within the 'always taxable' category on page 105, or are claiming deductions other than the £30,000 exemption, read the Inland Revenue help sheet IR204

Figure 5.2: Employment page 1 (see Example 5.10)

Inland Revenue

Income for the year ended 5 April 2003

EMPLOYMENT

Fill in these boxes first

Name: MINDY MALONE

Tax reference: 12345 67890

If you want help, look up the box numbers in the Notes.

Details of employer

Employer's PAYE reference - may be shown under 'Inland Revenue office number and reference' on your P60 or 'PAYE reference' on your P45

1.1 A1111234

Employer's name

1.2 DUSTY MILLER BAKERIES

Date employment started (only if between 6 April 2002 and 5 April 2003)

1.3 / /

Date employment finished (only if between 6 April 2002 and 5 April 2003)

1.4 / /

Employer's address

1.5 CRUSTY HOUSE
FRIARY ROAD
CRUNCHESTER

Postcode XX9 1AB

Tick box 1.6 if you were a director of the company

1.6

and, if so, tick box 1.7 if it was a close company

1.7

Income from employment

■ ***Money*** - *see Notes, page EN3*

		Box	
• Payments from P60 (or P45)		1.8	Before tax £ 29,500
• Payments not on P60 etc.	- tips	1.9	£
	- other payments (excluding expenses entered below and lump sums and compensation payments or benefits entered overleaf)	1.10	£
• **Tax deducted** in the UK from payments in boxes 1.8 to 1.10		1.11	Tax deducted £ 8,613

■ ***Benefits and expenses*** - *see Notes, pages EN3 to EN6. If any benefits connected with termination of employment were received, or enjoyed, after that termination and were from a **former** employer you need to complete Help Sheet IR204, available from the Orderline. Do not enter such benefits here.*

	Box	Amount		Box	Amount
• Assets transferred/ payments made for you	1.12	£	• Vans	1.18	£
• Vouchers, credit cards and tokens	1.13	£	• Interest-free and low-interest loans *see Note for box 1.19, page EN5*	1.19	£
• Living accommodation	1.14	£	*box 1.20 is not used*		
• Excess mileage allowances and passenger payments	1.15	£	• Private medical or dental insurance	1.21	£ 1,200
• Company cars	1.16	£ 5,400	• Other benefits	1.22	£
• Fuel for company cars	1.17	£ 2,850	• Expenses payments received and balancing charges	1.23	£ 1,024

SA101

Figure 5.3: Employment page 2 (see Example 5.10)

Income from employment continued

■ ***Lump sums and compensation payments or benefits including such payments and benefits from a former employer***
Note that 'lump sums' here includes any contributions which your employer made to an unapproved retirement benefits scheme

You must read page EN6 of the Notes ***before*** *filling in boxes 1.24 to 1.30*

Reliefs

- £30,000 exemption — 1.24 £
- Foreign service and disability — 1.25 £
- Retirement and death lump sums — 1.26 £

Taxable lump sums

- From box B of *Help Sheet IR204* — 1.27 £
- From box K of *Help Sheet IR204* — 1.28 £
- From box L of *Help Sheet IR204* — 1.29 £
- Tax deducted from payments in boxes 1.27 to 1.29 - *leave blank if this tax is included in the box 1.11 figure.* — Tax deducted 1.30 £

■ ***Foreign earnings not taxable in the UK in the year ended 5 April 2003*** - see Notes, page EN6 — 1.31 £

■ ***Expenses you incurred in doing your job*** - see Notes, pages EN7 to EN8

- Travel and subsistence costs — 1.32 £ 840
- Fixed deductions for expenses — 1.33 £
- Professional fees and subscriptions — 1.34 £ 96
- Other expenses and capital allowances — 1.35 £
- Tick box 1.36 if the figure in box 1.32 includes travel between your home and a permanent workplace — 1.36

■ ***Foreign Earnings Deduction*** (seafarers only) — 1.37 £

■ ***Foreign tax for which tax credit relief not claimed*** — 1.38 £

Student Loans

■ ***Student Loans repaid by deduction by employer*** - see Notes, page EN8 — 1.39 £

- Tick box 1.39A if your income is under Repayment of Teachers' Loans Scheme — 1.39A

1.40 ***Additional information***

Now fill in any other supplementary Pages that apply to you.
Otherwise, go back to page 2 in your Tax Return and finish filling it in.

Lump sums and compensation payments to help you work out the taxable amount to the Revenue's satisfaction. To sum up:

- Box 1.27 is for payments received under the terms of your employment – the 'always taxable' category on page 105.
- Box 1.28 is for lump sums from non-approved retirement schemes, minus any tax-free amounts (which should be entered in box 1.26).
- Box 1.29 is for other payments in the 'sometimes taxable' category on page 106, including redundancy, minus deductions for foreign service or disability (box 1.25) and minus the £30,000 exemption (box 1.24).

Note, though, that the £30,000 exemption is per job, so if you received payments relating to one job in more than one tax year you may already have used part of the exemption. If so, you should use help sheet IR204.

Boxes 1.32 to 1.36 Expenses

Enter here work expenses for which you are claiming tax relief (see Table 5.5 on page 111). Note that box 1.36 ('includes travel between your home and a permanent workplace') is a bit of a trap. You cannot usually claim tax relief for home-to-work travel, and if you tick box 1.36 prepare to justify your claim to your tax office.

Boxes 1.31, 1.37 and 1.38 Foreign earnings and foreign tax

If you have included income from working abroad in boxes 1.8 to 1.10 you may be able to claim deductions:

- in box 1.31 depending on whether or not you are a UK resident for tax purposes, and where the job was done (see Inland Revenue help sheet IR211 *Employment – residence and domicile issues*)
- in box 1.37 if you were a seafarer working outside the UK – see Inland Revenue help sheet IR205 *Foreign earnings deduction: seafarers*)
- in box 1.38 to account for any foreign tax you have paid. Note, though, that 'tax credit relief' may be a better option – if so, you will need to complete the Foreign supplementary pages (see page 210).

Boxes 1.39 and 1.39A Student loans and Teachers' Loan Scheme

If you have an 'income-contingent' student loan (see page 6) and your employer has deducted loan repayments from your pay, enter the total deductions here. The amount will be shown on your P60, but if you change jobs you should also check the amounts shown on your payslips. Tick box 1.39A if you have a loan, but the government is paying it for you under the Teachers' Loan Scheme and your employer has been notified of this.

Example 5.10: **Filling in the Employment pages**

Mindy is a personnel manager. In her Employment pages (shown in Figures 5.2 and 5.3), she enters the 'Pay' figure (£29,500) from her P60 in box 1.8, and the 'Tax' figure (£8,613) in box 1.11. (She contributes to the company pension scheme, but the 'pay' figure in her P60 has taken account of this.)

Mindy takes the figures for her benefits and expenses from her P11D. These add £10,474 to her pay, but on page 2 she can claim tax relief for some expenses – £840 for travel expenses and £96 for her subscription to her professional institute. Her taxable pay is £29,500 + £10,474 – £936 = £39,038. Her fringe benefits have pushed her into the higher-rate tax band, which starts (in 2002–03) once your taxable income exceeds £29,900.

Record-keeping

Here are some of the key records you should keep.

Your pay

- Your P60 or P45 as evidence of your taxable pay, and your P11D or P9D showing taxable benefits and expenses.
- A note of any tips or gratuities, or any other taxable pay. Record these as soon as you get them, rather than estimating them later.
- Correspondence relating to any lump sum payment.

Your expenses

- Copies of expense claims and foreign travel itineraries.

- Records of business mileage and other motoring expenses.
- Receipts, credit statements and other purchase records. If you have given these to your employer, copies of your expense claims may help.
- Notes of cash payments for which you have not got a receipt.

If you are in a share scheme or receive share-related benefits

- Any related correspondence from your employer.
- The price you paid for your shares or options, and the relevant dates.
- The market value of the shares at relevant dates, such as when you receive them (or options to buy them) or exercise your option to buy.
- A copy of each share option certificate or exercise notice.
- Notes of any benefits received, or alteration in the rights or restrictions attached to your shares.

Tax-planning hints

1 Beware of the IR35 rules if you are a director or partner in your own business providing services (see page 90).
2 Make life easy – keep your P60, P45 and P11D carefully. And keep your own records of expenses, particularly business mileage.
3 If you use your own car for work, you can claim tax relief at the approved mileage rates even if your employer pays less (see page 109).
4 You can claim tax relief on home-to-work travel if you are working at a temporary but not a permanent workplace (see page 108).
5 Free fuel for your company car is now heavily taxed, particularly if you end up paying National Insurance on fuel bills reimbursed by your employer (see page 94). Consider paying for your private fuel yourself (but you have to pay for the whole cost of private use, not just part).
6 A more fuel-efficient company car will save you tax (and see page 99 for cheaper alternatives).
7 If you are in an approved share scheme, check the rules – you may have to pay tax if you breach the conditions.
8 Capital gains tax may be payable when you sell shares from some share schemes. You may avoid this if you transfer the shares to an ISA first.

9 If you get a pay-off on leaving a job, negotiate with your employer to make sure it is paid in a way that minimises your tax bill (see page 105).

10 Your own contributions to a pension scheme are liable to National Insurance, but your employer's are not. You save National Insurance if you sacrifice salary for higher employer's pension contributions.

11 Don't forget to enter on your Employment supplementary pages *all* the tax you have paid or had deducted.

6

Income from your business

As the 'job for life' moves towards extinction, more people are experiencing self-employment for at least part of their working lives. However, becoming self-employed also means taking responsibility for sorting out your own tax, and organising your cashflow so that you can pay your tax in two instalments, on 31 January and 31 July each year.

When you are starting up on your own, sorting out your tax may be a less immediate concern than meeting your first orders. However, it cannot be ignored. You must notify the Inland Revenue within three months of starting up, or risk a £100 penalty.

On the plus side, making full use of the various types of tax relief available to the self-employed can keep your tax bill low.

Does this affect you?

This chapter affects you if you are self-employed, either as a sole trader or in a partnership. If you are a director of your own company, you are also 'in business', but strictly speaking you are an employee and your tax is covered in Chapter 5. The company has its own tax return and is subject to corporation tax – not covered in this book.

This chapter does not affect you if receive odd bits of freelance income – e.g. from writing an article – but have not set up in business to do this. Income of this type is taxed separately and should be reported under 'All other income' in Question 13 of the tax return. However, if your income of this type becomes substantial, you might be regarded as trading – if in doubt, contact your local tax office.

Sole traders

A 'sole trader' is what you are if you simply start up on your own, without creating (or buying into) a partnership or setting up a company (a separate legal entity). The whole of any profits or losses counts as your income, on which you are liable to pay income tax and Class 2 and Class 4 NICs.

Partners

As a partner, you have a share in the partnership's profits or losses, as set out in the partnership agreement. The partnership has its own tax return, but is not itself taxed – you pay income tax and National Insurance on your share of profits as if you were a sole trader. And you can make your own choices about how you use your share of any losses – your choices may be different from those of other partners.

Other taxes to consider

As a sole trader or partner, you may have to pay capital gains tax (see Chapter 11) on profits from disposing of business equipment or property, although there are special tax reliefs which businesses can claim. If you are a partner, you are taxed only on your share of any capital gains (or losses). However, transfer of the assets between partners can also create a taxable capital gain.

There is also VAT to consider. You have to register for VAT only if your turnover over the previous 12 months (excluding exempt sales) is above a threshold, or you expect your turnover to be above in the next 30 days. The threshold was £55,000 in 2002–03, rising to £56,000 from 10 April 2003. You may want to register even if you are below the threshold as you can reclaim VAT on what you buy, but the VAT will put up your prices to retail customers. There are special schemes that make the paperwork simpler for small businesses, such as the flat rate scheme (see page 135).

Sole trader, partner or company?

The legal form your business should take depends on your individual situation and the nature and needs of your business – and may shift over time as tax rules change (company tax law is under review) and as your business develops. Get specialist advice, but do not be driven by tax considerations alone – companies have to meet many more legal requirements than sole traders.

Are you really self-employed?

Problems can arise if your tax office decides you are not self-employed, but are an employee of your client, liable to PAYE and employee's National Insurance. This may also affect you if you are a director of your own company, and your tax office seeks to apply the special 'IR35' rules (see page 90).

There is no simple definition of self-employment, but there have been many relevant court cases, and a number of 'tests' have developed. (See Table 6.1, but note that it is the overall picture that counts, and each test cannot be looked at in isolation.) If you are not sure how the tests apply to you, you can ask your tax office for a written decision about your 'employment status', as it is called, but note that you can be employed for one piece of work and self-employed for another – it all depends on the circumstances. (See Inland Revenue leaflet IR56 *Employed or self-employed?*.)

How income tax on your business is worked out

You are taxed on your business profits (or losses) for a 'basis period'. Normally, your basis period is the accounting period ending in the tax year in question. So if you make up your accounts to the end of December each year, say, in the 2002–03 tax year you pay tax on your profits for the period for 1 January 2002 to 31 December 2002.

Inland Revenue help sheet IR222 *How to calculate your taxable profits* explains basis periods.

Table 6.1: Tests for self-employment

These suggest employment	*These suggest self-employment*
Control Your client has the right to tell you at any time what to do, or when and how to do it	**Right to subcontract** You can choose whether to do the work yourself or hire (and pay) someone else to do it for you
Location You work at your client's premises, or at a place or places he or she decides	**Providing your own equipment** You supply the main items needed to do your job
Payment You are paid by the hour, week or month, receive overtime pay and benefits (e.g. sick pay or expenses) and work set hours or a given number of hours a week or month	**Risking your own money** You bear the cost of overheads, working on a fixed price, spending significant amounts on skills training for use in future work
Part and parcel of the organisation You are someone taken on to manage a client's staff, for example	**Risk of losses** You have to correct unsatisfactory work in your own time and at your own expense
Right of dismissal You have the right to notice of a set length	**Personal factors** You may be, for example, a skilled worker working for several clients in a year
Long periods working for one client	**No right to work and pay** Your client has no obligation to provide work or pay when no work is available
Intention Whether you and your client intend you to be self-employed only comes into play if all other tests are neutral	

Working out your taxable profits

You must work out your profits on an 'earnings' basis – i.e. income is included in your accounts from the date it is earned, not when you receive it, and expenses on the date you incur them, not the date you pay the bill.

- *Step 1: add up your business income (i.e. turnover)* (see next page).

- *Step 2: deduct your business expenses,* adjusted to take account of any expenses in your accounts not allowed for tax, such as depreciation on cars and business equipment (see opposite).
- *Step 3: deduct capital allowances,* you can claim these instead of depreciation (see page 132).

The result of steps 1 to 3 is your net business profits (or losses) for an accounting period for tax purposes. But there are further adjustments that look beyond your latest set of accounts:

- *Step 4: adjustments if your basis period is not the same as your accounting period.* This usually affects you in the first year or so you are in business or in your final year of trading (see page 136 for how it works).
- *Step 5: deduct losses from previous years* – the result is your taxable profit for a basis period.
- *Step 6: add on any other taxable business income.* This includes business start-up allowances, taxable payments from the New Deal scheme and incentives received if you take a lease on business property. You cannot deduct anything from it for expenses and so on.

The result gives you your taxable income from self-employment, which is taxed at 10 per cent, 22 per cent or 40 per cent, according to what falls into the lower-, basic- and higher-rate bands (see page 5).

A partner in a partnership? Steps 1 to 3 all take place in the partnership's tax return. The business profits (or losses) are then shared out according to the partnership agreement, and the adjustments covered in steps 4 to 6 are made in your own tax return. Joining a partnership counts as starting in business, and leaving counts as closing down.

Business income

Your income from self-employment consists of the turnover from your trade or profession, i.e. your trading income. (Note that a rental business may be classified as a trade – see Chapter 8.) There is no tax-free income to ignore. If you take things from stock for your own or your family's use, remember that this counts as a sale.

What expenses can you deduct?

The law concentrates on what you *cannot* do rather than what you can – in particular, you cannot deduct expenses which are not 'wholly and exclusively' for your trade.

However, there are many expenses that the Revenue will commonly accept. And if an expense is partly for business, partly private, you can usually claim a proportion in line with the business use. For example, you can claim some expenses for using your car or home for work. Table 6.2 summarises the main items, but there is more detail in the notes to the Self-employment or Partnership pages of the tax return.

The main expenses you cannot deduct

- The cost of buying or improving fixed assets, or depreciation (you can claim capital allowances instead).
- Costs and fines for breaking the law (parking fines, say).
- Business hospitality – you can claim the cost of entertaining staff, but not if this arises as part of business hospitality (e.g. if an employee takes a customer out to lunch, the whole cost is business hospitality).
- The non-business part of any expense.
- Tax (but you can deduct employers' NICs and, if you are not VAT-registered, VAT).
- Your own pay, benefits, pension contributions and NICs.

Raw materials and goods bought for resale

If you make or sell things, you will need to carry out a stock-take at the end of each accounting period. You should value your stocks (including your work in progress) at their cost to you or, if lower, the amount they would fetch. Include things that you have received but not yet paid for.

To work out what you have used during the period:

- take the value of your stock and work in progress at the start of the period
- *add* anything you bought during the period
- *deduct* what you have left at the end of the period.

Table 6.2: Summary of business expenses you can claim

Advertising and promotion	Newspaper advertisements, mailshots, non-consumable gifts with a prominent advertisement worth £50 or less per person
Bad debts	Amount of money included in turnover but written off at end of accounting period (not a general bad debts reserve)
Employee costs	See opposite
General administrative costs	Phone bills, postage, stationery, printing, office expenses, insurance, papers and publications
Interest and other finance costs	See page 131
Legal and professional costs	Fees of accountant, solicitor, surveyor, stocktaker etc., professional indemnity insurance, costs of debt recovery (but not legal costs of buying or selling fixed assets)
Premises costs	See opposite
Raw materials and goods bought for resale	See page 127
Business costs of cars and other vehicles	See page 130
Other business travel costs	Rail, air and taxi fares, hotels, meals when away overnight on business
Pre-trading expenditure	Allowable expenses are treated as if incurred on the date you start trading
Research and development costs related to a trade (not a profession)	Excludes costs of acquiring rights to research – you may be able to claim capital allowances instead
Subscriptions to relevant trade and professional associations	Also contributions to local enterprise agencies and other such bodies

Employee costs

You can deduct all the costs of hiring other people, whether they are permanent, temporary or casual staff, or subcontractors. This includes pay, pension contributions, employer's NICs and all other staff-related costs, such as fringe benefits and training.

However, you cannot deduct your own pay, National Insurance, benefits or pension contributions. You can claim the cost of your own training if this is to update your existing skills, but you may have difficulty justifying your claim if the result is a completely new specialisation or qualification.

If you take on an employee, you will have to comply with the requirements for operating PAYE (see Chapter 2). The Revenue have a new employer's helpline with which you can register (see the Fact File).

Premises

If you have business premises, you can claim rent, business rates, water rates, light, heat, power, maintenance and repairs (but not improvements), property insurance, security costs and so on. For leases of 50 years or less, you can claim part of any premium you have to pay. You cannot claim the cost of buying property, although you may be able to claim capital allowances for some industrial buildings or hotels.

If you work from home, you can claim the same types of expense (including mortgage interest and council tax), in line with the proportion of your home that you use for business purposes. The basis for any claim should be explained – and records kept to support it.

Using part of your home exclusively for work

If part of your home is used exclusively for business, part of any gain when you sell the house is liable to capital gains tax (see Chapter 11). You can avoid this by ensuring that there is some private use – e.g. by using your office as a guest room as well. And even if part of your home does become liable to capital gains tax, the gain would be reduced by taper relief for business assets, and possibly roll-over relief.

Example 6.1: **Using your home for work**

Paul runs a software business from home. He has one of the eight rooms set aside as an office, and he claims one-eighth of his mortgage interest as a business expense. At the end of the tax year he asks his lender for a 'certificate of interest paid' and claims one-eighth of the interest shown (he can't claim capital repayments).

Cars and other vehicles

You can claim running costs of a car or other vehicle you use for work, including fuel, servicing, repairs, road tax, insurance, parking charges (but not fines) and the cost of rescue services.

If you use the car for private purposes as well as for business, there are two methods of claiming vehicle costs:

- you can claim a proportion of the costs, in line with the amount of business mileage you do, plus capital allowances
- *or* if your turnover is below the level at which you need to register for VAT (see page 123), whether or not you have registered, you can claim a set figure per business mile, using the mileage rates shown in Table 5.4 on page 109. If you do this, you cannot also claim capital allowances.

Note that you can only change between the two methods when you acquire a car – you cannot chop and change. Whichever method you use, you can claim interest on a loan to buy the car, or other finance costs (see below).

Example 6.2: **Claiming your car as an expense**

About 20% of Leah's mileage is for business. She can either claim 20% of the running costs of her car, plus a £600 capital allowance for the cost of buying it (see Example 6.4), or she can claim just the Revenue-approved mileage rate (40p per mile in Leah's case). In either case, she can also claim 20% of the interest on her car loan.

Interest and other finance costs

You can claim bank charges, credit card charges and overdraft interest. You can also claim interest on a loan to buy something you use in your business (or a proportion of the interest if you use it partly for business, partly privately). This includes hire purchase interest (but not capital repayments) and finance lease rentals.

However, if you lease a car (but not a van) worth more than £12,000 when new, you can claim only part of the hire charge. The percentage you can claim is the car's price plus £12,000, divided by twice the car's price – this works out at 90 per cent if the price is £15,000, 80 per cent with a £20,000 price, and 70 per cent with a £30,000 price.

Employing family members

You can claim tax relief on the pay and National Insurance of a family member you employ, but you must be able to show that the work is needed for the business, the family member actually does it and is formally paid for doing it, and that you are paying the National Minimum Wage. There is no National Insurance on earnings below £4,615 (see Chapter 2), but if you pay at least £77 a week your employee will become entitled to contributory state benefits such as the retirement pension.

Get your expenses established early

When you start up, even if you are intending to keep your own books, it is worth getting help in establishing what expenses you can claim and what records you need to back them up. You can use an accountant, or ask your tax office about the Revenue's business support service.

What to do about VAT and your expenses

If you are VAT-registered, your profits are usually worked out excluding VAT on both your income and your expenses (although you can use VAT-inclusive figures). If you are not VAT-registered, you can claim expenses and capital allowances including the amount of any VAT.

Capital allowances

If you buy plant and machinery (capital assets) for use in your business, such as cars, vans, tools, computers and office equipment, you can claim capital allowances to be deducted from your profits. Only part of the allowance can be claimed if an asset is used partly for private purposes.

You can also claim capital allowances on some industrial or agricultural buildings and hotels, and on things like patents and scientific 'know-how'. However, here we concentrate on plant and machinery. You cannot claim capital allowances on houses or (except in an enterprise zone) on shops or offices, but you can claim them on some fixtures and fittings and the costs of converting flats over shops (see Chapter 8).

Working out allowances on plant and machinery

The basic principle of capital allowances is that you claim 25 per cent of the cost of an item each year, and so write it off over a period of time. However, in the accounting period in which you buy something, you may be able to claim a higher 'first-year allowance'.

Small and medium-sized businesses can claim 40 per cent in the first year on most plant and machinery and 100 per cent on most items for use in Northern Ireland acquired before 12 May 2002. Small businesses can claim 100 per cent in the first year on computer and communication technology, including WAP mobile phones, acquired before 1 April 2004. And businesses of any size can claim 100 per cent on some energy-saving plant and machinery – *including* new cars with CO_2 emissions of 120g per kilometre or less. The scheme is being extended during 2003 to cover equipment to improve water use. (There is a special Inland Revenue website listing items that qualify – see the Fact File.)

The cost of each new item, after deducting any first-year allowance, is added to a 'pool' of expenditure. Some things have to be kept in separate pools, but everything else goes in one main pool – see Figure 6.1.

At the end of each accounting period you work out your writing-down allowance on each pool as follows:

1. Take the value of the pool at the end of the previous accounting period and add the cost of any new purchases, excluding those which qualify for a first-year allowance.
2. Deduct the proceeds of any sale from the value of the pool, or the original cost of the item if less. (The market value is deducted if you gave the item away or started to use it for non-business purposes.) If the sale proceeds are more than the value of the pool, the difference is a *balancing charge*.
3. Multiply the result by 25 per cent. This is your *writing-down allowance* on the pool. Deduct the writing-down allowance from the value of the pool so far.
4. Add the cost of any new purchases which qualified for a first-year allowance (after deducting first-year allowance). The result is the value of your pool at the start of the next accounting period.

The total of your first-year allowances and writing-down allowances is *deducted* from your taxable profits. If you sell something in the pool for more than the value of the pool so far, the difference is a balancing charge and it is *added* to your profits.

Your allowance or balancing charge must be adjusted if:

- You use an item partly for business, partly privately. The capital allowance (or balancing charge) is restricted in line with the proportion of any business use (see Example 6.4 on page 136) and you must keep it in a separate 'pool'.
- Your accounting period is not 12 months (e.g. when starting up in business). If your accounting period is eight months long, say, you get eight-twelfths of the full writing-down allowance. But first-year allowances are not adjusted in this way.

Figure 6.1: What happens in the year you buy a new item

1 Can you claim a 100% first-year allowance?

Claim the whole of the cost. The item is still added to your pool in case there is a balancing charge when you sell it. If it is used partly privately, put it in its own pool, otherwise put it in your main pool.

2 Is the item a car, something you bought to lease out, or something that you have brought into your business after using it privately?

No first-year allowance (you can claim a 25% writing-down allowance instead). Put each car worth over £12,000 in its own pool, all other cars in one separate pool. The maximum writing-down allowance for cars over £12,000 is 25% or £3,000 if less.

3 Deduct a 40% first-year allowance.

4 Do you want to claim that this is a 'short-life' asset (one you expect to dispose of within five years)?

YES →

Put it in its own pool and claim it as a short-life asset on your tax return. If you dispose of it within five years, you can claim an immediate allowance for anything left in the pool. If you don't scrap it within five years, its remaining value is added to your main pool.

5 Used partly privately?

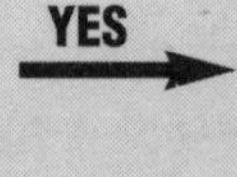

Put it in its own pool. Your allowances are restricted in line with the business use.

6 Any remaining costs are added to your main pool of expenditure.

Buying on credit

You can claim capital allowances for things bought with a loan or on hire purchase. The allowances are based on the original cost of the item. You cannot claim capital allowances on items you bought with a finance lease (the lessor gets the capital allowance, not you).

Capital allowances don't always save tax

You can choose not to claim part or all of your allowances. If you don't claim them in full one year, you have more value remaining in your pool to claim in future. Don't claim if:

- you wouldn't have to pay tax on your profits anyway
- they reduce the value of your pool to less than any sale proceeds (in which case you would have a balancing charge added to your profits).

When a pool ends

If you sell an item that is kept in a separate pool, or you close down your business, you can claim the whole of any value remaining in your pool as a 'balancing allowance'.

Flat rate VAT

If you are VAT-registered, you normally have to keep track of the VAT on each item you buy and each item you sell. However, small businesses (with turnover up to £150,000) can opt to pay tax instead on a percentage of turnover, ranging from 5 per cent to 14.5 per cent depending on your trade. Ask your VAT office or the Customs & Excise National Advice Service (see the Fact File) whether you qualify.

Example 6.3: **Working out capital allowances**

In his accounting period ending on 31 December 2002, Noah spent £8,000 on new office equipment, including £1,500 for a new computer on which he gets a 100% first-year allowance. He sold his old equipment for £2,450. This is how he works out his allowances on his main pool of expenditure.

		Allowances £	*Pool £*
Pool at start of period			4,250
Sales			−2,450
			1,800
Writing-down allowance	£1,800 × 25%	450	−450
			1,350
Purchases			
New computer £1,500	× 100% first year allowance	1,500	0
Other purchases £6,500	× 40% first year allowance	2,600	3,900
Pool to carry forward			5,250
Total allowances		4,550	

Example 6.4: **Capital allowances on a car**

Leah's car has a written-down value of £13,000. As it cost over £12,000, the maximum allowance she can claim in any one year is 25% or £3,000 if less – £3,000 in Leah's case. However, as her business mileage in the car is only 20% of the total mileage, she can only claim 20 per cent of the full allowance: £3,000 × 20% = £600.

Adjustments for your basis period

Your profits are calculated for an accounting period, but you are taxed on your profits for a 'basis period'. After you have been in business for two or three years, the two periods will coincide. Until then, you may need to make an adjustment to your profits for your first, and possibly your second, accounting period. You may also have to make adjustments if you change your accounting date.

If your basis period is shorter than the period covered by one set of accounts, you pay tax on only part of the profits in your accounts. If it is longer, you add in part of the profits of the next set of accounts. Splitting up your profits is done according the number of days, weeks or months in each period.

A partner in a partnership? You have your own basis period, which may differ from that of the other partners in the first year or so after you join the partnership. Otherwise, the rules are the same as for sole traders.

First tax year you are in business

Your 'basis period' is the period between the date you start up and the next 5 April.

Example 6.5: **Your first tax year in business**

Archie starts up on 5 January 2003 and ends his first accounting period on 5 January 2004. His basis period for the 2002–03 tax year is 5 January 2003 to 5 April 2003 – three months. However, as his first accounts cover a 12-month period, he pays tax for 2002–03 on 3⁄12 of the profits of his first accounting period.

On his tax return for 2002–03 he reports his profits for the whole of his first accounting period, but then (in box 3.77) he enters a negative adjustment of 9⁄12 of his profits.

Give yourself time to work out your profits

If your first accounting period ends just before 31 January (the last date for sending in your return), you might have to work out your tax on the basis of provisional figures. The Revenue allow this if your accounting period ends within three months of 31 January, but you will have to pay interest if you underestimate your tax.

Second tax year you are in business

Your basis period depends on the length of your first accounting period:

- *less than 12 months:* you are taxed on 12 months' profits, beginning on the date you started
- *12 months or more:* you are taxed on the profits of the 12 months to your accounting date
- *no accounting period ending in the tax year:* you are taxed on the profits of the 12 months from 6 April in one year to 5 April in the next.

Example 6.6: **First accounting period 12 months or longer**

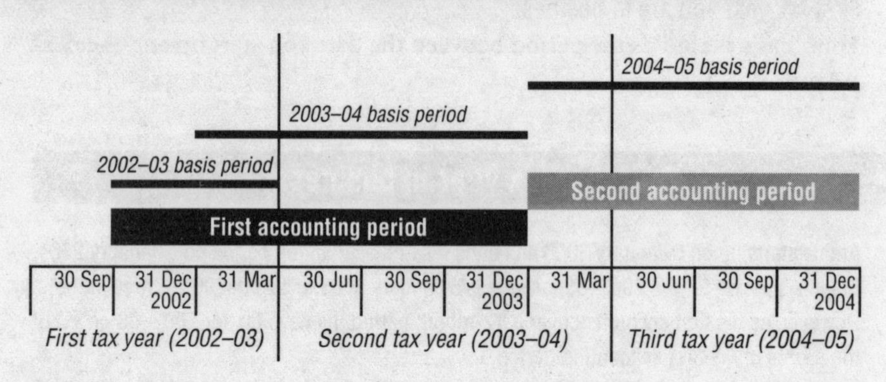

Andrew starts in business on 1 October 2002 and ends his first accounting period on 31 December 2003 – 15 months later – with a profit of £25,000. For the 2003–04 tax year (his second in business) his basis period is the 12 months up to 31 December 2003. The profits for this basis period are $^{12}/_{15}$ of the profits in his first accounting period – i.e. £25,000 × $^{12}/_{15}$ = £20,000. He must enter a negative adjustment of £25,000 – £20,000 = £5,000 in box 3.77 of his 2002–03 tax return.

Three months of the profits in Andrew's 2003–04 basis period have also been included in his 2002–03 basis period, i.e. £25,000 × $^{3}/_{15}$ = £5,000. These are called 'overlap profits'.

Example 6.7: **First accounting period less than 12 months**

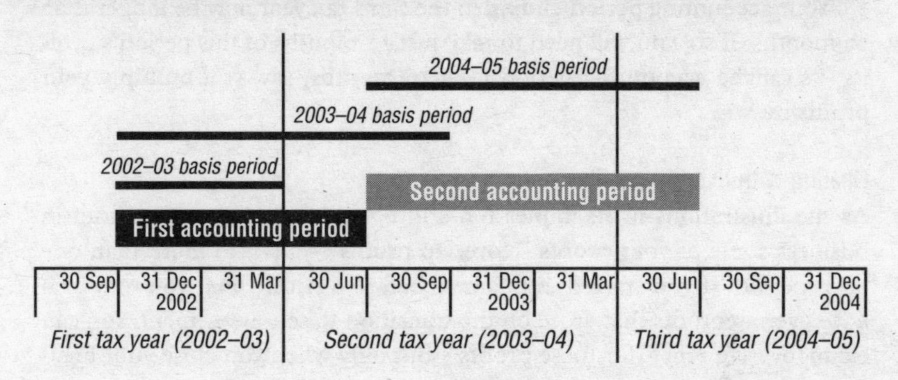

Belinda also starts in business on 1 October 2002, but she ends her first accounting period after 9 months, on 30 June 2003. Her basis period for her second tax year in business (2003–04) is the 12 months from the day she started up, i.e. 1 October 2002 to 1 October 2003. Her profits were:

1 October 2002 – 30 June 2003	£18,000
1 July 2003 – 30 June 2004	£40,000

To make up the profits of her 2003–04 basis period, Belinda is taxed on the 9 months' profit from her first accounting period (£18,000), and 3 months of the profits from her second accounting period – i.e. £40,000 × 3⁄12 = £10,000. She will be taxed on £18,000 + £10,000 = £28,000.

Six months of these profits overlap with those included in the 2002–03 basis period (£18,000 × 6⁄9 = £12,000), and three months overlap with those included in the 2004–05 basis period (£40,000 × 3⁄12 = £10,000). Belinda's 'overlap profits' are £12,000 + £10,000 = £22,000.

Third tax year you are in business

From this tax year on, your basis period is the 12 months running up to your accounting date in that year – so if, for example, if you make up your accounts to 30 September each year, your basis period for the 2003–04 tax year would be the period of 30 September 2002 to 30 September 2003.

Your accounting period ending in the third tax year may be longer than 12 months. If so, you will need to take just 12 months of this period's profits – so if the accounting period lasts 16 months, say, you multiply your profits by 12/16.

Dealing with overlap profits

As the illustrations in Examples 6.6 and 6.7 show, when you start up in business some of your profits – 'overlap profits' – fall into more than one basis period. If you started in business before 6 April 1994, you may also have overlap profits that arose on the transition to self-assessment. You can claim 'overlap relief' for these profits – but only when you close your business or change your accounting date.

Overlap profits look as though they have been taxed twice. In practice, at the end of each tax year you will find that the number of months' profit on which you have been taxed, including the overlap period, is the same as the number of months in which you have been in business so far.

Note that if you make a loss in an overlap period, you cannot claim the whole loss in each overlapping basis period. Instead, part of the loss belongs to one tax year and the rest to the next tax year. (So if Belinda in Example 6.7 made a loss, six-ninths of it would belong to 2002–03 and three-ninths to 2003–04.)

Keeping things simple

You have no overlap profits if you end your accounting period with the end of the tax year – which doesn't necessarily mean 5 April. If your accounting period ends on any date from 31 March to 4 April, you can treat it as ending on 5 April.

When is your first tax bill due?

If you haven't received a tax return, you must tell your tax office that you have taxable profits by 5 October after the end of your first year in business. (You should in any case tell them within three months of the end of the month when you become self-employed.) If you have any taxable profits in your first basis period (running up to 5 April), you will have to pay the tax on them by the following 31 January.

You may have to start making payments on account on 31 January following the end of your first tax year in business, but as Chapter 3 explains, you have to do this only if less than 80 per cent of your tax bill for the previous tax year was met from tax paid at source, or if the tax *not* deducted at source was £500 or more.

Planning your tax

Depending on your tax outstanding after the first tax year in business, you will have to start making payments on account from about 10 to 22 months after the end of your first tax year in business. A long delay could leave you with a large bill to pay in one go, so make sure you put aside enough cash to pay it.

Choosing your accounting date

- Depending on the date you choose, you may have a lot of overlap profits or none at all.
- Overlaps work in your favour if your profits are rising, against you if your profits are high in the first year and then drop.
- The simplest option is to end your first accounting period at the end of a tax year.
- Ending your accounting period as early as possible in the tax year means that you have longer to work out your tax bill before you have to submit your return.

When your business ends

You are taxed on your profits between the end of your last basis period and the date you stop trading or leave the partnership. If you have any profits when you close down, you can deduct any overlap relief carried forward. If you close with a loss, it is increased by the amount of any overlap relief. See Figure 6.2 for how you get tax relief on a loss.

Figure 6.2: Your choices for claiming a loss

Losses on starting up
Losses in the first four years of trading can be set against your overall income of the previous three tax years (earliest year first).

Losses of any year
can be set against the overall income of the previous tax year. If the loss is bigger than your income, you can set the rest against any capital gains.

Losses on closing down
Losses in the final 12 months of trading can be set against the profits of the previous three tax years (latest year first).

CARRY BACK

Loss-making year
(start here)

'Sideways' relief
is set against the overall income of same tax year. If the loss is bigger than your other income, you can set the rest against your capital gains.

CARRY FORWARD

Losses of any year
can be carried forward indefinitely and set against the first profits arising from the same business.

Losses

If you make a loss, you can claim tax relief for the loss in a number of ways. (See Figure 6.2, and Inland Revenue help sheet IR227 *Losses*.)

Subject to claiming within the time limits (see below) you can carry the loss back to set against the income of earlier years. If so, the tax saved is worked out using the rates of tax that applied in the earlier year, and given as a credit against your statement of account. Alternatively, you can choose to set your losses against your overall income of the same tax year (e.g. from investments or another job), and, if you still have losses left over, your capital gains. But you cannot claim only part of a loss.

Otherwise, once you have claimed your losses by entering them in your tax return, they are carried forward indefinitely and used in the first year in which you have profits from the same business – even if those profits are not taxable because they are less than your personal allowances, say.

A partner in a partnership? Any losses are shared out according to the partnership agreement, and each partner can use them as he or she prefers.

Using your losses

It often makes sense to set your losses against other income or carry them back, rather than carry them forward against profits that may never arise. But this depends on your tax bill in the earlier and current years, and your likely profits in future.

Watch out for time limits

If you want to carry back losses, or claim sideways relief, you must claim on your tax return (or tell your tax office) within 22 months from the end of the tax year in which you made the loss, i.e. by 31 January 2005 for losses made in 2002–03. The time limit is longer – 5 years and 10 months – for losses on closing down or losses carried forward.

Example 6.8: **Claiming a loss**

Anji made a loss of £5,000 in her first year in business and expects her profits for the next year to be low. She does not have any capital gains.

Anji has the following options: carrying her loss forward, or setting it against the overall income of the current tax year or any of the previous three tax years. Anji has some income from investments in the current tax year, but she will only pay basic-rate tax on this, whereas in the previous three tax years (before she left her job to set up on her own) she was a higher-rate taxpayer. She will save most tax by carrying back her loss: £5,000 × 40% = £2,000.

Special rules for some trades

If you are in the following industries you should get further information:

- Agriculture – see Inland Revenue help sheets IR224 *Farmers and market gardeners* and IR232 *Farm stock valuation.*
- Art and literature – see help sheet IR234 *Averaging for creators of literary or artistic works.*
- Legal – see help sheet IR233 *The 'true and fair view' for professions.*
- Maritime – see Inland Revenue leaflet CA11 *National Insurance for share fishermen.*
- Medicine – see help sheet IR231 *Doctors' expenses.*
- Construction – see leaflet HMCE (MISC5) *Help for your business in the construction industry.*

National Insurance contributions

As a self-employed person, you may have to pay both Class 2 and Class 4 National Insurance contributions. (See Inland Revenue leaflet CWL2 *National Insurance contributions for self-employed people. Class 2 and Class 4.*)

If you have a job as well as being self-employed, you may also have to pay Class 1 employees' NICs, but there is an overall maximum. You can apply to defer paying Class 2 or Class 4 contributions (see page 30).

Class 2 NICs

These are flat-rate contributions of £2 a week in 2002–03 and 2003–04. When you start up in business, you must register with the Inland Revenue within three months of the end of the month in which you start trading, and then, if you are liable, payments are usually made by monthly direct debit. You will be sent a separate bill for any contributions between registering and the first direct debit. However, you do not have to pay once you are over state pension age (65 for men, 60 for women).

You can claim exemption from NICs if your profits are low

If your profits are less than £4,025 in 2002–03 (£4,095 in 2003–04), you can apply not to pay Class 2 contributions. But this could affect your right to state retirement pension and some other state benefits, so you may want to continue paying voluntarily. (Full details and an application form are in leaflet CA02 *National Insurance contributions for self-employed people with small earnings.*)

Class 4 NICs

You do not have to pay Class 4 NICs for any tax year if, on the first day of that year, you are over state pension age. Otherwise, you pay a percentage of your profits. Table 6.3 shows the rates payable. So if your taxable profits were £35,000 in 2003–04, say, you would pay nothing on the first £4,615, 8 per cent on the next £26,325 (i.e. £2,106) and 1 per cent on anything over £30,940 (i.e. on £35,000 − £30,940 = £4,060). This comes to £2,106 + £40.60 = £2,146.60 in total.

Class 4 NICs are collected with your income tax through your payments on account. If you have more than one business, the rate payable depends on the total profit from all your businesses. If you are a partner in a partnership you pay Class 4 NICs on just your share of the partnership's profits. You do not have to pay them if you are a sleeping partner, contributing to, but not working in, the partnership.

Table 6.3: Class 4 NICs for 2002–03 (2003–04 figures in brackets)

Slice of taxable profits	*Rate payable*
First £4,615 (£4,615)	Nil
Next £25,805 (£26,325)	7% (8%)
Anything above £30,420 (£30,940)	Nil (1%)

Use your losses

You can use losses to reduce your Class 4 NICs in the same way as for income tax. However, if you choose to set your losses against non-trading income (which is not liable to Class 4 contributions), you will have unused losses for National Insurance purposes. You can carry them forward to set against future profits when working out Class 4 NICs.

Example 6.9: **How losses can reduce Class 4 NICs**

Anji (from Example 6.8) had a loss of £5,000 that she set against her non-trading income of an earlier year – but this income wasn't liable to Class 4 NICs. So she still has the whole £5,000 available to reduce her Class 4 NICs in future years.

What to tell the Inland Revenue

The most important thing is to register as self-employed, or a partner, within three months of the end of the month in which you start trading. If you don't, you may have to pay a penalty of £100 unless you can show that the annual equivalent of your earnings so far is below the threshold for Class 2 NICs (£4,095 in 2003–04).

There is a helpline for the newly self-employed with which you can register (see the Fact File). Also see leaflet P/SE/1 *Thinking of working for yourself?*, which has a registration form. This includes a box to tick if you think you will have to register for VAT. The Revenue have business support teams that give practical advice and run free local workshops.

Once you have registered, you should receive tax returns. Start on page 2 of the main return and tick:

- Question 3 if you were self-employed – you will need to complete the Self-employment supplementary pages.
- Question 4 if you were a partner in a partnership – you will need to complete the Partnership supplementary pages.

A partner in a partnership? The partnership gets its own tax return which covers all the business profits received by the partnership. It also contains a 'partnership statement' that tells the Revenue how the income and gains have been shared out between the partners. Individual partners also get Partnership supplementary pages for their own tax returns, covering their share of the profit or loss, and any adjustments claimed by them as individuals (e.g. losses).

Filling in the Self-employment or Partnership pages

The Self-employment pages and most of the Partnership tax return are very similar, so you can use the information below to help you fill in both forms. (See also the Revenue's notes to the forms.)

Boxes 3.1 to 3.13 Business details

Enter the business or partnership's name and address and the date the business started up or ceased. If you (or the partnership) have more than one trade you will need to complete a separate form for each.

You will also need to complete separate forms if the figures of more than one accounting period are included in your basis period for the 2002–03 tax year – e.g. if you have just started in business. If you have included one set of figures in last year's tax return you do not have to give them again, but tick 3.10 if this applies to all your accounts.

Box 3.9 applies only if you are a foster carer or adult carer, or if you run a business completely overseas and are taxed on a remittance basis (see Chapter 9). If so, you only need to complete a few boxes in the form. (Note that most income received by foster carers after 5 April 2003 is tax-free.)

The other boxes in this section give your tax office the information it needs to check your basis period.

Boxes 3.14 to 3.23 Capital allowances

See page 132 for how to work out the figures to enter in this section. Balancing charges are amounts that have to be added to your income when you make a profit on selling something for which you have previously claimed capital allowances.

Short-life assets

If you bought something in this period that you want to treat as a 'short-life asset' (so that you can claim immediate relief if you scrap it within five years), remember to add a note to this effect under 'Additional information'.

Boxes 3.24 to 3.26 Income and expenses – annual turnover below £15,000

If your *annual* turnover is below £15,000, you don't need to fill in boxes 3.27 to 3.73 of the form – instead, just enter here your overall income, expenses and net profit and move on to box 3.74. These are called 'three-line accounts'. Don't forget to include your capital allowances with your expenses, and any balancing charges with your income.

Common mistake

You complete boxes 3.24 to 3.26 only if your turnover is below £15,000 for a full year. This means that if the accounting period you are reporting here is shorter or longer than 12 months, you must adjust the £15,000 proportionately. So if it is 8 months, say, the threshold is £15,000 × $\frac{8}{12}$ = £10,000; if it is 14 months, it is £15,000 × $\frac{14}{12}$ = £17,500.

Boxes 3.27 to 3.73 Income and expenses – annual turnover £15,000 or more

Leave this page blank if you have already completed boxes 3.24 to 3.26. Otherwise, transfer the necessary information from your accounts or other records.

You may have to make the following adjustments:

- You should enter non-trading income relating to your business in the relevant pages of your basic tax return (e.g. Question 10 if you receive interest from a business bank account). If you include such income in box 3.50 (other income/profits), also enter it in box 3.71 as a deduction, or you will be taxed on it twice.
- If your expenses include amounts that do not qualify for tax relief, enter the disallowable part in boxes 3.30 to 3.45. These are added to your profits at box 3.69. (See the table of allowable and disallowable expenses in the Revenue's notes.) This is unlikely to apply, however, if you are keeping records only for tax purposes, not formal accounts.
- Goods taken out of your business for private use count as a sale for tax purposes and should be added back in at box 3.67.
- Add in your capital allowances and balancing charges at box 3.70 or 3.68.

Dealing with VAT

You do not need to tick box 3.27 or 3.28 (which ask whether your figures include VAT) if you were not VAT-registered during this period, but be sure to include any VAT paid in your expenses, so that you can get tax relief on it.

If you are VAT-registered, as well as ticking the relevant box, check the Revenue notes for what to enter if:

- you give figures including VAT, or supply zero-rated goods, or are partly exempt
- you are registered for the VAT flat rate scheme
- you registered or deregistered for VAT during this period.

Figure 6.3: Self-employment pages (see Example 6.10)

Income and expenses - annual turnover £15,000 or more

You must fill in this Page if your annual turnover is £15,000 or more - read the Notes, page SEN2

If you were registered for VAT, do the figures in boxes 3.29 to 3.64, include VAT? **3.27** [ ] or exclude VAT? **3.28** ✓

Sales/business income (turnover) **3.29** £ 42,302

	Disallowable expenses included in boxes 3.46 to 3.63	Total expenses	
• Cost of sales	3.30 £	3.46 £ 12,002	
• Construction industry subcontractor costs	3.31 £	3.47 £	
• Other direct costs	3.32 £	3.48 £	box 3.29 *minus* (boxes 3.46 + 3.47 + 3.48)
		Gross profit/(loss)	3.49 £ 30,300
		Other income/profits	3.50 £ 434
• Employee costs	3.33 £	3.51 £ 8,013	
• Premises costs	3.34 £	3.52 £ 3,020	
• Repairs	3.35 £	3.53 £	
• General administrative expenses	3.36 £	3.54 £ 540	
• Motor expenses	3.37 £ 320	3.55 £ 775	
• Travel and subsistence	3.38 £	3.56 £	
• Advertising, promotion and entertainment	3.39 £	3.57 £ 330	
• Legal and professional costs	3.40 £	3.58 £ 150	
• Bad debts	3.41 £	3.59 £	
• Interest	3.42 £	3.60 £	
• Other finance charges	3.43 £	3.61 £ 85	
• Depreciation and loss/(profit) on sale	3.44 £ 3,150	3.62 £ 3,150	
• Other expenses	3.45 £	3.63 £ 64	total of boxes 3.51 to 3.63
	Put the total of boxes 3.30 to 3.45 in box 3.66 below	Total expenses	3.64 £ 16,127
			boxes 3.49 + 3.50 *minus* 3.64
		Net profit/(loss)	3.65 £ 14,607

Tax adjustments to net profit or loss

• Disallowable expenses	boxes 3.30 to 3.45 3.66 £ 3,470	
• Adjustments (apart from disallowable expenses) that increase profits. Examples are goods taken for personal use and amounts brought forward from an earlier year because of a claim under ESC B11 about compulsory slaughter of farm animals	3.67 £	
• Balancing charges (from box 3.23)	3.68 £	
Total additions to net profit (deduct from net loss)		boxes 3.66 + 3.67 + 3.68 3.69 £ 3,470
• Capital allowances (from box 3.22)	3.70 £ 4,450	
• Deductions from net profit (add to net loss)	3.71 £ 434	boxes 3.70 + 3.71 3.72 £ 4,884
Net business profit for tax purposes (put figure in brackets if a loss)		boxes 3.65 + 3.69 *minus* 3.72 3.73 £ 13,193

Example 6.10: **Filling in pages 2 and 3**

When Archie transferred his figures from his accounts to his Self-employment pages, he had some adjustments to make. The 'other income' in box 3.50 is interest on a bank account; as he has also entered this elsewhere in his tax return, he deducts it at box 3.71 to avoid being taxed on it twice (see Figure 6.3).

Archie made a profit of £13,193 in this, his first accounting period. As this is a 14-month period (1/11/01 to 31/12/02), he must deduct two months' profits at box 3.77, £13,193 × 2 ÷ 14 = £1,885, leaving profits for this basis period of £13,193 − £1,885 = £11,308. As his basis period for the 2002–03 tax year overlapped with that for the 2001–02 tax year, he has overlap profits of £2,827 to carry forward in box 3.80 (see Figure 6.4 on page 152). Archie is also liable to pay Class 4 NICs of (£11,308 − £4,615) × 7% = £468.

Boxes 3.74 to 3.81 Adjustments to arrive at taxable profit or loss

These boxes appear only in the Self-employment pages, but if you are a partner you will see the same questions at boxes 4.5 to 4.21 of the Partnership pages that go with your personal tax return.

- The 'Adjustments to arrive at profit or loss' (box 3.77) applies if your basis period is not the same as your accounting period. This may also have created overlap profits to enter in box 3.78. (See page 140 for how to work out these figures.) Note that you can claim to deduct overlap relief this year (at box 3.79) only if your business has closed down or you have changed your accounting date.
- Boxes 3.81 and 3.82 apply only if you are a farmer or market gardener, writer or artist, or barrister who has previously been taxed on a 'cash' basis (see page 144 for where to find more information).
- Use boxes 3.85 to 3.89 to keep track of your losses from this business. (See Figure 6.2 on page 142 for the choices you have.) The first three boxes tell your tax office what you want to do with any losses from the current year. If you made a profit, and have losses from previous years, you must deduct them at box 3.89.
- 'Any other business income' (3.91) is explained at step 6 on page 126. Enter the amount received in the tax year, not the accounting period.

Figure 6.4: Self-employment pages (see Example 6.10)

Adjustments to arrive at taxable profit or loss

	Box	
Basis period begins	3.74	01 11 01
and ends	3.75	31 / 12 / 02
Profit or loss of this account for tax purposes (box 3.26 or 3.73)	3.76	£ 13,193
Adjustment to arrive at profit or loss for this basis period	3.77	£ (1,885)
• Overlap profit brought forward	3.78	£
• Deduct overlap relief used this year	3.79	£
• Overlap profit carried forward	3.80	£ 2,827
Averaging for farmers and creators of literary or artistic works *(see Notes, page SEN9, if you made a loss for 2002-03)*	3.81	£
Adjustment on change of basis	3.82	£
Net profit for 2002-03 (if you made a loss, enter '0')	3.83	£ 11,308
Allowable loss for 2002-03 (if you made a profit, enter '0')	3.84	£
• Loss offset against other income for 2002-03	3.85	£
• Loss to carry back	3.86	£
• Loss to carry forward (that is allowable loss not claimed in any other way)	3.87	£
• Losses brought forward from earlier years	3.88	£
• Losses brought forward from earlier years used this year	3.89	£
Taxable profit after losses brought forward (box 3.83 *minus* box 3.89)	3.90	£ 11,308
• Any other business income (for example, Business Start-up Allowance received in 2002-03)	3.91	£
Total taxable profits from this business (box 3.90 + box 3.91)	3.92	£ 11,308
• Tick box 3.93 if the figure in box 3.92 is provisional	3.93	

Class 4 National Insurance contributions

	Box	
• Tick box 3.94 if exception or deferment applies	3.94	
• Adjustments to profit chargeable to Class 4 National Insurance contributions	3.95	£
Class 4 National Insurance contributions due	3.96	£ 468

Subcontractors in the construction industry

	Box	
• Deductions made by contractors on account of tax (please send your CIS25s to us)	3.97	£

Tax deducted from trading income

	Box	
• Any tax deducted (excluding deductions made by contractors on account of tax) from trading income	3.98	£

Boxes 3.94 to 3.96 Class 4 National Insurance contributions (4.23 to 4.25 on Partnership pages)

See page 144 for how these contributions are calculated. If you are sending your return back by 30 September and want the Revenue to calculate your tax, leave 3.96 blank – otherwise, you need to work it out yourself using the Revenue's tax calculation guide and (if relevant) Inland Revenue help sheet IR220 *More than one business*.

However, you do not need to pay contributions at all, and can tick box 3.94, if you are over state pension age or exempt (i.e. because you are not resident in the UK, or you are a professional diver or a trustee). The 'adjustments' in box 3.95 are business losses carried forward from earlier years (see Example 6.9 on page 146), and interest that you have entered with your trading income (on which contributions do not have to be paid).

Boxes 3.97 to 3.98 Tax deducted (4.75 to 4.75A on Partnership pages)

Box 3.97 (4.75) applies only if you are a subcontractor in the building trade, and you have received payment with tax already deducted. The CIS25 vouchers showing the deductions should be sent in with your return.

It is very unlikely that you will have anything to enter in box 3.98. If you have, you may not be self-employed and should contact your tax office.

Boxes 3.99 to 3.115 Summary of balance sheet

Complete these boxes only if you actually have a balance sheet in your accounts for this accounting period.

Common mistakes

- Failing to complete the Self-employment pages in full, particularly on page SE3 from box 3.74 onwards.
- Including in expenses the amount you have spent on plant and machinery, instead of claiming capital allowances.
- If you are working out your own tax, forgetting to include in boxes 18.4 and 18.5 of the main tax return any adjustment from carrying back business losses, or from averaging your income if you are a farmer, writer or artist.

Record-keeping

You do not need to send a copy of your accounts to your tax office, although you can if you wish. But you must keep records to back up your entries, and you must keep all records for at least five years and ten months from the end of the tax year (so records for the 2002–03 tax year must be kept until 31 January 2009). Inland Revenue booklet SA/BK3 *Self Assessment. A guide to keeping records for the self-employed* gives examples. As well as records of all income and expenses (including receipts and invoices) remember to keep:

- If you are starting up, a note of when you register as self-employed.
- Records of transactions between your business and your private finances (it is usually simplest to keep separate bank accounts).
- A record of stock and work in progress at the end of the accounting period.
- Payments to employees, including (if you are in the building trade) records of any tax deducted from payments.
- Records of business mileage in a car used both privately and for work (and running expenses if you are not using the Revenue-approved mileage rates).
- Records of how much of any losses you set against your profits for Class 4 National Insurance purposes (see Example 6.9).

If you keep your records on computer you must also keep your original paper records unless you microfilm them or use an optical imaging system.

Tax relief on pre-trading expenses

You can claim tax relief on business expenses incurred before you formally start in business. Make sure you keep records of all possible expenses. If you register for VAT, you can also claim back VAT on some pre-registration expenses, but you will need a receipt showing the supplier's VAT registration number.

Avoiding an enquiry

Unusual or unexplained items in your Self-employment pages may trigger an enquiry. Explain in the 'Additional information' box anything that might look odd and make sure that your records support your explanations, for example:

- the basis on which you split expenses between private and business use
- reasons for any 'blips' in turnover or expenses – e.g. increased premises costs
- rounded numbers which might look like estimates.

Tax-planning hints

Starting up in business

1 When you start up, spend some time getting your records set up to make filling in your tax return (and VAT returns if applicable) easy. Do get help to establish what expenses you can claim – and on accounting periods and whether you should set up a company or partnership rather than operating as a sole trader.

2 You can claim tax relief on some pre-trading expenses.

3 See page 141 for guidance on choosing your accounting period. The simplest option is to end it at the end of the tax year.

4 In the January after the end of the tax year in which you first make taxable profits, you may have to pay an instalment of tax in advance, as well as tax owed so far. Put cash aside to meet the bill.

5 If you make a loss, you have a number of options that might be better than setting it against a future year's profits – but you must claim within the time limits (see page 143). Keep separate records of your losses for Class 4 National Insurance purposes (see page 146).

6 You can claim exemption from Class 2 National Insurance if your profits are low – but this will affect your right to state benefits.

Expenses and allowances you can claim

7 If you use part of your home for work, you can claim a proportion of your household expenses, but if you use part exclusively for work,

there may be capital gains tax when you sell the property (see page 129).

8 Buying a new car for business and personal use? You will need to decide whether to use the Revenue-approved mileage rates, or split the actual expenses in line with your business use (see page 130).

9 Remember to claim the VAT portion of any expense if you are not registered for VAT.

10 You can claim tax relief on the pay and National Insurance of a family member you employ – but it must be a proper job.

11 You can claim capital allowances on equipment you buy for the business – but see page 135 for cases when this might not save you tax.

12 You can get a 100 per cent first-year capital allowance on computers and other IT and communications equipment bought before 1 April 2004.

13 You can also get a 100 per cent capital allowance on cars with very low CO_2 emissions and some energy-saving and water-efficient equipment (see page 132).

7

Pensions and state benefits

In most cases, money going into a pension is tax-free; money paid out, however, is usually taxable. This includes most state pensions.

Most other state benefits, but not all, are tax-free, and the introduction of the new Child Tax Credit and Working Tax Credit heralds a new interaction between state benefits and the tax system. This chapter covers:

- tax relief on private pension contributions
- the tax you might have to pay on an income from your pension
- taxable state benefits, such as state retirement pension
- tax credits.

Does this affect you?

The state retirement pension counts as taxable income, although if it is your only income it may be below your personal and any other allowances you are entitled to.

Private pensions fall into the following categories, each with its own tax rules for the money you pay in and the money you draw out:

- *Occupational pension schemes*. Run by your employer, these may be either 'final salary' (you earn a pension of say, one-sixtieth of your final salary for each year of membership) or 'money purchase' (the benefits depend on the investment performance of contributions).

- *Personal pension schemes and stakeholder pensions*. These are individual pension plans taken out with a pension company, usually an insurance company. Stakeholder pensions are a form of personal pension with low minimum contributions, low cost transfers to and from other pension schemes, and a 1 per cent cap on charges. Both types may be arranged through your employer, in the form of group personal pensions and employer-sponsored stakeholder pensions.
- *Retirement annuity contracts*. These are no longer available – they were superseded by personal pensions in 1988 – but if you have one you can continue to pay in provided you have the right sort of earnings.

In addition to the state retirement pension, other taxable state benefits are:

- *Bereavement allowance* or *widowed parent's allowance*.
- *Industrial death benefit pension*. This is no longer available to new claimants, but may still be paid to widows and dependants of people who died before 11 April 1988 as a result of an accident at work.
- *Jobseeker's Allowance*. The taxable amount is capped: in 2003–04, the maximum taxable amount is £43.25 a week for a single person aged 18 to 24, £54.65 a week for a single person aged 25 or over, and £85.75 for a couple both aged 18 or over. (See Inland Revenue leaflet IR41 *Income tax and job seekers*.)
- *Statutory sick pay* and *statutory maternity or paternity pay*.
- *Invalid care allowance*. This is paid to people who spend at least 35 hours a week caring for a disabled person.
- *Incapacity Benefit*. This is taxable after the first 28 weeks of incapacity (but is not taxable if you previously claimed invalidity benefit for this disability continuously since 12 April 1995).

Child Tax Credit and Working Tax Credit are not themselves taxable, but the amount to which you are entitled is gradually withdrawn once your income rises above a certain amount. In effect, tax credits are state benefits administered by the Revenue, but families with an annual income up to £58,000, or even more, can benefit from them.

Changes on the way

The government are proposing sweeping changes to the tax rules for private pensions (from a date yet to be announced). Instead of different rules for each type, a 'lifetime limit' of £1.4 million on the maximum value of your pension fund is proposed. The new system looks much simpler, but if your pension fund is substantial, advice from a financial adviser specialising in pensions may be worthwhile.

Tax-free income

Tax-free pensions

- Pensions to employees disabled at work – but only if this is more than you would get had you retired on the grounds of ill-health.
- Some compensation for personal pensions that were mis-sold to you.
- War widows' pensions. (See Inland Revenue help sheet IR310 *War Widow's and dependant's pensions.*)
- Wound and disability pensions to members of the forces.
- 10 per cent of an overseas pension.
- German and Austrian pensions for victims of Nazi persecution.

Tax-free state benefits for families

- Additions to benefits paid because you have a child.
- Bereavement payment (a one-off lump sum on bereavement).
- Child benefit, Child Tax Credit and Guardian's Allowance.
- Maternity allowance (for women who are not eligible for statutory maternity pay, which is taxable).
- Working Tax Credit (Working Families' Tax Credit or Disabled Person's Tax Credit before 6 April 2003).

Tax-free state benefits if sick or disabled

- Attendance allowance (for people over 64 who need care).
- Disability living allowance.
- Incapacity Benefit paid during the first 28 weeks of incapacity at the short-term rate.

- Industrial injury benefits (except industrial death benefit pension).

Other tax-free state benefits

- £10 Christmas bonus paid with state pension and some other benefits.
- Some employment grants, e.g. New Deal training allowance.
- Cold weather payments and winter fuel payments.
- Council tax benefit and housing benefit.
- Income support (unless you are on strike) and the minimum income guarantee (replaced by the pension credit in October 2003).
- Jobseeker's Allowance above the taxable maximum (see page 158).
- Social fund payments.

How the tax is worked out

Tax relief for money going into a pension

Paying the right sort of National Insurance contributions will entitle you to a state retirement pension. You can get a forecast of how much you will get by asking your local social security office for form BR19.

Contributions to private pension schemes that have been approved by the Revenue qualify for tax relief at your top rate of tax, but there is a limit on how much you can contribute, depending on the type of scheme (see Table 7.1 on page 162 and Example 7.1). Almost all schemes are approved.

Inland Revenue leaflet IR78 *Looking to the future* and help sheet IR330 *Pension payments* give details of tax relief on pension contributions. The Financial Services Authority and the government's Pension Service also have a number of useful leaflets.

If your employer contributes

- Your employer's contributions to an approved occupational pension scheme are a tax-free fringe benefit for you.
- Your employer may contribute to your personal or stakeholder pension. Its contributions are included with yours when working out your maximum contributions.

How the tax relief is given

- With an *occupational pension*, your employer deducts the pension contributions from your pay and then works out the tax on what's left. This gives you tax relief at your highest tax rate.
- *Personal and stakeholder pension contributions* are paid net. This means that you hand over the amount that is due after basic-rate tax relief. See Example 7.2 on page 164. The pension company claims the basic-rate relief from the government (even if you are a non-taxpayer). If you are a higher-rate taxpayer you can then claim higher-rate relief either on your tax return or through your PAYE code (ask your tax office for form PP120). If you want to contribute more than £3,600 a year, you must give the pension company evidence of your earnings (e.g. your accounts).
- *Retirement annuity contributions* are paid gross. You get tax relief either on your tax return or through your PAYE code – if you are a taxpayer.

Maximising tax-free pension contributions

If you want to contribute the maximum to your personal or stakeholder pension, you can choose to base your contributions on your earnings for any of the previous five tax years. The year you nominate is called your 'basis year'. So if your earnings go down – or if you have no earnings at all – you can carry on contributing at the same rate for up to five years. If your earnings rise within the five years, you can nominate a new basis year.

Example 7.1: **How much tax relief?**

Brandon is keen to contribute the maximum to his personal pension. He is 42 and not in an occupational pension, so as Table 7.1 shows he can contribute either £3,600, or 20% of his earnings.

Brandon's earnings in 2003–04 are £50,000. On this basis, he can contribute £50,000 × 20% = £10,000. However, Brandon can choose to base his contributions on the earnings of any of the previous five years. His earnings for 2001–02 were £55,000, so if he nominates this as his 'basis year', he can contribute £55,000 × 20% = £11,000.

Table 7.1: Paying in to a pension – a summary

Type of pension	*Who can contribute?*
Occupational plan	Employees eligible to join (depends on scheme)
Personal/ stakeholder pension plan	Anybody under 75. If you are also in an occupational scheme, you can only pay in if: 1 Your earnings are £30,000 or less in the current year or any year since 2000–01, and you are not a *controlling director*[1] *or* 2 You have *relevant earnings*[2] from other work, or the occupational scheme provides only death benefits, or the personal/stakeholder pension is *rebate-only*[3]
Retirement annuity contracts	New plans are no longer available but if you already have one you can continue to pay in, provided that you have *relevant earnings*[2]. You can have both a retirement annuity contract and a personal/stakeholder pension, but the retirement annuity relief reduces the personal pension relief available. Inland Revenue help sheet IR330 *Pension payments* includes a calculator.

1 *Controlling director*. In this context, these are directors who on their own, or with their family and associates, own or control more than 20 per cent of the ordinary shares of the company that employs them.

2 *Relevant earnings*. If you are an employee, these are your taxable earnings from a job in which you have not joined an occupational pension, including the taxable value of any fringe benefits, but minus any expenses. If you are self-employed, they are your business profits minus capital allowances and losses.

How much each year?

Up to 15% of earnings, with an *earnings cap*[4] if you joined after May 1989. If your normal scheme contributions are less than 15%, you can make additional voluntary contributions (AVCs), either into the scheme itself or your own 'Free-standing' (FSAVC) scheme with a separate pension company.

Up to £3,600 (but you hand over £2,808 after basic-rate relief) *or*
Up to the following percentages of your *relevant earnings*[2] (below the *earnings cap*[4]) but you hand over less than the full percentage because you deduct basic-rate tax relief. Note that you cannot pay in more than £3,600 if (1) left applies.

Age at start of tax year	*% of earnings*
35 or less	17.5
36 to 45	20
46 to 50	25
51 to 55	30
56 to 60	35
61 to 74	40

Up to the following percentages of your *relevant earnings*[2]:

Age at start of tax year	*% of earnings*
50 or less	17.5
51 to 55	20.0
56 to 60	22.5
61 to 74	27.5

3 *Rebate-only*. If you are an employee, you can have a personal or stakeholder pension instead of building up benefits under the State Earnings Related Pension Scheme (SERPS). If you 'contract-out' of SERPS in this way, the government pays a rebate of part of your National Insurance contributions into your private pension. Pensions can be set up on a 'rebate-only' basis, with no other contributions going in.

4 *Earnings cap*. This affects you only if your earnings are more than £97,200 in 2002–03, £99,000 in 2003–04. If so, these are the maximum earnings on which you can make contributions.

Example 7.2: **How the tax relief is given**

Brandon's maximum contribution is £11,000 (see Example 7.1 on page 161), but this is the gross (before tax relief) amount. He can deduct 22% basic-rate tax relief before making the payment, so he actually hands over £11,000 × 78% = £8,580. His pension company claims the rest from the Revenue. Brandon claims higher-rate tax relief of £11,000 × 18% = £1,980 on his tax return or through his PAYE code.

'Carrying back' contributions

You can have contributions to a personal pension, stakeholder pension or retirement annuity contract treated as if made in the previous tax year. This allows you to confirm your earnings for the year before you decide your contributions. You get tax relief at the rate for the previous year.

If you want to do this, you must pay the contributions and notify the pension company that you are 'carrying back' by 31 January after the end of the tax year in which you want the payments to be treated as paid. So you can have contributions paid between 6 April 2003 and 31 January 2004 treated as if paid in the 2002–03 tax year provided that you tell your pension company when or before you make the payment. You will need to complete a form PP43 (the pension company can supply this) and send it to your tax office, or make the claim in your tax return. Form PP43 needs to be dated on or before the time of payment.

Note that the rules for retirement annuity contracts are slightly different. (See Inland Revenue help sheet IR330 *Pension payments*.)

Carrying back doesn't reduce your payments on account

If you have to pay your tax twice-yearly as a 'payment on account' (see Chapter 3), do not count on carrying back pension contributions to reduce your payments. You get tax relief as if the payment were made in the previous year, but this is treated as a credit on your statement of account. It does not reopen your tax calculation for the previous year.

Example 7.3: **Carrying back contributions**

Barbara runs her own florist's shop. She pays £200 a month (before tax relief) into a stakeholder pension, and when she inherits £10,000 in July 2003 she decides to pay in extra. She is 49 so the maximum is 25% of her earnings (see Table 7.1 on page 162).

Barbara's relevant earnings are £20,000, so her maximum contributions are £20,000 × 25% = £5,000.

Maximum contributions (£20,000 × 25%)	£5,000
Regular contributions (£200 × 12)	£2,400
Unused relief	£2,600

Barbara pays in an extra £5,200. Half of this uses up her remaining relief for 2003–04, and she carries back the remaining £2,600 to use up her unused relief for 2002–03. Note, though, that Barbara actually hands over £5,200 × 78% = £4,056 after basic-rate tax relief.

Tax on a private pension

You get tax relief on what goes into an 'approved' private pension. However, the money coming out is generally taxable, and there are various checks to stop people contributing just to get the tax relief. The main checks to be aware of are:

- *You cannot draw money from a pension scheme before a minimum age* (currently 60 for an occupational scheme or retirement annuity contract, 50 for a personal or stakeholder pension scheme, although the government plans to increase this to 55). Once you reach the relevant age you can draw your benefits even if you are still working.
- *Limits on the amount of benefits payable by 'final salary' occupational schemes.* The overall maximum the tax rules allow you is a pension of two-thirds of your final salary. Benefits payable by 'money purchase' schemes are naturally limited by what your investment will buy.
- *Most of your pension money must be used to buy an annuity when you retire.* An annuity is a guaranteed income for life, provided by an

insurance company. You can take part of your benefits as a tax-free lump sum instead, but the amounts are limited (see Table 7.2).

In practice, you do not usually have to worry about these limits – the pension scheme administrator will ensure that you do not exceed them – but they do present you with a number of choices. Table 7.2 gives a brief summary, but for more information see the leaflets available from the Department for Work and Pensions (DWP) and the Financial Services Authority.

Note that even though the tax rules may permit the various options, the pension scheme you are in may not. You may have to transfer your money to a different scheme that does provide the option you want.

Getting your money out of a pension

You cannot get your money out of a pension before you reach the minimum age laid down unless you become incapacitated, you are in some jobs such as professional sport, or you have been a member of an occupational scheme for under two years (in which case refunds will be paid with 20% tax deducted).

Annuity or income withdrawals?

The cost of an annuity fluctuates with conditions in the financial markets, and once you have bought one you cannot get your money back (although you can pay extra to ensure a minimum return). Instead, you can leave your money in the pension fund provided that you draw an income of at least 35 per cent of the annuity that your fund would otherwise have bought. If you do this, you must buy an annuity when you reach 75.

Not all schemes offer income withdrawals, there is a cost involved, and there is an element of risk. This makes such schemes unsuitable for many people. An alternative might be phasing your retirement, which you can achieve by splitting your pension plan into separate segments. See the Financial Services Authority *Guide to annuities and income withdrawal.*

Table 7.2: Your options on retirement

Type of scheme	*Tax limits (scheme limits may be less generous)*
Occupational pension (final salary)	■ Pension of up to two-thirds of final earnings, depending on length of service. ■ Part of pension may be taken as an optional tax-free lump sum of up to 1½ times final earnings. If you joined scheme after 16 March 1987, maximum lump sum is capped at around £150,000, and no lump sum may be taken from additional voluntary contributions if you started paying them after 7 April 1987.
Occupational pension (money purchase)	■ As above, but dependent on value of fund. ■ You may be able to defer taking your pension until age 75, and take income withdrawals instead.
Personal/stakeholder pension plan	■ Optional tax-free lump sum of up to one-quarter of your fund and ■ *either* annuity bought with balance of fund ■ *or* income withdrawals from the fund, with annuity taken by age 75.
Retirement annuity contracts	■ Optional tax-free lump sum of up to three times the annual value of the remaining annuity. Maximum of £150,000 for plans taken out after 16 March 1987. ■ Annuity bought with balance of fund.

Shop around for your annuity

With a money purchase pension, you can choose to buy your annuity from a different company from the company with which your pension is invested (the so-called 'open market option'). Always shop around – annuity rates vary hugely.

How money from a private pension is taxed

- Any lump sum is tax-free. If you invest the money, the interest or dividends arising will be taxable in the same way as any other income from savings and investments.
- The pension or annuity income from an occupational pension, personal pension or stakeholder pension counts as taxable income, taxed in the same way as earnings from a job. Tax will be deducted under PAYE, and you will receive a PAYE code (see Chapter 2).
- The annuity income from a retirement annuity contract is also taxable. The income will be paid with basic-rate tax deducted, unless you are a non-taxpayer, when you can ask your pension provider to pay the income before tax (ask your pension provider for form R89).
- Any income withdrawn from a pension fund, as an alternative to an annuity, is taxed in the same way as the income from an annuity.

Investing your lump sum

Note that *purchased life annuities* bought with funds which do not come from a pension fund are taxed differently from pension scheme annuities and are covered in Chapter 10.

Tax on state pensions and benefits

Taxable state pensions and benefits are listed at the start of this chapter.

When it comes to working out the taxable amount of a state retirement pension, the following additions to your pension are taxable:

- any addition for invalidity or for an adult dependant (but not a child)
- the age addition you get if you are over 80
- any additional pension from the State Earnings Related Pension Scheme (SERPS) or the state second pension
- any graduated pension earned before SERPS was introduced
- any increases paid by the DWP to uprate your guaranteed minimum pension if you are contracted out of SERPS.

Non-taxable additions are the £10 Christmas bonus and any cold weather payments. The minimum income guarantee or pension credit are also non-taxable, but you are unlikely to be a taxpayer if you qualify for them.

A state pension is taxed as yours if it is payable to you, even if you are a married woman claiming a pension on your husband's contributions.

How the tax is paid

State pensions are always paid out before tax, even when they are taxable, and so are most other state benefits.

The Revenue's preferred way of collecting any tax due on state pensions and benefits is to adjust your PAYE code for another source of income taxed under PAYE, such as a private pension – see Chapter 2. This will mean that more of your private pension (or other income from which the PAYE is deducted) goes in tax.

There are two state benefits that get special treatment:

- *Incapacity Benefit*. If you receive taxable Incapacity Benefit (in most cases, benefit paid after the first 28 weeks) and have no other income taxed under PAYE, the DWP deduct tax before paying you. (See Inland Revenue leaflet IR144 *Income tax and incapacity benefit.*)
- *Jobseeker's Allowance*. Tax is not deducted, but you must give your P45 to the jobcentre, which keeps track of your tax liability over the year. You will get a statement of taxable Jobseeker's Allowance from your jobcentre at the end of the tax year. Any tax you owe is normally collected by adjusting your PAYE code when you get a new job. If you have paid too much tax you will usually get a refund, from either the jobcentre or your new employer. (See Inland Revenue leaflet IR41 *Income tax and job seekers.*)

Could you claim a refund?

If your only income comes from benefits, you are unlikely to be a taxpayer. Indeed, you might be entitled to a tax refund when you start claiming benefits – ask your tax office for a repayment claim form P50.

Child Tax Credit and Working Tax Credit

Child Tax Credit and Working Tax Credit were introduced in April 2003, replacing the old Children's Tax Credit and Working Families' and Disabled Person's Tax Credits.

This section deals with the new credits. If you want help claiming Children's Tax Credit for earlier years, see Chapter 4. (Working Families' Tax Credit cannot be claimed in arrears, and so is not covered.) If you have been receiving Children's Tax Credit, you should have received a claim form TC600 for the new credit. If not, contact your tax office.

The Child Tax Credit and Working Tax Credit are interlinked. The maximum credit depends on your circumstances, but it is then withdrawn by a certain amount once your income exceeds a certain limit.

Can you claim?

See Table 7.3 on page 173 to check your entitlement to the various 'elements' that make up the credits. Note that if you are married, or living with someone as husband and wife, you have to claim jointly – you cannot claim separately. If you have a child who lives with an ex-partner for some of the time, you must either decide between you who will claim Child Tax Credit, or the Revenue will decide which of you has 'main responsibility'.

If you have been getting state benefits with child additions in the past, the new child credit replaces the child additions. You can continue to claim child benefit, which is now also administered by the Revenue.

Contact the Revenue's tax credits helpline for further information and a claim form. The Revenue's website has a calculator to help you work out how much you can claim; you can also claim online.

How much credit?

This depends on your income – or, if you are married, or living with someone as husband and wife, on your *joint* income. This is broadly the same as your income for tax purposes, but excluding:

- Most taxable perks from your job, except the taxable value of a company car and car fuel, mileage allowances, vouchers and cheap or free goods.

- Pension income, investment income, property income and foreign income, if, altogether, they come to under £300.

You can increase your right to credit by making a pension contribution or Gift Aid donation, as these are deducted from your income for tax credit purposes.

If your annual income is above £5,060, you lose first your Working Tax Credit, then the child element of the Child Tax Credit – you only start to lose the family element once your income exceeds £50,000.

The full tax credit calculation is complex, and you do not have to do it yourself. Contact the tax credits helpline, or use the calculator on the Revenue website. But, to get a quick idea:

1. Work out your maximum Working Tax Credit (from Table 7.3).
2. Divide the answer at step 1 by 0.37, and add £5,060. This gives the maximum income you can have before your Working Tax Credit is reduced to zero.
3. If the result of step 2 is more than your income, you are entitled to all your Child Tax Credit, but your Working Tax Credit is reduced by 37 pence for each £1 of income above £5,060.
4. If the result of step 2 is less than your income, you get no Working Tax Credit, and the child element of your Child Tax Credit is reduced. To find the reduction, take your income, and deduct either £13,230 or, if larger, the figure from step 2. Multiply the result by 0.37.
5. Your child element entitlement is £1,445 for each child (more for a disabled child), minus the result of step 4.

Next, work out the family element of the Child Tax Credit:

- If your household income is below £50,000, you get the full family element (£545, or £1,090 if you have a new baby).
- If your household income is above £58,175 (or £66,350 if you have a new baby), you get nothing.
- If your household income is between £50,000 and £58,175 (or £66,350), deduct £50,000. Divide the result by 15 and deduct it from £545 (£1,090 if you have a new baby). This tells you how much family element you can claim.

Example 7.4: **Working out tax credits**

Susie and Simon have two children, aged two and four. They work full-time and earn £34,000 between them. They pay £7,500 a year for childcare. They are entitled to Working Tax Credit of:

Basic element for people with children	£1,525
Extra for couples	£1,500
Extra for people working 30+ hours	£620
Childcare: £7,500 x 70%	£5,250
Total	£8,895

To work out their maximum income before their Working Tax Credit is reduced to zero, they divide this amount by 0.37, and add £5,060, to get £8,895 ÷ 0.37 = £24,040 + £5,060 = £29,100. As this is less than their income they get no Working Tax Credit.

The child element of their Child Tax Credit is reduced by 37 pence for each pound of income above £29,100 (or £13,230 if greater):

£34,000 − £29,100 = £4,900 × 0.37 = £1,813.

As the child element is £1,445 for each child, i.e. £2,890, this works out at £2,890 − £1,813 = £1,077 child element. They qualify for the full family element, so their Child Tax Credit comes to £545 + £1,077 = £1,622.

How tax credits are decided and paid out

Initially, your claim is decided on the basis of your income for the previous tax year. In the first year of tax credits (2003–04), however, your credit will depend on your income for 2001–02. Even if your income has changed since then, claim anyway, and notify the Revenue of any changes since 2002.

After the end of the tax year, you will receive an annual renewal form. If, based on this form, it turns out that you have received too little credit, the amount owed will be paid to you as a lump sum. If you have received too much, the overpayment will be collected by adjusting next year's

Table 7.3: Child and Working Tax Credits for 2003–04

Working Tax Credit	*Annual amount*
Basic element for:	
■ People with children or a disability who work at least 16 hours a week; other people aged 25 or over who work at least 30 hours a week	£1,525
■ Extra for couples and lone parents	£1,500
■ Extra for people with children or a disability who work at least 30 hours a week (including couples who work 30 hours between them, provided one works at least 16 hours)	£620
■ Extra for disabled workers	£2,040
■ Extra for people aged 50-plus who have moved into employment from benefits in the last 3 months	£1,045 if working 16+ hours a week, £1,565 if working 30+ hours
■ Extra for workers with a severe disability	£865
Working Tax Credit childcare element	
■ People paying for approved childcare – worth up to 70% of the first £200 you pay per week (£135 a week for one child)	Maximum £4,914 for one child, £7,280 for two or more

Child Tax Credit	*Annual amount*
Child Tax Credit child element	
■ Amount for each child	£1,445
■ Extra for each disabled child	£2,155
■ Extra for each child with severe disability	£865
Child Tax Credit family element	
■ Families with children up to 16 or up to 19 and in full-time education	£545
■ Extra in year of baby's birth	£545

credit, or through your PAYE code (from 2005), or by you making a payment direct to the Revenue.

The annual renewal form will also form the basis of the next year's award, but if you expect your income to fall, you can ask for the credit to be based on your estimated income.

How the credit is paid depends on the type:

- Child Tax Credit and the childcare element are paid directly into the current account of the main carer, in the same way as Child Benefit.
- Any other Working Tax Credit will be paid by your employer, or direct by the Revenue if you are self-employed.

When things change

Changes will be picked up at the end of the tax year through your annual renewal form. However, you must tell the Revenue during the tax year if:

- you marry, start living with someone, split up or there is any other change in the adults leading the household
- you are claiming the childcare element and reduce your childcare.

The first £2,500 of any increase in income in the tax year is ignored in working out whether you have received too much credit. Any increase above that will reduce your credit. So out of a rise of £3,500, only £3,500 – £2,500 = £1,000 is taken into account.

Tell the Revenue promptly if things change

If a change increases your right to credit (e.g. you have a baby), the increase is backdated to the date of the change only if the Revenue are told within three months. However, if the change is due to a Revenue mistake, it can still be made up to five years after the end of the tax year in question.

Changes that reduce your credit are always backdated, and you could end up having to repay a large sum if you don't notify the Revenue as soon as possible.

What to tell the Inland Revenue

Pension contributions

If you are a basic-rate taxpayer paying into a personal or stakeholder pension, or making free-standing additional voluntary contributions, you don't need to do anything to claim your tax relief – you get it by paying less. Tax relief on occupational pension contributions is also given at source.

With a retirement annuity contract or if you are a higher-rate taxpayer contributing to a personal or stakeholder pension, you will have to take some action. If you get a tax return, complete Question 14 of the main tax return. If you do not get a return, write to your tax office with the details or ask for form PP120.

Receiving a pension or state benefits

Make sure your tax office knows in good time if you expect to start receiving a pension in the next few months so that they can sort out your PAYE code, if relevant. You may be asked to complete a 'pension enquiry' form P161. With state benefits, your tax office should not need notifying.

If you get a tax return, enter the taxable amount of any UK pension, state or private, or state benefits, in Question 11 on page 4.

To claim Working Tax Credit or Child Tax Credit, contact the Revenue's tax credits helpline or claim through the Revenue's website (see the Fact File), or get the forms from your tax office or jobcentre.

Filling in your tax return

Question 11 – Did you receive a taxable UK pension, retirement annuity or Social Security benefit?

Tick this if you received a pension from an ex-employer or other private pension, or if you received a state retirement pension or other taxable state benefit listed in the question. Don't tick it if you received an overseas pension or benefit – these go on the Foreign supplementary pages.

Boxes 11.1 to 11.9 State pensions and benefits

Generally, you should enter the taxable amount to which you were entitled between 6 April 2002 and 5 April 2003, whether or not you received it. And note that you should enter the total of your weekly entitlements, even if you received the income monthly or quarterly. See 'Record-keeping' on page 179 for documents that show taxable amounts.

Mistakes to avoid when entering state benefits

- Additions to state benefits and pensions for children are not taxable. Do not include them.
- If you received Jobseeker's Allowance for more than one period in the tax year, remember to add together the taxable amounts given on each of the P45U forms you received, plus that shown on the P60U you get if still claiming on 5 April 2003.
- Don't confuse bereavement allowance with the lump sum bereavement payment. The allowance is taxable – the payment is not.
- Don't include statutory maternity, paternity, or sick pay in this section unless they have been paid to you directly by the Revenue. If paid by your employer, enter them on the Employment supplementary pages.
- If you received the minimum income guarantee or pension credit in addition to your state pension, only the pension itself is taxable.

Boxes 11.10 to 11.14 Other pensions and retirement annuities

Enter here any pension from a UK occupational pension, personal or stakeholder pension, free-standing additional voluntary contributions (FSAVC) plan, or retirement annuity contract. If instead of buying an annuity with your pension fund you took an income withdrawal, include the amount of income withdrawn. Do not include:

- any tax-free cash lump sum from your pension
- a taxable lump sum from an unapproved pension scheme – this is taxed as income from employment (see Chapter 5)
- any tax-free amount, such as an addition to your pension paid because of a work-related accident or illness

- a purchased life annuity (see page 167). This goes in box 10.14.

Note that box 11.13 for 'Deduction' applies only if you have a UK pension, paid through an overseas government, for public service in the Commonwealth or other UK protectorate.

If you have more than one private pension, you need to give details of each. Use 'Additional information' at the end of the return if there is not enough room in box 11.14.

Question 14 – Do you want to claim relief for your pension contributions?

Don't tick the 'Yes' box if you only paid into an occupational scheme, except in the rare situation that you paid contributions out of your after-tax income (e.g. if you make an extra contribution direct, rather than by deduction from your pay). Such contributions go in box 14.10.

You should enter in this section any contributions you paid into a personal pension, stakeholder pension, retirement annuity contract or free-standing additional voluntary contributions (FSAVC) scheme. Start by entering the gross amount actually paid:

- between 6 April 2002 and 5 April 2003 in box 14.1, box 14.6, or box 14.11, as relevant
- after 5 April 2003 but before 31 January 2004, if you want to 'carry back' the contributions and have them treated as if paid in 2002–03. Enter the gross contribution, in box 14.4 or box 14.8, as relevant. You cannot carry back FSAVC contributions.

Remember to include contributions your employer paid into your plan. And for personal pension, stakeholder pension and FSAVC contributions, you must enter the gross amount you paid, that is the amount you handed over plus the basic-rate tax relief the pension company claims from the Revenue. To work this out, divide the amount you paid by 0.78. (Don't do this to your employer's contributions, you don't get tax relief on these.)

By now you should have entered everything you actually paid. Next, you can deal with any contributions paid between 6 April 2002 and 5 April

2003 that you want to 'carry back' and treat as if paid before 6 April 2002. For personal or stakeholder pensions, enter the carried-back amount in box 14.7 (remembering that you should enter the gross amount).

For retirement annuity contracts, you need to divide up the carried-back contributions into:

- amounts that you have already claimed to carry back (before sending in your tax return) – these go in box 14.2
- amounts that you want to carry back but for which you have not yet put in a carry-back claim – these go in box 14.3.

For both types of pension, follow the instructions on the form to work out the amount on which you will actually get tax relief for the 2002–03 tax year, in boxes 14.9 and 14.5. These do not include any contributions made after 5 April 2003 that you are claiming to carry back to 2002–03 because they do not affect your 2002–03 tax bill (see page 164).

Figure 7.1: Question 14 (see Example 7.4)

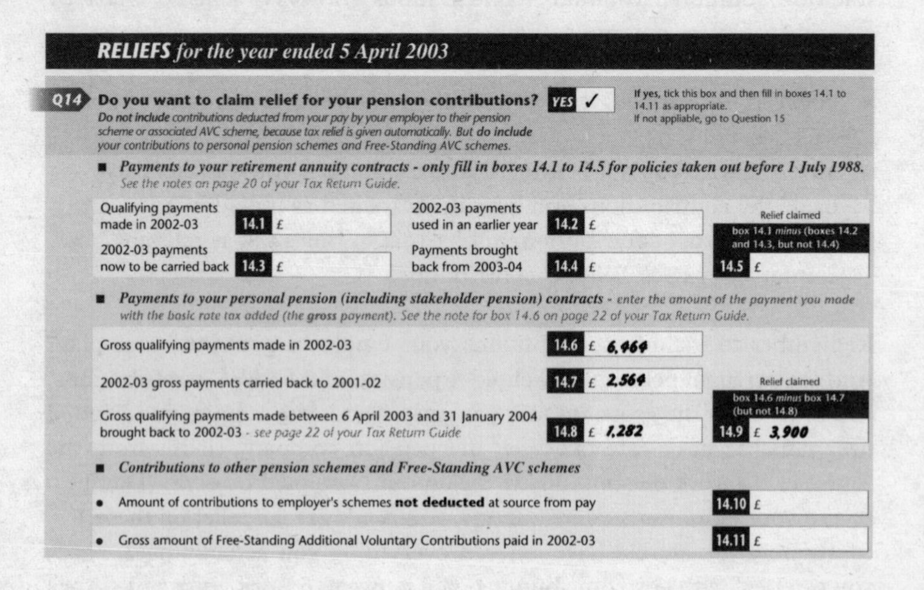

RELIEFS *for the year ended 5 April 2003*

Q14 Do you want to claim relief for your pension contributions? YES ✓

If yes, tick this box and then fill in boxes 14.1 to 14.11 as appropriate.
If not appliable, go to Question 15

Do not include contributions deducted from your pay by your employer to their pension scheme or associated AVC scheme, because tax relief is given automatically. But do include your contributions to personal pension schemes and Free-Standing AVC schemes.

■ ***Payments to your retirement annuity contracts - only fill in boxes 14.1 to 14.5 for policies taken out before 1 July 1988.***
See the notes on page 20 of your Tax Return Guide.

Qualifying payments made in 2002-03	14.1 £	2002-03 payments used in an earlier year	14.2 £	Relief claimed box 14.1 *minus* (boxes 14.2 and 14.3, but not 14.4)
2002-03 payments now to be carried back	14.3 £	Payments brought back from 2003-04	14.4 £	14.5 £

■ ***Payments to your personal pension (including stakeholder pension) contracts*** *- enter the amount of the payment you made with the basic rate tax added (the **gross** payment). See the note for box 14.6 on page 22 of your Tax Return Guide.*

Gross qualifying payments made in 2002-03	14.6 £ 6,464	
2002-03 gross payments carried back to 2001-02	14.7 £ 2,564	Relief claimed box 14.6 *minus* box 14.7 (but not 14.8)
Gross qualifying payments made between 6 April 2003 and 31 January 2004 brought back to 2002-03 - *see page 22 of your Tax Return Guide*	14.8 £ 1,282	14.9 £ 3,900

■ ***Contributions to other pension schemes and Free-Standing AVC schemes***

• Amount of contributions to employer's schemes **not deducted** at source from pay	14.10 £
• Gross amount of Free-Standing Additional Voluntary Contributions paid in 2002-03	14.11 £

Mistakes to avoid when entering pension contributions

- Entering the amount you actually paid into a personal or stakeholder pension or FSAVC plan (the net amount), rather than the gross payment.
- Forgetting to include contributions carried back to a previous year with the other payments actually made in the tax year. Enter all the payments made first, and then enter separately any payments to carry back.
- If you are working out your own tax and are carrying back contributions, forgetting to complete boxes 18.5 or 18.8 on page 8 (see Example 3.4 on page 54).

Example 7.5: **Entering your pension contributions**

Oscar is a member of a group personal pension scheme. He contributes £156 a month, to which his employer adds £125. The pension company reclaims basic-rate tax relief on Oscar's contributions, but not on his employer's, so the total regular payment into his plan is £156 ÷ 0.78 = £200 + £125 = £325 a month, or £3,900 each year.

Oscar also pays in his annual bonus as a lump sum – £2,000 (£2,564 gross) in May 2002, and £1,000 (£1,282) in May 2003. Because the bonus arrives close to the end of the tax year, he makes the payment in the new tax year and carries it back to the previous one.

On his tax return, Oscar enters in box 14.6 his total contribution for 2002–03: £3,900 + £2,564 = £6,464. In box 14.7 he enters the May 2002 payment (included in box 14.6) that he has carried back to 2001–02. He has already claimed relief for this in last year's return, so he deducts it from his total payments for the year and enters the result (£3,900) at 14.9. At 14.8 he claims to carry the May 2003 payment (£1,282) back to 2002–03. He is due higher-rate relief of £1,282 × 18% = £231, which he enters in box 18.8.

Record-keeping

You must keep records for at least 22 months (five years and ten months if your return includes trade or letting income) from the end of the tax year to which they relate.

Pension contributions

- Keep records of all your contributions – e.g. receipts or contribution certificates. (Inland Revenue help sheet IR330 *Pension payments* has useful worksheets for keeping track of your contributions.)
- If you are carrying back contributions, you will need form PP43 (from your pension provider), or form 43 if you are contributing to a retirement annuity contract.
- If you are contributing more than £3,600 to a personal or stakeholder pension, you will need proof of your earnings for the year that you are using as your 'basis year'.

Receiving a pension or state benefits

- Keep the letter you receive from the DWP each year giving the value of your basic pension, and details of other state benefits. If you are not sure how much taxable state pension you have received, ask your benefit office for form BR735 for the relevant tax year.
- If you have been claiming Jobseeker's Allowance, you should have received a statement of taxable amounts on either a P45U (when you stopped claiming) or P60U (at the end of the tax year). For incapacity benefit, you should receive a P45 (IB) or P60 (IB).
- If you have a pension from someone other than the state, you should receive a P60 or other certificate at the end of the tax year, showing the taxable amount and any tax deducted. It is also sensible to keep any PAYE Coding Notice (P2).

Tax-planning hints

1. You pay no tax or National Insurance on contributions your employer makes to your pension – worth remembering when negotiating pay.
2. If you are a director of your own company, you can reduce your taxable profits by making a contribution to your own pension.
3. With a personal or stakeholder pension, you can choose to base your contributions on earnings for any of the previous five years, and you don't have to have an income to have one. If you buy one for a low-income family member, they will get basic-rate tax relief.

4 'Carrying back' pension contributions to the previous tax year allows you to maximise your contributions – and you will get more tax relief if your tax rate has fallen from the higher to basic rate. But you must make the carry-back election on or before the date you make the contribution.
5 When entering pension contributions in your tax return, don't forget to add the basic-rate tax relief you have already received.
6 Doctors and dentists can contribute to a private pension as well as the NHS pension scheme. Ask your tax office for details.
7 Always shop around for an annuity – rates vary hugely. Alternatively, consider 'income withdrawals' – but see page 166 for some risks.
8 If you have a retirement annuity contract, you may be able to transfer your money to a personal or stakeholder pension if you want to make use of the newer rules – but check that you aren't affected by less favourable changes (e.g. the earnings cap).
9 If you want to pay more into an occupational pension scheme, a stakeholder pension may be a cheaper alternative to free-standing AVCs.
10 If your only income comes from benefits, you might be entitled to a tax refund in the year you start claiming benefits.
11 You can defer drawing your state retirement pension – this may be worthwhile if it would push you into a higher tax bracket or affect your age-related allowances (see Chapter 4).
12 If your income is just at the level where you lose Child Tax Credit, paying a pension contribution or Gift Aid donation could reduce your income enough to qualify.
13 If you are not sure whether your income in 2003–04 will entitle you to tax credits, claim anyway. You may not get anything now, but the credit depends on your annual income and you cannot backdate your claim beyond three months. You can be sure of getting tax credit for the whole of 2003–04 only if you claim by 6 July 2003.

8

Income from property

You take in a lodger to help with your mortgage or rent. You let out – or sublet – part of your home. You get posted abroad and let your home. You've joined the growing number of buy-to-let landlords. You rent out a holiday property.

However you make money from property – whether you own it or not – if you make more than you spend on servicing the property (in Inland Revenue-speak, 'your rents and receipts from the exploitation of your land or property exceed your business expenses incurred in earning the income'), you'll usually be liable for income tax. And if you make a profit when you sell a property that you have let, there may also be a capital gains tax bill.

Does this affect you?

You don't need to worry about income tax if you let a room in the home you are living in to a lodger and your letting income for the tax year is less than the limit for tax-free income under the Rent-a-Room scheme (see opposite). You *will* be liable to income tax if the income you get from letting a room in your home exceeds that limit and/or you have other income from property. However, tax is not charged on the whole amount of the income because of the deductions you can make.

Capital gains tax becomes an issue only when you sell a property you have let. You don't have to worry about capital gains tax if you let a room to a lodger who shared your living space and the home qualifies for 'private residence relief' (see Chapter 11). But there may be a capital gains tax bill if the part of your home you let was self-contained (a 'separate dwelling house'), or you made major structural alterations to create the accommodation that you let. However, you can reduce your gain – and so the capital gains tax bill – by claiming 'lettings relief' (see page 257). If you sell property which you let but never used as your own home, the whole of the gain is subject to capital gains tax, although what you have to pay (if anything) depends on what you can claim to reduce the gain (see Chapter 11).

Tax-free income from property

In the 2002–03 and 2003–04 tax years, under the Rent-a-Room scheme, the first £4,250 of income from letting a room (or rooms) in your home is tax-free. This limit – which hasn't changed since 1997 – applies to owner-occupiers and those who sublet a room in a home they rent.

If you share a home, the person who lets the room gets the whole exemption of £4,250. If two (or more) share the rental income, or you rent out separate rooms in a joint home, each gets an exemption of £2,125.

If the money your lodger pays is more than the exempt amount that you're entitled to, you pay tax on the excess. So if you receive £5,000 in rent and are entitled to the full exemption of £4,250, you'll pay tax only on £5,000 – £4,250 = £750.

Rent-a-Room is usually the best option

If you claim an exemption under the Rent-a-Room scheme, you cannot claim any expenses. You do not have to claim Rent-a-Room relief, but unless you have expenses of more than £4,250 (£2,125 if you let jointly) from letting a room in your home (which is unlikely in most cases), you will always be better off – and have less paperwork to deal with – if you do claim.

What counts as income from property

Although you still have to pay tax on it, some property-related income is excluded when working out the taxable profit from your rental business. Yearly interest on a business bank account – which counts as savings income (see Chapter 10) – is one example. Another is income from property abroad which counts as foreign income (see Chapter 9) even though the taxable profits from property overseas are calculated in broadly the same way as those on non-holiday property in the UK.

If the way you make money from your land or property counts as a trade, the tax you pay on it is worked out using the rules described in Chapter 6 and you should include details of the income on the Self-employment pages of the tax return rather than on the Land and Property pages. Trading income includes income from:

- using your home to run a guest house or to provide B&B
- charging tenants (in a property you don't live in) for services – such as providing meals, cleaning and laundry – which are well beyond the services normally provided by a landlord; for tax purposes, you should separate these charges from the rents you receive (which *do* count as rental business income) even if you include the cost of these services in the rent rather than charging for them separately
- farming and market gardening
- exploiting the natural resources on your land – this includes things like mining, quarrying and cutting timber from woodland
- allowing roads, railways, canals and so on to pass through your land.

Rent-a-Room for traders

Although the income you get from using your home to run a B&B, guest house or small hotel counts as trading – rather than rental – income, you can still claim Rent-a-Room relief. (For more information on whether this is worthwhile for you, see help sheet IR223 *Rent a Room for traders.*)

How the tax is worked out

As far as the Revenue are concerned, the money you make from property – whether you merely take in a lodger or you are a buy-to-let tycoon – is treated as income from a rental business and you are taxed on the profits from that business. Tax is based on the profits from rental income due to you in a tax year even if you don't actually get some of the income until after the end of the tax year and even if you have accounts that cover a different 12-month period.

After ignoring income that is tax-free under the Rent-a-Room scheme and income that doesn't count as income from a rental business, the taxable profit on your rental business is worked out as follows:

- *Step 1:* total all income from letting holiday property which qualifies for special treatment (see next page).
- *Step 2:* subtract expenditure on letting holiday property in the form of allowable expenses (see page 187) and capital allowances (see page 190).
- *Step 3:* add the total of rents from letting part of your home and/or other properties which don't qualify for special treatment and all other income from property (see page 190).
- *Step 4:* subtract the total of allowable expenses on all other properties (see page 191) and/or any exempt amount you're entitled to under the Rent-a-Room scheme (if applicable).
- *Step 5:* subtract any qualifying losses (see page 192) to arrive at your taxable profit for the year.

Inland Revenue booklet IR150 *Taxation of Rents* is a detailed guide.

If you have made a taxable profit, it is added to your other non-savings income and taxed according to what falls into the lower-, basic- and higher-rate income tax bands (see Chapter 1).

A simpler way of working out your profits

Strictly speaking, when working out your taxable profits, you should include rent (and other income from property) which is earned from the tenant's use of the property in a tax year – called the 'earnings basis' – irrespective of when you actually got the money. However, you may be able to work out your profits using the simpler 'cash basis' where you base your figures on the cash paid and received in the tax year provided that:

- your gross rental business income is less than £15,000
- you always use the cash basis when working out your profits
- using the cash basis doesn't mean that your profits are substantially lower than they would be if you had used the stricter earnings basis to calculate them.

Tell the Revenue under 'Additional information' in your tax return if you are doing this.

Working out profits on holiday homes

You don't *have* to calculate the profits from letting holiday property separately from your other rental business income, but if the property passes the 'furnished holiday lettings' test (see opposite), you can:

- claim capital allowances on furniture and furnishings
- use any losses from the property to reduce tax on other income
- claim special reliefs from capital gains tax when you sell the property.

Rental income can increase your pension contributions

If you make profits from holiday property which passes the furnished holiday lettings test you can pay more into a stakeholder or personal pension – and so get more tax relief on your pension contributions. This is because such profits count as 'relevant earnings' for working out how much you can pay into your pension (see Chapter 7).

The furnished holiday lettings test

You can take advantage of the special rules for holiday property provided it is furnished and all of the following conditions are met in the 12 months covered by the tax year. However, in the first year of letting, the 12 months run from the date the property is first let; in the final year of letting the 12 months run to the date of the last letting. Whichever time period applies, the property must:

- be in the UK – the special rules don't apply to foreign property
- be available for letting at a commercial rent for a minimum of 140 days
- be let for at least 70 days – or, if you have more than one property, at least 70 days on average for the properties involved (see Example 8.1)
- not be occupied for more than 31 days by the same person in any period of seven months.

If the holiday property you let doesn't pass the 'furnished holiday lettings' test, you work out your profits according to the rules for other property given on pages 190 to 192.

Example 8.1: **Dealing with multiple properties**

Ryan lets out three holiday cottages. One of them fails the 70-day test, but otherwise they all meet the tests to qualify as furnished holiday lettings. Each property is let for:

Cottage 1: 90 days   Cottage 2: 78 days   Cottage 3: 66 days

Ryan divides the total (234 days) by the number of properties (3) to arrive at an average of 78 days, so all three properties still pass the furnished holiday lettings test.

Allowable expenses for holiday property

You don't pay tax on all the income you receive from letting holiday property (which qualifies for special treatment) because, when calculating your taxable profits, you can deduct the expenses involved in letting it. You cannot deduct 'capital expenditure' which includes the cost of buying the property and the cost of any improvements to the property – although you may be able to claim capital allowances for some things.

To be able to deduct the full amount of other costs, they must be incurred 'wholly and exclusively' in letting the property. The Revenue divide deductible expenses into six main categories.

Rent, rates, insurance, ground rents etc.

- rent if you lease a property which you then sublet
- buildings, contents and rental guarantee insurance
- business rates, council tax, water rates, ground rents, feu duties (in Scotland), service charges (for flats)
- gas and electricity bills, less any amount your tenants contribute towards them

Repairs, maintenance and renewals

- repairs and maintenance, excluding improvements – but see opposite
- painting and decorating – inside and out
- other work necessary to prevent the property from deteriorating – e.g. stone-cleaning and damp treatment
- renewing and replacing moveable objects such as furniture, domestic appliances, cutlery and crockery – unless you claim capital allowances instead (see page 190)

Finance charges, including interest

- interest on a mortgage or another type of loan to buy the property and any charges involved in taking out the loan, such as arrangement fees or booking fees for fixed-rate loans
- bank charges and overdraft interest on a separate business account

Legal and professional costs

- legal fees for renewing a lease (provided it is for less than 50 years) or evicting a tenant
- fees charged by an accountant for drawing up your accounts
- management fees for the cost of letting – e.g. you employ an agent to deal with the business of letting the property

Costs of services provided, including wages

- costs of services you provide such as cleaning and gardening, but only if you pay someone else to provide them; you cannot claim the cost of your own time

Other expenses

- advertising costs
- stationery, phone calls and other incidental expenses
- travel costs provided travel was solely for business purposes – travelling to inspect your holiday cottage and then coming straight back will count but travelling to inspect your holiday home while taking a holiday in it will not
- expenses incurred before you started letting, provided they would have been allowable if incurred once the letting had begun.

If you incur an expense partly for private use (e.g. you use a holiday property for your own holidays or let friends and family use it rent-free), you can deduct only the proportion of the expense which relates to the commercial letting of it. So if you use the property for your own holidays for a month each year, you will be able to claim only $^{11}/_{12}$ of the expenses.

Combining repairs with improvements

If you combine repair work with improvements to the property none of the cost of the work can be claimed as an allowable expense. Similarly, if you replace fixtures and fittings, such as kitchen units and bathroom suites, and upgrade them at the same time – you rip out cheap units and replace them with designer versions, for example – the cost counts as capital expenditure and so is not allowable (but in holiday property, you may be able to claim a capital allowance). However, if an 'improvement' occurs because you have used the nearest modern equivalent to what you replaced so that you meet modern-day building standards, the cost is an allowable expense. A good example is replacing single-glazed windows with double-glazed equivalents. So keep good records of your maintenance work and try to keep any 'improvements' separate.

Capital allowances for holiday property

The main advantage of having a holiday property treated for tax purposes as a furnished holiday letting is that you can claim capital allowances (explained in detail in Chapter 6) for the cost of furnishing and equipping the property. This makes good financial sense, but remember that when you replace items, you must claim capital allowances for the replacements *instead of* claiming the cost of such renewals (see above) as an allowable expense.

You can also claim capital allowances for equipment you need to run the letting business. This includes things like ladders, lawnmowers, tools, fax machines, computers, filing cabinets and other business furniture.

As with expenses, if you claim a capital allowance for something used partly for business and partly for your own personal use, you can claim only a proportion of the allowance.

Working out the profits on other property

Other income from property is lumped together, so if you have more than one property, you don't need to work out the profit (or loss) separately for each one. As well as rents, income from other property includes:

- rent charges, ground rents and feu duties (Scotland)
- income from sporting rights such as fishing and shooting permits
- income from allowing waste to be buried or stored on your land
- payments for allowing other people to use your property – e.g. to store things in your shed or as a location for a film
- grants from local authorities or others for repairs (but not improvements) to a property
- income from caravans or houseboats which never go anywhere
- service charges
- refunds of running costs you claimed previously as allowable expenses
- payments from rental guarantee insurance (which provides cover against non-payment of rent)
- lump sums you received when you grant a lease of less than 50 years.

How you arrive at the profit (or loss) figure for other property is the same as how you calculate profits on holiday property, but there are important differences in the tax reliefs you can claim.

Allowable expenses on other property

All the expenses which are allowable as deductions for holiday property (see page 188) are allowable as deductions for other property. However, if you let furnished property, instead of claiming the actual cost of renewal and replacement of furniture and so on, you can choose to claim a 'wear and tear' allowance. This is worked out as 10 per cent of the rent you receive after subtracting council tax and other bills which you, rather than your tenant, pay. Once you have chosen the way in which you are going to get tax relief on renewals, you can't change your mind.

Wear and tear advantage

The advantage of choosing to claim a wear and tear allowance rather than deducting the cost of replacement items is that you can make the deduction every year even if you haven't actually replaced anything. It also makes record-keeping simpler.

Capital allowances on other property

You cannot claim capital allowances for furnishing and equipping the property. But you can claim them for equipment needed to run your rental business as you can for holiday property.

Flats over shops

If you buy a flat above a shop to rent out, you can claim the cost of renovations as a 100% capital allowance even though such expenditure is not normally allowable. The same allowance is available for the cost of converting vacant or underused space above business premises into a flat to let. (See Inland Revenue leaflet IR2007 *Capital allowances for flats over shops*.)

Using losses

A loss you make on letting out any type of property can be used to reduce the size of your taxable profit. And all losses can be carried forward if you can't make use of them in the current tax year. However, losses carried forward can be set only against future profits from your rental business. A loss on qualifying holiday property is treated as a business loss, so you have the options shown in Figure 6.2 on page 142, including setting it against other income in the same tax year, or even the income of earlier years. Any loss left over is carried forward to set against rental income in future years.

What to tell the Inland Revenue

If you don't get a tax return and your only income from property is rent that falls within the tax-free Rent-a-Room scheme limit, you don't need to tell the Revenue anything. But you are required to tell your tax office if any of the following apply:

- you have been receiving Rent-a-Room relief but no longer qualify e.g. you have moved but are still receiving the lodger's rent, or the rent has risen above the tax-free amount
- you receive any other income from property.

You must notify your tax office by 5 October after the end of the year in which you received the income – i.e. by 5 October 2003 for income received in the 2002–03 tax year. You will usually be sent a tax return, but if you are taxed under PAYE and the amount of rental income is small, the tax may be collected by adjusting your PAYE code. Otherwise you will have to make payments on account (see Chapter 3).

If you have not been sent a tax return, 5 October is also the deadline for telling your tax office if you have sold a property you let and have made a taxable capital gain (see Chapter 11).

If your income from property counts as trading income (see page 184), you must register as self-employed (see Chapter 6).

If you get a tax return and receive any income from property, you should tick Question 5 in the main tax return and fill in the Land and Property supplementary pages *unless*:

- the way you make money from your home counts as a trade (see page 184), in which case you should tick Question 3 in the main tax return and fill in the Self-employment supplementary pages
- you receive rent (or other income) from property abroad, in which case you should tick Question 6 in the main tax return and fill in the Foreign supplementary pages.

Filling in the Land and Property supplementary pages

The Land and Property supplementary pages ask for details of all your income from property in the UK. If the only income you receive is money from a lodger who shares your home and this amounts to less than £4,250 (£2,125 if you let jointly), all you have to do is tick 'Yes' in answer to the first question.

Furnished holiday lettings

Complete the rest of this page only if you let out holiday property that passes the 'furnished holiday lettings' test (see page 187). If the property you let fails this test (even if it is a holiday property), go to page 2.

Boxes 5.1 to 5.9 Income from furnished holiday lettings

Enter in box 5.1 the total amount of income you received from letting holiday property that passes the 'furnished holiday lettings' test. If this is £15,000 or less over a whole year, you can:

- *either* break down your expenses according to the Revenue's headings in boxes 5.2 to 5.7 (see page 188 for what comes under each heading) and then total them in box 5.8
- *or* you can simply enter the total figure for all your expenses in box 5.7 and again in box 5.8 without giving any details.

If your total income from letting furnished holiday property is more than

£15,000, you must fill in boxes 5.2 to 5.7 and give the total in box 5.8.

Relating income and expenses to a tax year

Unless you are using the 'cash basis' (see page 186) for working out your profits, you must give details of income due to you in a tax year and expenses which relate to a particular tax year even if you incurred expenses at an earlier or later date. For example, if you had your holiday property repainted in March 2002 but didn't pay the bill until the end of April, the expense still belongs to the 2002–03 tax year. In addition, if you have an expense that straddles two years, you need to divide the payment between the two tax years, in line with the number of days between the date you incurred the expense and the end of the tax year (see Example 8.2).

Example 8.2: **Splitting expenses between tax years**

Lucy's buildings insurance on her rental property runs from 5 October 2002 to 5 October 2003 and she pays a lump-sum premium of £300: half of the premium belongs to the 2002–03 tax year (which ends on 5 April 2003), and half to the 2003–04 tax year.

Boxes 5.10 to 5.14 Tax adjustments

Before you arrive at the figure for your taxable profit from letting holiday property, you may need to:

- add back the proportion of your expenses which relate to private use in box 5.10, unless you have already taken this into account in the expenses figures entered in boxes 5.2 to 5.7
- add any 'balancing charges' in box 5.11, if you have made a profit from selling something on which you previously claimed capital allowances
- subtract capital allowances you can claim in box 5.13 (see Chapter 6 for how to calculate them). Note that you can claim enhanced allowances if you buy energy-saving equipment – if you have done this, tick box 5.13A.

Unless you have made a loss in this tax year, filling in box 5.14 completes this part of the Land and Property pages and you should now turn the form over and copy the figure from box 5.14 to box 5.19.

Boxes 5.15 to 5.18 Losses

If you have made a loss at box 5.1, you need to tell your tax office what you want to do with the loss. If you want to use it to reduce your tax bill on:

- *non-property income and/or capital gains*, enter the loss in box 5.16 (remember to include it in box 8.5 of the capital gains tax supplementary pages if you're using it to reduce that tax)
- *income from earlier tax years*, enter the loss in box 5.17 and give the amount and the tax year you want the loss to be used for in box 23.5 in the main tax return
- *other income from property*, enter the amount in box 5.18 and copy it to box 5.38.

Other property income

The second page of the Land and Property supplementary pages deals with property that doesn't pass the 'furnished holiday lettings' test. You must give details of not only rents you receive but also all other property income (see page 190).

Boxes 5.19 to 5.23 Income

- Ignore box 5.19 unless you filled in the first page of the form. If so, copy the figure you entered in box 5.14.
- In box 5.20 give a total figure for all your income from property in the UK which hasn't already been accounted for.
- Box 5.21 applies only to landlords who are resident abroad – their tenants may be required to deduct basic-rate tax from the rent and pay the tax to the Revenue.
- The 'chargeable premiums' referred to in box 5.22 apply only if you received a lump-sum payment from your tenant when granting a lease of less than 50 years. If this applies, fill in the working sheet on page LN5 of the Land and Property notes to get the correct figure to enter.

- Ignore box 5.22A unless you sublet a leased property and received a lump-sum payment (a 'reverse premium') to encourage you to take on the lease. Check with your tax office if you think that this may apply.
- Total all the figures in this section and enter them in box 5.23.

Jointly owned property

If you receive income from jointly owned property, enter only your share of the income and expenses.

Boxes 5.24 to 5.30 Expenses

You don't need to fill in this part of the form if your income from property is made up solely of one or more of the following:

- income from a lodger who lives with you and you are claiming relief under the Rent-a-Room scheme (see page 183)
- rent from property which passes the 'furnished holiday lettings' test – you have already given details of expenses in boxes 5.2 to 5.8
- you have joint income from property and you know only your share of the income after expenses has been deducted.

Unless any of the above apply:

- if your property income is less than £15,000 over a full year, enter a total figure for all your expenses in boxes 5.29 and 5.30
- if your property income is more than £15,000, enter separate figures split according to the headings given in boxes 5.24 to 5.29 with a total of these figures in box 5.30. (See page 191.)

Boxes 5.32 to 5.35 Tax adjustments

Before you arrive at the figure for your taxable profit from UK property, you may need to:

- add back the proportion of your expenses which relates to private use in box 5.32, unless you have already taken this into account in the expenses figures entered in boxes 5.24 to 5.29 (see page 189)
- add any 'balancing charges' referred to in box 5.33 if you have made a profit from selling something on which you previously claimed capital allowances (see page 191)
- if you get rent which is tax-free under the Rent-a-Room scheme, enter in box 5.35 the amount of relief you are claiming – i.e. £4,250 (£2,125 if you let the property jointly) or the amount of rent to which the relief applies if less
- subtract any capital allowances you can claim in box 5.36 (see Chapter 6 for how to calculate them) and tick box 5.36A if you are claiming a 100 per cent allowance for a flat over a shop (see page 191) and box 5.36B if claiming for environmentally friendly expenditure
- subtract your 'wear and tear' allowance (see page 191) if you let furnished property and you have chosen not to claim the actual cost of repairing and replacing furniture and so on
- subtract any loss on holiday property which you have chosen to set against other income from property (from box 5.18).

Follow the instructions on the form to find your adjusted profit in box 5.40, or loss in box 5.41. Finally, subtract any losses made in an earlier tax year and so far unused and enter the result in box 5.43. However, if the brought-forward loss is bigger than your adjusted profit, don't forget to enter the difference in box 5.45 to carry it forward to future years.

Boxes 5.44 to 5.47 Losses etc.

- Box 5.44 applies only if you have made a loss – either partly or wholly – as a result of claiming capital allowances and you want to set this loss against other income rather than carrying it forward to set against future income from property. You cannot claim to do this for any other loss, unless it is a loss made on furnished holiday lettings.
- You will have losses to carry forward to a future year either if you made a loss in this year or if you made a profit but it was less than your loss brought forward from previous years. Enter in box 5.45 any losses brought forward and not used this year, plus any loss made this

year, minus any loss which you are claiming to use against other income in box 5.44.
- Tick box 5.46 only if you have given details of income from jointly owned property of any type. If you have not given details of expenses because your co-owner deals with that side of things and so you only know your profit after expenses have been deducted, give the name and address of your co-owner in box 23.5 in the main tax return.
- Tick box 5.47 if this is the last tax year in which you expect to receive taxable income from property (this may affect your PAYE code).

Example 8.3: Filling in the Land and Property pages

Edgar has rent of £5,250 from a buy-to-let property and £3,000 from a lodger (see Figure 8.1). He enters the total – £8,250 – in box 5.20. As he is claiming Rent-a-Room relief on his lodger's rent, he can claim expenses only on his buy-to-let property, which come to £3,500. His rent is less than £15,000 over a full year, so he doesn't need to break down his expenses and he enters the total in box 5.29. He claims the tax-free amount of rent from his lodger in box 5.35, and 10% wear and tear for his buy-to-let property in box 5.37. This gives him a total profit at box 5.40 of only £1,225. However, his buy-to-let property was empty for part of 2001–02 and he made a £1,845 loss, which he enters in box 5.42. This wipes out his profit and leaves £1,845 – £1,225 = £620 of unused loss to carry forward to 2003–04.

Record-keeping

The records you have to keep if you have income from property are similar to those you have to keep if you run any kind of business (see Chapter 6). You must keep them for at least five years and ten months after the end of the tax year. However, in addition to keeping documentary evidence of all your income and relevant expenditure, you should keep a record of the number of days:

- a property was not available to let at a commercial rent (so that you

Figure 8.1: Land and property, Questions 5.19 to 5.47 (see Example 8.3)

Other property income

■ *Income*

• Furnished holiday lettings profits (copy from box 5.14)	5.19	£		
• Rents and other income from land and property	5.20	£ 8,250	5.21 (Tax deducted)	£
• Chargeable premiums	5.22	£		
• Reverse premiums	5.22A	£	5.23 (boxes 5.19 + 5.20 + 5.22 + 5.22A)	£ 8,250

■ *Expenses* (do not include figures you have already put in boxes 5.2 to 5.7 on Page L1)

• Rent, rates, insurance, ground rents etc.	5.24	£		
• Repairs, maintenance and renewals	5.25	£		
• Finance charges, including interest	5.26	£		
• Legal and professional costs	5.27	£		
• Costs of services provided, including wages	5.28	£		
• Other expenses	5.29	£ 3,500	5.30 (total of boxes 5.24 to 5.29)	£ 3,500
Net profit (put figures in brackets if a loss)			5.31 (box 5.23 *minus* box 5.30)	£ 4,750

■ *Tax adjustments*

• Private use	5.32	£		
• Balancing charges	5.33	£	5.34 (box 5.32 + box 5.33)	£
• Rent a Room exempt amount	5.35	£ 3,000		
• Capital allowances	5.36	£		
• Tick box 5.36A if box 5.36 includes a claim for 100% capital allowances for flats over shops	5.36A			
• Tick box 5.36B if box 5.36 includes enhanced capital allowances for environmentally friendly expenditure	5.36B			
• 10% wear and tear	5.37	£ 525		
• Furnished holiday lettings losses (from box 5.18)	5.38	£	5.39 (boxes 5.35 to box 5.38)	£ 3,525
Adjusted profit (if loss enter '0' in box 5.40 and put the loss in box 5.41)			5.40 (boxes 5.31 + 5.34 *minus* box 5.39)	£ 1,225
Adjusted loss (if you have entered '0' in box 5.40)	5.41 (boxes 5.31 + 5.34 *minus* box 5.39)	£		
• Loss brought forward from previous year			5.42	£ 1,845
Profit for the year			5.43 (box 5.40 *minus* box 5.42)	£ 0

■ *Losses etc*

• Loss offset against total income (read the note on page LN8)	5.44	£
• Loss to carry forward to following year	5.45	£ 620
• Tick box 5.46 if these Pages include details of property let jointly	5.46	
• Tick box 5.47 if **all** property income ceased in the year to 5 April 2003 **and** you don't expect to receive such income again, in the year to 5 April 2004	5.47	

Now fill in any other supplementary Pages that apply to you.
Otherwise, go back to page 2 of your Tax Return and finish filling it in.

can work out the proportion of an expense that counts as personal use – see page 189)

- a holiday property was let so that you can check whether it passes the 'furnished holiday lettings' test (see page 187).

Tax-planning hints

1. If you take in a lodger, you pay no tax on the income you receive if you charge less than the Rent-a-Room limit, £354 a month or less, or £177 if letting jointly.
2. If you are claiming Rent-a-Room relief you cannot deduct expenses. If you are just over the threshold of £354 a month, get your lodger to pay some bills separately. If you include them in the rent, the money for bills counts as income and you'll have to pay tax on it.
3. A holiday property in the UK may qualify for favourable tax rules if it is available for letting for at least 140 days in the year, and is actually let for at least 70 days (see page 187).
4. If you make a loss on letting holiday property which passes the test above, try to set it against other income and/or capital gains in the same tax year as you made the loss. If you carry the loss forward, it can only be used to reduce future income from property.
5. There are also favourable tax rules if you buy a flat above a shop (or other commercial premises) to rent out (see page 191).
6. You can claim tax relief on a mortgage to buy a property you let out, but not on a mortgage on your own home.
7. Consider employing your spouse or children to do the cleaning or gardening at the properties you let. You'll be able to claim the money you pay them as an allowable expense – you can't do this if you do the work yourself. But they must actually do the work and be paid for it at a realistic rate.

9

Income from abroad

You still have to think about UK tax if you go overseas to work, or have an income from overseas property, investments or pensions. If you are resident in the UK, overseas income and capital gains are taxed in much the same way as other income or gains. Even if you are not a UK resident, UK tax may affect you.

For tax purposes, the Channel Islands and Isle of Man count as 'overseas'; the UK covers England, Wales, Scotland and Northern Ireland.

Does this affect you?

This chapter affects you if you are resident or 'ordinarily resident' (see page 203 for definitions) in the UK, but you have income from outside the UK, or you own property or other assets abroad. If so, you will have to declare your foreign income and capital gains, and may have to pay tax on them.

Non-residents do not have to pay UK tax on foreign income. But they may still have to pay it on UK income, and (if temporarily non-resident), UK capital gains. This is covered on page 209.

Whether resident or non-resident, you may still have to pay overseas tax on any foreign income. The UK has 'double taxation agreements' with many countries which may reduce the overall tax bill.

Fuller information is given in Inland Revenue booklet IR20 *Residents and non-residents*, and there are flow-charts to help you work out your residence status in the notes to the Non-residence pages of the tax return. The Revenue's Centre for Non-residents also has a helpline (see the Fact File).

Tax-free foreign income and gains

Table 9.1 on page 206 shows which types of income and gains are tax-free if you are not resident or not domiciled in the UK.

If you are a UK resident, the same types of income and capital gains that are tax-free in the UK are tax-free if they come from overseas. So, for example, foreign social security benefits that correspond to tax-free UK social security benefits are also tax-free. But some special tax reliefs, such as the Rent-a-Room scheme (see Chapter 8) do not apply overseas.

Foreign pensions are favourably taxed

Ten per cent of the income from a foreign pension is tax-free for UK residents. See Chapter 7 for other tax-free pensions, and note that a UK pension might also be partly or fully tax-free if it came from a job that involved working overseas. (See Inland Revenue help sheet IR204 *Lump sums and compensation payments.*)

How the tax is worked out on foreign income and gains

- *Step 1: check your residence status* (see opposite).
- *Step 2: check how much of your foreign income and gains is taxable in the UK.* You may not have to pay tax on all of it (see Table 9.1).
- *Step 3: check whether any special rules apply,* if you are working abroad, or have investments or a property overseas (see page 207 onwards).
- *Step 4: convert to sterling.* Use the rate of exchange at the time the income arose, unless it is taxable only when you bring it in to the UK (if so, use the rate at the time it is brought in). You can use the average exchange rates on the Revenue website (see page 299).
- *Step 5: claim relief for any foreign tax already paid* (see page 210).

Any taxable foreign income or gains are then taxed at the same rate as any UK income or gains of the same type.

Checking your residence status

There are three types of 'residence' that might affect your tax: residence, 'ordinary' residence, and 'domicile'. The effect that they have is summarised in Table 9.1 on page 206, and see Example 9.1.

Are you non-resident?

If you are non-resident, your foreign income is not taxable in the UK. You can claim to be non-resident if:

- *either* you go abroad to work full-time as an employee (or accompany a husband or wife who is working abroad)
- *or* you show that you have gone abroad to live permanently, or for at least three years – e.g. by buying a permanent home abroad and selling your UK home. If you have no such evidence, you may still be able to claim if you have gone for a particular purpose that is likely to cover an extended period of time.

And you meet both of the following conditions:

- you are away from the UK for at least one whole tax year
- your visits to the UK since leaving have totalled less than 183 days in any tax year and averaged less than 91 days in a tax year. (The average is worked out over four tax years, or the period of your absence if less, and excludes days in the UK for exceptional reasons, such as illness.)

If you become non-resident during the tax year

You may be able to claim 'split-year' treatment – you will still need to declare your non-UK income, but you are taxable on only the amount arising before you left the UK.

Are you ordinarily resident?

If you are not resident, you are usually not ordinarily resident as well. But you might be classed as non-resident but ordinarily resident if, say, you are away for a whole tax year but not working abroad and cannot show that you have gone abroad permanently. If so, your foreign income is not taxable in the UK but any foreign capital gains will be.

If you come to the UK, you may become resident but remain not ordinarily resident, for example if it is clear that you intend to stay less than three years (four years for students). If so, your foreign income and capital gains may become taxable in the UK, but this depends on whether you are 'domiciled' in the UK – see below.

Example 9.1: **Claiming non-residence**

Nigel and Ben both go abroad to work full-time for 15 months and both spend only 42 days in the UK during their absence. However, only Nigel is treated as non-resident. That's because he left in February 2002 and returned in May 2003, and so was away for the whole of the 2002–03 tax year. Ben, however, left, in May 2002 and returned in August 2003 – so he did not meet the condition of being away for a whole tax year.

Are you non-domiciled in the UK?

Broadly speaking, your domicile is the country regarded as your permanent home. It will normally be the country in which your father was domiciled at the time of your birth (not necessarily the country where you were born), or, for women married before 1974, their husbands' domicile. You can change your domicile but it is difficult.

If you are not UK-domiciled, foreign income and capital gains are taxable here only if you bring them into the UK. Your overseas assets may also be free of UK inheritance tax.

Note that the residence and domicile rules are currently under review, and in particular how they affect non-domiciled individuals living in the UK, though no proposals were published in the 2003 budget.

Long-term planning for inheritance tax

You cannot escape UK inheritance tax on your overseas property by a last-minute move abroad, because you are still treated as UK-domiciled for inheritance purposes if you were domiciled in the UK in the previous three years, or if you were a UK resident in 17 of the previous 20 years. (See Inland Revenue leaflet IHT18 *Inheritance tax. Foreign aspects.*)

How much of your foreign income is taxable in the UK?

If you are a UK resident, all your income and gains from abroad are normally liable to UK tax from the date they become yours, even if they stay overseas. This is called the 'arising' basis. However, there are two cases in which you might not have to pay tax on the income immediately:

- If you are not domiciled in the UK, you may only have to pay UK tax when you actually bring the money into the UK. This is called the 'remittance' basis (see Table 9.1).
- Whatever your residence status, if you cannot bring the money into the UK, because of exchange controls, say, you can claim that it is 'unremittable'. You pay tax on it when it does become possible to transfer it to the UK (even if you choose to leave it where it is).

Special rules

You may get special treatment and should contact the Inland Revenue Centre for Non-residents (see the Fact File) if you are:

- working at sea, or in the gas and oil industries, or in entertainment or sport
- an employee of the Crown or European Union, or a citizen of the Commonwealth, Republic of Ireland, Isle of Man or Channel Islands.

Table 9.1: Summary of how foreign income is taxed in the UK

If you are	*Taxable on amount arising*	*Taxable only if remitted to UK*	*Not taxable in UK*
Resident and			
■ ordinarily resident, domiciled	all foreign income (minus 10% of foreign pensions); foreign capital gains		
■ ordinarily resident, non-domiciled	earnings from working abroad for a UK-resident employer	all other foreign income and capital gains	
■ not ordinarily resident, domiciled	all foreign income except earnings (minus 10% of foreign pensions); foreign capital gains	foreign earnings as an employee	
■ not ordinarily resident, not domiciled		all foreign income and capital gains	
Not resident and			
■ ordinarily resident, domiciled	foreign capital gains		all foreign income
■ ordinarily resident, non-domiciled		foreign capital gains	all foreign income
■ not ordinarily resident, (domiciled or non-domiciled)			all foreign income; foreign capital gains unless only temporarily non-resident

Working abroad

Provided that you go to live and work abroad for at least a whole tax year, and your visits back do not average more than 91 days in a tax year, you will be non-resident. All your earnings abroad will be free of UK tax from the day after your departure until the day of your return.

If you are a non-resident employee, but your job involves working partly abroad and partly in UK, your UK earnings (allocated on daily rate) are taxable unless they are 'incidental' to your work abroad. However, you may be able to claim full relief under a double taxation agreement with the other country involved. If you are self-employed, your business has to be completely overseas for the profits to be tax-free.

If you are UK-resident, your foreign earnings are taxable in the UK. However, you may be able to claim the following extra deductions:

- At the start or end of the job, travel costs between the UK and your workplace abroad, provided that your employer is UK-resident.
- During the course of the job, travel to and from the UK, provided that your employer pays or reimburses you.
- The cost of board and lodging overseas, provided that this is paid or reimbursed by your employer, who must be UK-resident.
- If your job keeps you abroad for 60 days or more, travel costs for your spouse and children, provided that your employer bears the cost.
- Seafarers who are out of the UK for a 'qualifying absence' of 365 days or more can claim to have their foreign earnings tax-free.
- If you are not domiciled in the UK, a deduction for earnings you do not bring into the UK (see Inland Revenue help sheet IR 211 *Employment – residence and domicile issues*).

National Insurance contributions while abroad

Generally, you pay social security contributions in the country in which you are working, and if you go abroad to work your UK National Insurance contributions usually stop. But if a UK employer sends you to work in another country, you may have to carry on paying UK contributions for up to 52 weeks or even longer. This depends on agreements between the UK and the country you are visiting.

Not paying UK contributions means that your right to some UK social security benefits, such as a state pension, may be affected. If you plan to return to the UK, it may be worth paying voluntary contributions in the UK to protect your pension rights. (See Inland Revenue Leaflet NI38 *Social Security Abroad* and DWP leaflet SA29 *Your social security insurance, benefits and health care rights in the European Community*.)

Frequent flyers

Even if you spend more than 183 days abroad, and are home for less than 91 days a year, the Revenue are unlikely to treat you as non-resident if you have no settled home abroad, no intention of staying abroad indefinitely, and return to a UK base and UK home at the end of each assignment.

Investing abroad

If you are a UK resident, income from an 'offshore' investment is still liable to UK tax.

You may be able to claim relief for any tax already deducted by the overseas government (see page 210). But this relief is not available for dividends from some countries, and foreign dividends do not qualify for the 10 per cent tax credit that applies to UK dividends.

Any foreign investment income you get is added to any UK income of the same type and taxed at the same rate – so interest is taxed at 20 per cent if you are a basic-rate taxpayer, and dividends at 10 per cent. The exception is investment income to which the remittance basis applies (see Table 9.1); this is taxed in the same way as non-savings income, e.g. earnings.

When you sell your overseas investments, you are liable to capital gains tax in the same way as if you sell UK investments, except for some offshore funds. With these, your gains when you sell are taxed as income, unless the fund has 'distributor status' (in which case part or all of the gain is subject to capital gains tax). The fund managers or the Centre for Non-residents can tell you if this applies. Note, though, that changes are likely to be introduced to the taxation of these funds in 2004.

Beware anti-avoidance rules

There are many tax rules designed to reduce the temptation for people to transfer money offshore to avoid tax. The Revenue also have information-sharing agreements with many countries. You are likely to need professional advice if you are involved in an offshore trust.

A property abroad

Your profits from renting out property overseas are worked out in the same way as your profits on UK property (see Chapter 8), except that Rent-a-Room relief and the special rules for holiday properties do not apply. As in the UK, if you have more than one overseas property, the income and expenses for all the properties are added together. You can claim tax relief for interest on a loan to buy the property, adjusted to allow for any private use.

Although the same *method* for working out your profits is used as for UK property, your overseas property is treated as a separate rental business. This means that overseas expenses cannot be deducted from UK rental income (or vice versa) and, if you make a loss on overseas property, you cannot use it to reduce your UK profits – instead, the loss must be carried forward to set against any future profits from overseas property.

Your UK tax if you are non-resident

If you are not resident in the UK for tax purposes, you still have to pay UK tax on income arising in the UK. But:

- *You cannot claim UK personal allowances* (see Chapter 4), unless you are a citizen of the Commonwealth or the EU, a missionary, a servant of the Crown, abroad for health reasons, or entitled to allowances under a double taxation agreement. However, you still get the first £7,700 (in 2002–03) or £7,900 (in 2003–04) of capital gains tax-free.
- *Your tax bill is capped.* The maximum is the amount deducted at source from your investment income (see next page) *plus* the tax due on any other income. But this is worked out without deducting any personal

allowances. If you can claim allowances, you may pay less tax by working out your tax as if you were a UK resident. (See Inland Revenue help sheets IR300 *Non-residents and investment income* and IR304 *Non-residents – relief under Double Taxation Agreements.*)

- *You may still have to pay UK capital gains tax* if you are away for less than five years and part with UK or overseas assets that you owned before you left. (See Inland Revenue help sheet IR 278 *Temporary non-residents and capital gains tax.*)
- *If you let out your UK property*, your tenant or letting agent may have to deduct basic-rate tax from the rent before paying you. You can apply to receive rent before tax. (See Inland Revenue leaflet IR140 *Non-resident landlords, their agents and tenants.*)

Tax-free interest

If you are not ordinarily resident in the UK, you can receive interest from a bank, building society, unit trust or OEIC without having tax deducted by completing form R105 (from the financial organisation or your tax office). Interest from British Government Stock is also tax-free if you are not ordinarily resident.

Claiming relief for foreign tax

You may find yourself having to pay tax on foreign income and gains both in the UK and in the country from which they arise. You can claim tax relief for foreign tax in one of two ways:

- *Tax credit relief* – a special credit against your UK tax bill. Usually, the credit is equal to the amount of UK tax on the foreign income or gain, or the amount of the foreign tax if less (so overall your foreign income is taxed at the higher of the two national rates – see Example 9.2).
- *Deducting the foreign tax from the foreign income* before you work out the UK tax – so that if, say, you paid £50 overseas tax on income of £500, you pay UK tax on £450.

Usually, tax credit relief saves you most money because it credits you with the whole amount of the tax. Deducting the tax just saves you the UK tax payable on the foreign tax. But:

- If the UK has a double taxation agreement with the other country, the amount of foreign tax on which you can claim tax credit relief may be restricted. Agreements in force are summarised in the notes to the Foreign pages of the tax return.
- If there is no double taxation agreement, you can claim relief only if the foreign tax corresponds to UK income tax or capital gains tax.
- You can claim tax credit relief only if you are a UK resident.

If you cannot claim tax credit relief, your only option is to claim relief for your foreign tax by deducting it from the income.

Example 9.2: **Claiming relief for foreign tax**

Hannah has interest of £860 from a foreign bank account, from which tax at 15% (£129) was deducted before she received it. However, as she is a basic-rate taxpayer, the interest is liable to 20% tax in the UK: £860 × 20% = £172. She can claim tax credit relief of either the UK tax (£172), or the foreign tax (£129), whichever is lower. So her tax credit relief is £129 and in the UK she pays tax of £172 − £129 = £43.

Claiming tax back from the overseas tax authority

If more tax has been deducted from your foreign income than allowed for under any double taxation agreement, reclaim the excess from the foreign tax authorities. If you have already claimed relief for the excess tax in the UK, you will have to tell the Revenue and repay the relief. Ask the payer if the income can be paid gross in future.

What to tell the Inland Revenue

If you have any foreign income or gains that are taxable in the UK, and are not sent a tax return, you need to declare them to the Revenue by 5 October after the end of the tax year. You will usually be sent a tax return and may have to make payments on account (see Chapter 3).

If you are claiming to be non-resident or non-domiciled in the UK, it is up to you to 'self-certify' yourself as not resident or not domiciled, if relevant, by ticking the boxes on the Non-residence pages of the tax return, and Question 9 on page 2 of the main tax return. The Revenue may then decide to start an 'enquiry' into your tax return – it will not issue formal rulings on your residence status in advance. But you may be able to anticipate any problems by sending a form P85 to your tax office when you leave the country. You may also have to complete form P86 (on your arrival in the UK) or DOM1 (if you are claiming non-domicile).

You do not need to declare foreign income or gains that are not taxable in the UK (though you should make a note under 'Additional information' in your tax return if you have non-taxable foreign earnings). Otherwise enter:

- *Income from a job abroad* on the Employment pages (see Chapter 5). If you want to claim tax credit relief on this income, you must enter the relief in box 6.9 of the Foreign pages.
- *Taxable overseas capital gains* on the Capital Gains pages (see Chapter 11). Again, if you want to claim tax credit relief on your gains, you must enter the relief in box 6.10 of the Foreign pages.
- *Any other foreign income* on the Foreign pages. Remember to tick Question 6 on page 2 of the main tax return.

Filling in the Foreign supplementary pages

First, enter separately the income from each overseas source – e.g. each foreign savings account – in the relevant category on pages F1 or F2. However, if you have foreign property income, fill in pages F4 and F5 first (see page 215) and just enter the total on page F2. Finally, work out the tax credit relief you are claiming and enter it on page F3.

Pages F1 and F2 – Foreign savings and income etc.

Broadly the same information is needed for each type of income.

Column A Country

Enter the name of the country from which the income comes. In the section for 'Interest and other income from overseas savings' at the top of page F1 you should also write in [I] if the income is interest, and [O] if it is any other type of overseas savings income.

Tick box if income is unremittable

No tax is payable on income that you are prevented from transferring to the UK, but you still need to declare it and tick this box. Enter the amount of income and any tax in the currency in which you received it (cross out the £ sign) but leave column E ('Amount chargeable') blank.

Column B Amount before tax

Enter the amount before deducting any UK or foreign tax. Generally, you should enter the income earned, even if you left it in the overseas country, reinvested it, or received it late. But if part of the income was unremittable, or taxed on the remittance basis, enter only the amount you brought into the UK. Enter the amount in sterling, unless it is unremittable.

Column C UK tax

If some types of foreign income are paid through someone in the UK, UK tax might have been deducted – enter the amount of tax in this column.

Column D Foreign tax

Enter the amount of any foreign tax paid on the income, but if a double taxation agreement applies, make sure that what you enter does not exceed the maximum allowed under the agreement (see the Revenue's notes to the Foreign pages). Enter the amount in sterling (or in the overseas currency if the income is unremittable).

Column E Amount chargeable

This is the amount that is included in your taxable income.

- *If the income is unremittable* – leave this column blank.
- *If part of the income is tax-free* (e.g. 10 per cent of a foreign pension) – only include the taxable amount.
- *If you are claiming tax credit relief* – copy the figure from column B, minus any tax-free amount, and tick the 'foreign tax credit relief' box.
- *If you are not claiming tax credit relief* – enter the amount in column B, minus the foreign tax in column D, and minus any tax-free amount.

Boxes 6.3, 6.3A, 6.4, 6.4A, 6.5A Overseas trusts, companies and other entities

These boxes (and the reference to overseas trusts and companies in box 6.5) appear so that the Revenue can apply various anti-avoidance rules. Read the Revenue's notes carefully before you enter anything.

Box 6.5 Disposals of holdings in offshore funds

If you have sold part or all of an offshore fund, your gain may be liable to income tax, rather than capital gains tax – check with the fund manager.

Boxes 6.6 to 6.8 Gains on foreign life insurance policies

A foreign policy is one issued by an insurer from outside the UK, or by an overseas branch of a UK insurer. A policy issued by the UK branch of an overseas insurer is *not* usually a foreign policy. If in doubt, check with the insurer. You will need to read Inland Revenue help sheet IR321 *Gains on foreign life insurance policies* to find what to enter in these boxes.

Page F3 – Foreign tax credit relief

You need to complete the two tables on this page if you are claiming tax credit relief on income or capital gains that you have entered elsewhere in the tax return, e.g. the Employment or Capital Gains pages.

If you are working out your own tax, you must enter the amount of tax credit relief to which you are entitled in boxes 6.9 and 6.10 – otherwise leave these boxes empty. The relief is worked out separately for each item of foreign income, starting with the item on which you have paid the highest rate of foreign tax. The notes to the Foreign pages include a working sheet, and there is one for capital gains in Inland Revenue help sheet IR261 *Foreign tax credit relief: capital gains.* Non-residents should see IR304 *Non-residents: relief under Double Taxation Agreements.*

Pages F4 and F5 – Income from land and property abroad

The general principle is that you fill in a separate page F4 for each foreign property you let, because tax credit relief has to be worked out separately for each. However, if no foreign tax has been deducted, or if all your properties are in the same country, or if no foreign tax has been deducted, and you are not claiming that any income is unremittable, you can enter all the information on one page F4.

Your taxable profit is worked out in the same way as for rental income in the UK, so see Chapter 8 for how to complete page F4.

Page F5 pulls together your taxable profits from all your overseas let properties, to enter on page F2.

Example 9.3: **Filling in the Foreign pages**

Hannah (from Example 9.2) is a UK resident with £860 income from an offshore savings account, on which she paid £129 foreign tax. She enters the income on page 1, writing [I] after the country to show that it is interest. She is claiming tax credit relief, so the chargeable amount in column E is also £860. As she is working out her own tax, she claims tax credit relief of £129 in box 6.9 on page F3 (she does not need to complete the table above box 6.9 because she has already entered the details on page F1).

Record-keeping

Keep the same records as for UK income of the same type, plus:

- Dividend counterfoils from overseas companies.
- Records of any overseas tax deducted.

Figure 9.1: Foreign supplementary pages (see Example 9.3)

Foreign savings

Fill in columns A, B, D and E, and tick the box in column E if you want to claim foreign tax credit relief.

	Country A	tick box if income is unremittable	Amount before tax B	Foreign tax D	Amount chargeable E	tick box to claim foreign tax credit relief
■ *Interest, and other income from overseas savings* - see Notes, page FN4	RURITANIA [1]		£ 860	£ 129	£ 860	✓
			£	£	£	
			£	£	£	
			£	£	£	
			£	£	£	
			£	£	£	
			£	£	£	
			£	£	£	
			£	£	£	
			£	£	£	
			£	£	£	
					total of column above 6.1 £ 860	
■ *Dividends* - see Notes, page FN4			£	£	£	
				£		

Foreign tax credit relief for foreign tax paid on employment, self-employment and other income

See Notes, page FN14

Enter in this column the Page number in your Tax Return from which information is taken. Do this for each item for which you are claiming foreign tax credit relief	Country A	Foreign tax D	Amount chargeable E	tick box to claim foreign tax credit relief
		£	£	
		£	£	
		£	£	
		£	£	
		£	£	
		£	£	
		£	£	

- If you are calculating your tax, enter the total foreign tax credit relief on your income in box 6.9 · *see Notes, pages FN15 and FN16.*

6.9 £ 129

- Notes of exchange rates used in converting between currencies, and, if taxed on the remittance basis, the dates on which income was received in the UK.
- Records of any calculations you carried out to arrive at the figures entered in the Foreign pages (e.g. tax credit relief working sheets).
- Records to support any claim to be non-resident or non-domiciled in the UK, such as records of living overseas and the dates of travelling to and from the UK, and employment contracts.

Tax-planning hints

1 If you can organise your overseas visits so that you are classed as non-resident in the UK, your foreign earnings will be free of UK tax. Note that a move abroad may not save UK inheritance tax or capital gains tax (see pages 205 and 210).
2 If you are not ordinarily resident, you can register to have your UK interest paid without tax deducted. Interest from British Government Stock is also tax-free.
3 Foreign pensions qualify for a 10 per cent deduction, but part or all of a UK pension may also be tax-free if it arose from work overseas.
4 Some extra expenses are tax-free if you work abroad (see page 207).
5 Even if you do not have to pay UK National Insurance contributions, it may still be worth doing so to protect your rights to UK benefits.
6 If you want to claim non-residence, sending in Inland Revenue form P86 when you leave and asking for confirmation that you will be regarded as non-resident may reduce the chance of problems later.
7 Tax credit relief can save you UK tax if you have already paid foreign tax (see page 211).
8 Don't invest offshore just in the hope of saving tax. Any foreign investment income is still liable to UK tax.

10

Income from your savings

Everybody with savings and investments needs to take tax into account: a 6 per cent interest rate is worth only 4.8 per cent to you if you are a basic-rate taxpayer, 3.6 per cent if you pay higher-rate tax. Even non-taxpayers may find themselves paying tax.

Fortunately, there are several tax-free schemes, which are covered in this chapter, to encourage you to save. See also Chapter 7 for the generous tax rules on pension contributions. If the income came from overseas see Chapter 9. And capital gains tax may be an issue if you disposed of investments – see Chapter 11.

Does this affect you?

You will need to read this chapter if you have:

- interest – e.g. from a bank or building society account
- dividends from companies, unit trusts, investment trusts and open-ended investment companies (OEICs – a modern form of unit trust)
- taxable gains from a life insurance policy
- income from a purchased life annuity
- income from a trust that is taxed as yours (a trust is a legal arrangement for holding investments or other assets)
- income from the estate of someone who has died.

Investing for children

- Children are taxed the same way as adults. The first slice of their income is tax-free (£4,615 in 2002–03 and 2003–04) but they pay tax on any income above that.
- Children are normally non-taxpayers so if yours have savings accounts make sure you register for the interest to be paid gross – i.e. without tax deducted.
- To stop parents investing in their children's name purely to use their allowances, any income arising from gifts to your own child is taxed as yours, *unless* it comes to less than £100 a year (per parent per child). If this is likely to affect you, choose a tax-free investment for your child. The rule doesn't apply to gifts from grandparents.

Child Trust Fund

All children born from September 2002 will receive an 'endowment' of between £250 and £500 at birth, to be invested in special accounts and accessible at age 18. Details (including the tax treatment) have yet to be announced, and accounts are not expected to be available until 2005, but endowments will be backdated.

Tax-free income from savings and investments

You can save tax only on money you put *in* a savings or investment scheme if you invest in a pension plan (see Chapter 7), Community Investment schemes (see Chapter 4) or Venture Capital Trusts and Enterprise Investment Schemes (see page 235). However, the interest or dividends coming *out* of the following investments is tax-free:

- ISAs (Individual Savings Accounts), TESSAs (Tax-Exempt Special Savings Accounts) and PEPs (Personal Equity Plans).
- Venture Capital Trusts.
- National Savings & Investments Ordinary Account (up to £70 per person per year – impossible to exceed at current interest rates).
- Savings Certificates from National Savings & Investments (both fixed-

interest and index-linked versions).

- Ulster Savings Certificates, if you normally live in Northern Ireland, and were living there when they were bought or repaid.
- Children's Bonus Bonds from National Savings & Investments.
- Premium Bond prizes, lottery prizes and other gambling winnings.
- Save As You Earn schemes (now available only in conjunction with share option schemes – see Chapter 5).
- Tax-exempt friendly society life insurance polices. In practice, you can usually avoid paying tax on other life insurance policies, but this is because the insurance company is taxed (see page 229).
- Income from a family income benefit life insurance policy.
- *Part* of the income from purchased life annuities (ones you buy independently, not in connection with a pension – see page 228).
- If you are not ordinarily resident in the UK (see Chapter 9), British Government Stock.

Individual Savings Accounts (ISAs)

ISAs offer tax-free saving in the following categories (or 'components'):

- cash, e.g. a savings account (see below if you already have a TESSA)
- stocks and shares, including unit trusts, OEICs, investment trusts, corporate bonds and British Government Stock.
- some life insurance policies.

Your ISA is run by an 'ISA manager', such as a bank, a building society or National Savings & Investments, and many investment firms.

You can withdraw all or part of your money at any time, although the ISA manager may impose a minimum investment period. Until April 2009, any money coming out of your ISA is free of income tax and capital gains tax. In addition, until 5 April 2004, the ISA manager can reclaim on your behalf the 10 per cent tax credit deducted from any dividends or distributions (individuals cannot reclaim this tax).

Full details are in Inland Revenue leaflet IR2008 *ISAs, PEPs and TESSAs*, but your choices are summarised opposite.

Your ISA choices

You can invest up to £7,000 in ISAs in each tax year (£5,000 from April 2006). Each year, you can choose either one 'Maxi-ISA' or up to three 'Mini-ISAs', but you cannot take out both a Maxi and a Mini in the same year. Investments must be in cash, so if you have investments that you want to move into an ISA, you will have to sell them and reinvest – except for shares from some employers' share incentive schemes (see Chapter 5).

Your choices start afresh the next tax year, so you can end up with a collection of Mini- and Maxi-ISAs. You can also transfer your ISA to a different ISA manager, or switch your money from one investment to another offered by the same ISA manager, provided that you keep your money in the same category (i.e. cash, stocks and shares, life insurance). However, these are only the tax rules; check whether your ISA manager imposes other restrictions.

Note that the only way you can put more than £3,000 in stocks and shares in a single tax year is to choose a Maxi-ISA with one ISA manager.

Figure 10.1: Your ISA choices

In each tax year you can invest up to £7,000 overall (£5,000 from April 2006). You can choose to invest through either of the two routes below:

Either	***Or***
THE MAXI ROUTE Put all your money in one Maxi-ISA, from one ISA manager, with: ■ Up to £3,000 in cash ■ Up to £1,000 in life insurance ■ The rest in stocks & shares, i.e. up to £7,000 (£5,000 from April 2006)	**THE MINI ROUTE** Split your money between three Mini-ISAs, one for each component, from separate ISA managers, and with: ■ Up to £3,000 in stocks & shares ■ Up to £3,000 in cash ■ Up to £1,000 in life insurance

Plus up to £9,000 in a TESSA-only ISA

Withdrawing money from an ISA

Think twice before withdrawing money from an ISA in the same tax year in which you invest it. If, say, you put the maximum £3,000 in a cash ISA in May 2003, and then withdraw £1,000 in July 2003, you will not be able to put in another £1,000 in the 2003–04 tax year.

Beware of exceeding the ISA limits

If you buy more than one Maxi-ISA in a tax year, or more than one Mini-ISA of the same component, or both a Mini-ISA and a Maxi-ISA, you have broken the rules and you will be liable for tax on the most recent ISA investment.

Example 10.1: **Your ISA choices**

James puts £5,000 a year into an ISA. In 2002–03 he put the maximum in cash (£3,000) and the remaining £2,000 in unit trusts. In order to get the best interest rate on his cash he chose to go down the Mini-ISA route and pick two Mini-ISAs from separate managers.

In 2003–04, James puts £5,000 in unit trusts, but to do this he has to follow the Maxi ISA route, with one ISA manager only. He also switches his 2002–03 Mini cash ISA to a new manager with better rates. The rules allow this, but he must keep the money in cash, he cannot switch it into shares.

TESSA-only ISAs

A TESSA is a tax-free way of saving in a bank or building society, similar to a cash ISA. The main difference is that you lose the tax advantages if you withdraw your savings (but not the interest) within five years of opening the account. TESSAs have not been available since April 1999, but if you have one that has not yet matured, you can continue to pay into it.

Once your TESSA has matured, any further interest or bonuses are taxable. However, you can transfer the money you put into your TESSA (but not any interest on it) into a cash ISA – either an existing ISA or a special 'TESSA-only' ISA. The latter has the advantage of allowing you to exceed the normal ISA limits, so that even if you have contributed the maximum £3,000 a year to a cash ISA, you can also open a TESSA-only ISA.

Do not delay transferring your TESSA money

If you want to move your money from a TESSA to an ISA, you must do so within six months of the TESSA maturing. If you want to switch bank or building society, ask them for a 'maturity certificate' to give to the new ISA manager.

PEPs

PEPs were the predecessor of the stocks and shares component of an ISA, and have the same tax advantages. They have not been available since April 1999. If you have one, you can keep it, but you cannot put more money in. You do not have to keep the PEP for a minimum length of time.

How tax is worked out on investment income

- *Step 1: deduct (or ignore) any tax-free income* (see page 219).
- *Step 2: sort income into categories.* Different types of investment income are taxed at different rates, so first your income is sorted into interest, dividends and life insurance gains.
- *Step 3: add any investment income from trusts or estates.* If you have received income from a trust, or the estate of someone who has died, the money may count as yours for tax purposes (see page 234).
- *Step 4: work out which tax band each type of investment income falls within.* Your income is taxed in this order: first your non-investment income, then your interest, then dividends, then any taxable life insurance gains. So first you need to work out how much of your allowances, lower-rate tax band and basic-rate tax band are used up by your non-investment income (see Figure 1.1 on page 5).

- *Step 5: decide how much tax you have to pay, taking into account any tax already paid.* Multiply each category of investment income by the appropriate rate of tax and then deduct any tax already paid (or treated as paid) on the income before you received it. You may be able to claim tax back – or you may have more to pay.

Read on to see how each category is taxed. A useful guide is Inland Revenue leaflet IR110 *Bank and building society interest. A guide for savers.*

Interest

As well as interest from a bank or building society, interest includes:

- income from taxable National Savings & Investments products
- income from lending money to people, organisations, or governments (for example, British Government Stock)
- interest distributions from a unit trust or OEIC.

Unless you have invested through an ISA, the interest is taxable. It is paid out to you either without any tax deducted (gross) or after the deduction of 20 per cent tax (i.e. 'net', 'with tax deducted at source').

If the income is paid out after tax, you have no further tax to pay provided that all your taxable income – including the interest, but after deducting your allowances – is less than £29,900 in 2002–03 (£30,500 in 2003–04). Indeed, if your taxable income is less than £1,920 (£1,960 in 2003–04), you will be able to claim part or all of the tax back, using form R40 if you do not get a tax return (see Chapter 2). On income above £29,900 (£30,500 in 2003–04), you will have a further 20 per cent tax to pay to bring the overall tax up to 40 per cent. This is done by adjusting your PAYE code or through your tax return.

Bank and building society interest

This is usually paid with 20 per cent tax deducted, unless you are a non-taxpayer and have registered to receive the interest gross by completing form R85, available from the bank or building society, or in leaflet IR110 *Bank and building society interest. A guide for savers.* With a joint account, the

Table 10.1: Total tax payable on different types of investment income

Type of income	*Non-taxpayer*	*Lower-rate taxpayer*	*Basic-rate taxpayer*	*Higher-rate taxpayer*
Non-savings income	0%	10%	22%	40%
Interest	0%	10%	20%	40%
Dividends	10%	10%	10%	32.5%
Life insurance	None – because the insurance fund is taxed			18% but only if the policy is 'non-qualifying'

other person must be a non-taxpayer too, unless the bank or building society agrees to pay half of the interest gross.

British Government Stock, corporate bonds and other loan stocks

The following types of investment are effectively interest-paying loans to various organisations. The interest you receive is taxable, but how it is paid depends on the investment:

- *British Government Stock* (or 'gilts'): the interest is normally paid gross, but you can opt to have it paid net – contact the Bank of England's Registrar department (see the Fact File).
- *Corporate bonds* (loans to a company): the interest is paid net.
- *Local authority stocks*: the interest is paid net but if you are a non-taxpayer you can apply to have it paid gross.
- *Permanent Interest Bearing shares* (PIBs – loans to a building society): the interest is paid gross.

Once issued, all these loan stocks can be bought and sold, which means that the price goes up and down to reflect demand. In particular, if you buy stocks after they are first issued, or sell them before they mature, part of the price may reflect the right to receive the next interest payment – i.e. the 'accrued' interest. The contract note for the sale should show the amount.

If the face value of all your stocks and bonds is below £5,000, the accrued interest will not affect your tax. Otherwise, you are within the 'accrued income scheme', which is a way of deciding whether the purchaser or the seller is taxed on the accrued interest. This is how it works:

1. Find the tax year in which the first payment of interest after the transaction falls. You must apply the rules if, at any point within that tax year or the preceding tax year, you owned stocks with a total face value (not 'price') of more than £5,000.
2. Check whether the accrued interest was added to the price, or deducted from it (this should be on the contract note).
3. If the accrued interest is added to the price (the normal practice), the accrued interest counts as the taxable income of the seller and is called a 'charge'. It is deducted from the income of the purchaser as a relief.
4. If the accrued interest is deducted from the price, the purchaser pays tax on the accrued interest and the seller gets relief on it.

Any tax is payable, or any relief is given, in the tax year of the first interest payment, not the tax year in which the sale took place. (See Inland Revenue leaflet IR68 *Accrued income schemes*.)

Example 10.2: **Dealing with accrued income**

In January 2003, Frances sold some British Government Stock with a face (or 'nominal') value of £4,000. She also has corporate bonds with a face value of £3,000, so she is within the accrued income scheme. The next interest payment is due in May 2003. Five months of accrued interest is added to the price she gets for her stock. This is a 'charge' on which she must pay tax but, as the next interest payment is not due until May 2003, she pays tax on it in 2003–04, not the tax year in which she sold her stock.

'Strips' and 'discounted securities'

The right to receive interest can sometimes be bought and sold separately from the right to the capital repayment when a stock or security matures. The process of separating the interest from the capital is called 'stripping'.

Alternatively, a security may be issued where little or no interest is paid and the return comes from the difference between the issue price and the amount payable on redemption. With such 'discounted securities' or 'strips', both the interest and any profit on the 'capital' element of the security or gilt are taxable as interest, but the exact rules depend on the type of security.

Credit union share interest

The 'dividend' from credit unions is paid gross but is taxable.

National Savings & Investments products

All of these are taxable, *except* for Savings Certificates, Children's Bonus Bonds, Premium Bonds and the first £70 of Ordinary Account income. The taxable products fall into two groups:

- The Investment Account, Deposit Bonds, Income Bonds, Capital Bonds, Pensioners' Guaranteed Income Bonds and Guaranteed Equity Bonds: income from all these products (plus any Ordinary Account interest above £70 a year) is paid out before tax. The income is still taxable, but any tax due is collected either by adjusting your PAYE code or through your tax return.
- Fixed Rate Savings Bonds: 20 per cent tax is *always* deducted from the income paid out by these bonds. You can reclaim overpaid tax, but non-taxpayers should pick more suitable products.

A downside of Capital Bonds

You are taxed each year on the income earned on National Savings & Investments Capital Bonds – even though it is not paid until the end of the five-year term.

Interest from a unit trust or OEIC

Unit trust or OEIC funds that are invested in gilts, loan stocks and other interest-producing investments pay out interest distributions instead of dividend distributions. The tax voucher will show what type of distribution you receive.

Unless you have invested through an ISA, 20 per cent tax will be deducted. You cannot register to have the interest paid gross, although you can reclaim any tax overpaid.

Purchased life annuities

A purchased life annuity is a fixed lifetime income payable by a life insurance company, in return for a cash lump sum. Do not confuse it with an annuity from a pension company – it is taxed completely differently.

Part of the income from a purchased life annuity – the 'capital element' which will depend on your age at purchase – is tax-free. The rest is taxable as interest, with 20 per cent deducted before it is paid. If you are a non-taxpayer you can get the interest paid gross by completing form R89 (or R86 for joint annuities).

Dividends

The main types of dividend income are cash payouts, such as:

- share dividends from UK companies
- dividend distributions from UK unit trusts and OEICs. (Note that 'cash' type unit trust funds pay out 'interest' distributions, see above.)

With both types, you are treated as if 10 per cent tax has been paid before you receive the dividend. This is called a 'tax credit'. The taxable amount is the dividend you received, *plus* the tax credit, but you can then set the tax credit against your tax bill. So if, for example, you receive a dividend of £90, the tax credit is £90 × 1/9 = £10: you are taxed on £90 + £10 = £100 but you can set the £10 tax credit against your tax bill.

If you are a lower-rate or basic-rate taxpayer, you have no further tax to pay on your dividend. But if you are a higher-rate taxpayer, you will have a further 22.5 per cent to pay, to bring the overall tax up to 32.5 per cent. So on a dividend of £90, with its £10 tax credit (a taxable amount of £100), you pay further tax of £22.50: £32.50 tax in total.

Non-cash payouts

The following non-cash payouts to shareholders also count as dividends:

- Dividends payable as extra shares instead of cash ('stock' or 'scrip' dividends).
- Bonus redeemable shares or bonus securities. These are potentially taxable both when they are issued (as 'non-qualifying distributions') and when they are redeemed (as a 'qualifying distribution').

You are treated as having paid 'notional tax' at 10 per cent on these payouts. This is effectively the same as a dividend tax credit: non-taxpayers cannot reclaim the tax and higher-rate taxpayers will have more to pay.

The tax voucher or other statement should make it clear what sort of payment it is, and whether you get a tax credit. If you receive a 'scrip' dividend the tax voucher will also show the taxable value of your extra shares ('the appropriate amount in cash').

Share-owning disadvantages for non-taxpayers

You cannot reclaim the tax credit on share dividends, even if you are a non-taxpayer. With investments held in an ISA, the ISA manager can reclaim the tax credit on your behalf, but only until 6 April 2004, when even this concession will stop.

Life insurance

The life insurance fund in which your money is invested is taxed. When the money is paid out to you, you are treated as if you have already paid 'notional tax' of 22 per cent of the amount received. If you are a non-taxpayer, lower-rate taxpayer or basic-rate taxpayer, you have no further tax to pay. But you will have more to pay if:

- You have a 'non-qualifying' policy *and*
- You make a taxable gain on the policy (such a 'gain' is liable to income tax, not capital gains tax) *and*

- You are a higher-rate taxpayer, or a basic-rate taxpayer but the taxable gain on your policy pushes you into the higher-rate tax band. Even so, a special 'top-slicing relief' may be due.

See Inland Revenue help sheet IR320 *Gains on UK life insurance policies*.

What is a non-qualifying policy?

This is one into which you are not expected to pay regular premiums over a period of at least ten years. So, for example, a life insurance bond into which you pay a single premium is non-qualifying. Your insurance company will be able to tell you if the policy does or doesn't qualify.

A savings-type insurance policy, e.g. an endowment policy or a 'whole life' policy, is usually qualifying and therefore tax-free. But it will become non-qualifying if you stop paying into the policy, sell it or receive benefits from it within the first ten years (or, if the policy is intended to last less than 13.4 years, within the first three-quarters of the intended term, for example 7.5 years for a ten-year policy).

Change on the way?

From 6 April 2004, the 'notional tax' on life insurance policies will fall to 20 per cent (instead of the current 22 per cent). However, the Revenue is currently reviewing life insurance taxation, so more radical changes cannot be ruled out.

Have you made a taxable gain?

You may make a gain during your lifetime when your non-qualifying policy matures, or if you surrender or sell it or withdraw money from it. There may be a gain when the policy pays out on your death – though the gain is worked out using the surrender value immediately before your death, which may differ from the amount actually paid out.

If you have made a taxable gain, the insurance company should issue a 'chargeable event' certificate which tells you the taxable amount.

At its simplest, a gain occurs when you get more out of a policy than you put in. So if you invest £10,000 in a policy that eventually produces £15,000, your gain is £5,000. But it is common to surrender only part of a non-qualifying policy – to top up your income, say. If so, you can put off paying any tax on these partial withdrawals until the policy finally ends.

You can put off paying tax if, in any one year, you withdraw less than 5 per cent of the amount you paid in to the policy *plus* any unused '5 per cents' from previous years. Note that 'year' in this context means years you have had the policy, not tax year.

If you make no withdrawals in the first year you have the policy, you can withdraw 10 per cent in the second year. The maximum you can withdraw without triggering a taxable gain is 100 per cent (i.e. the amount you put in) after 20 years (see Example 10.3). If you withdraw *more* than your accumulated 5 per cents, your taxable gain is the total amount withdrawn to date (on which you have not so far paid tax), minus the accumulated 5 per cent allowances.

When the policy comes to an end, you are taxed on your total benefits from it, minus the amount you paid in, and minus any taxable gains so far (i.e. withdrawals above your accumulated 5 per cents).

How much tax on your taxable gain on a non-qualifying policy?

Even if you make a taxable gain on a non-qualifying policy, you do not have to pay tax on it unless it falls within the higher-rate band. And you do not have to pay the full top rate of 40 per cent on any gain in the higher-rate band, because almost all policies are treated as if 22 per cent tax has already been deducted. So only a further 40 − 22 = 18 per cent tax is payable by you.

A problem with insurance policies is that the one-off lump sum paid out can push your income into the higher-rate tax bracket. Top-slicing relief compensates for this. It works by first dividing the total gain by the number of complete years you have had the policy to find the average annual gain. If the average annual gain, when added to the rest of your income:

- *falls within the basic-rate tax band* – the whole of your gain is tax-free
- *falls within the higher-rate band* – top-slicing relief does not save you any tax
- *falls partly in the basic-rate band, partly in the higher-rate band* – you do

not pay the full top rate of tax on your insurance gain. This is achieved by charging you higher-rate tax on the average annual gain and multiplying the tax by the number of complete years you have had the policy.

Example 10.3: **Tax on a non-qualifying insurance policy**

Ten years ago Patrick invested £10,000 in a single-premium insurance bond (a non-qualifying policy). From year 2 he withdrew £600 a year to top up his income, which he increased to £700 from year 7. In year 7 his total withdrawals so far came to more than his total 5% allowances so far, and he made a taxable gain of £200 in that year and the following year. He did not have to pay tax on these gains because they did not push him into the higher-rate tax bracket.

In year 9, Patrick cashed in his policy for £8,545. This, plus his regular withdrawals, made a total gain of £12,945. From this he can deduct the money he put in (£10,000) plus his taxable gains in years 7 and 8 (£400). His overall taxable gain is £12,945 – £10,000 – £400 = £2,545.

Patrick's other income in year 9 is just £400 below the top of the basic-rate band and the insurance gain would push him into the higher-rate band. But top-slicing relief comes to his rescue. His average annual gain is £2,545 divided by the 8 complete years he has had the policy – £318. As none of this falls within the higher-rate tax band, he has no tax to pay.

Year	*1*	*2*	*3*	*4*	*5*	*6*	*7*	*8*	*9*	*Totals*
Paid in	10,000									**10,000**
Annual 5% allowance	500	500	500	500	500	500	500	500		
Previous years' unused allowance		500	400	300	200	100	0	0		
Withdrawals		600	600	600	600	600	700	700	8,545	**12,945**
Taxable gains during policy							200	200		**400**

Tax relief for a loss on a non-qualifying policy

If you make a loss on a policy (because stock markets have fallen, say), you may qualify for a special tax relief called 'corresponding deficiency relief'. You can claim relief only if you have previously paid tax on the policy, and you are a higher-rate taxpayer. (See Inland Revenue help sheet IR320, *Gains on UK Life insurance policies.*)

Taxable insurance policies: points to remember

- The 5% allowance is just a way of putting off tax on an insurance gain – it is not a tax-free allowance.
- It might be better to draw more than 5% during the life of the policy if you are not a higher-rate taxpayer, rather than build up a big gain at the end of the policy.
- If you are receiving an age-related personal allowance, any taxable gain counts as income for the purposes of working out whether you are entitled to age-related allowance (see Chapter 4).
- The 5% withdrawals are 5% of the premium – not the policy value. If your policy has increased in value, cashing it in and reinvesting it will allow you to withdraw more while staying within the 5% limit, but you will have to pay any costs of reinvesting.

Investing as a couple

- If you are married and own investments jointly, you are normally each taxed on half of the income from it. However, married couples who contributed unequal proportions to the investment can opt to have the income taxed in line with the proportion each invested, by asking their tax office for Form 17.
- You can save tax by putting investments in the name of the partner who pays the lower rate of tax.
- Married couples can give each other investments without incurring inheritance tax or capital gains tax. Non-married couples should consult Chapters 11 and 12 to see whether these taxes are likely to affect them.

Income from trusts

A trust is a legal arrangement designed to hold investments or other assets in the care of trustees for the benefit of one or more 'beneficiaries'. The person who provides the assets is called the 'settlor'. If you are a beneficiary or a settlor of a trust, some or all of the income received by the trust may be taxed as yours – and, since trusts are often set up to hold investments, the income paid is often investment income. Life insurance policies are often held in trusts for inheritance tax purposes (see Chapter 12).

There are various types of trusts, to which different tax rules apply. As an individual, part or all of a trust's income may be taxed as yours if:

- You are a beneficiary of a 'bare' trust (one where you have an unconditional right to the trust's property and income). All the trust's income is treated as if it were yours. If the beneficiary is a child and the trust funds were provided by a parent, it will be the parent who pays the tax.
- You are the settlor of any type of trust (apart from a bare trust) and you or your husband or wife have any right to the trust's property and income (or 'retain an interest' in tax-speak).
- You are a beneficiary of any type of trust apart from a bare trust. The trust itself (or rather, the trustees) may pay tax and receive its own tax returns. Any income to which you are entitled is taxed as yours, but you get a credit for tax paid by the trust (see below).

The trustees should give you form R185 showing how much income is taxable as yours, and how much the tax credit is. Note that income from a discretionary trust (one where the income is not automatically paid out and the trustees have a right to decide who will benefit) is paid out with a tax credit of 34 per cent ('the rate applicable to trusts'). You can reclaim some or all of this tax, unless you are a higher-rate taxpayer.

Income from estates

When someone dies, there is a gap between the paperwork being completed and the distribution of the estate to the people named in the will. During this period, the estate may still be receiving income, such as interest on a bank account or dividends from investments. If you are a residuary beneficiary of the estate (i.e. entitled to what is left after all the legacies have been paid), some or all of this income may be taxed as yours.

If so, it is taxed in the same way as any other income within the same category – e.g. dividends or interest. Whoever is administering the estate should give you a form R185 stating how much income you have received in each category, and how much tax has been paid on your behalf.

Tax relief on investments

Only a few investments give you tax relief on the money you pay in. The most important is a private pension (see Chapter 7). The Enterprise Investment Scheme (EIS) and Venture Capital Trusts (VCTs) are ways of investing in unquoted companies. They give you tax relief at 20 per cent of the amount invested. If you sell your shares for a profit, there is no capital gains tax, but the rules differ if you make a loss.

See Inland Revenue booklets IR137 *The Enterprise Investment Scheme* and IR169 *Venture Capital Trusts (VCTs). A brief guide.* With both schemes, you can claim your tax relief either through your tax return, or by sending the certificate provided by the company or trust to your tax office. Note, though, that both schemes are under review.

Reinvesting to avoid capital gains tax

If you make a taxable capital gain on any asset, you can put off paying the tax by reinvesting the proceeds in the Enterprise Investment Scheme or Venture Capital Trusts. (See Inland Revenue help sheets IR297 *Enterprise Investment Scheme and Capital Gains Tax* and IR298 *Venture Capital Trusts and Capital Gains Tax.*)

Enterprise Investment Scheme (EIS)

You get tax relief either if you buy shares in an unquoted trading company that has been approved under the scheme, or if you invest via a special investment fund. You cannot use the scheme to invest in a company with which you are 'connected', for example as a paid director or as a major shareholder, unless, possibly, you come into the company after the shares are issued. You will also lose relief if you receive some benefit, apart from normal dividends, from the company.

You get tax relief of 20 per cent of the amount you subscribe for shares, up to a maximum of £150,000 per tax year. If the shares are issued in the first six months of the tax year, you can claim to have half of your investment (up to a maximum of £25,000) treated as though made in the previous tax year. But you lose tax relief if you part with your shares within three years (five years for shares issued before 6 April 2000).

If your shares become worthless, you can claim tax relief on the amount of your loss, *minus* the amount of tax relief received when you bought the shares. You can set the loss either against your taxable income for the year of the loss (or the preceding year), or against any taxable capital gains.

Venture Capital Trusts (VCTs)

With Venture Capital Trusts you invest through a company that is itself listed on the stock exchange. You get income tax relief of 20 per cent of the amount you invest in new ordinary shares, but not shares bought 'second-hand'. Whether the shares are new or second-hand, you do not have to pay any tax on the dividends, but the 10 per cent tax credit on the dividend cannot be reclaimed and does not count as tax paid.

Any profit on shares held for the minimum period (three years, or five if issued before 6 April 2000) is free of capital gains tax, but unlike the Enterprise Investment Scheme you cannot claim relief on any losses.

What to tell the Inland Revenue

If you do not get sent a tax return, you should contact your tax office if:

- You are a taxpayer receiving taxable investment income paid out before tax (for example, from British Government Stock) or a higher-rate taxpayer, and any tax due is not already collected through your

PAYE code. If so, you must tell your tax office by 5 October after the end of the tax year (that is, 5 October 2003 for income received in 2002–03).

- Tax on your investment income is collected through your PAYE code but your circumstances change – e.g. you expect to receive more or less investment income in future.
- You want to claim tax relief for an investment in an EIS or VCT.
- You have a tax-free investment and somehow breach the conditions – e.g. if you withdraw money (other than interest) from a TESSA within the first five years.
- You are a lower-rate taxpayer or non-taxpayer, and think you might be able to claim tax back. In this case, there is also a special Taxback helpline (see the Fact File). You might be asked to fill in a form R40 to claim a tax repayment. (There is more about this in Chapter 2.)

If you do get a tax return, it will guide you through what you need to disclose about your investment income. There are special supplementary pages if you receive foreign investment income (see Chapter 9) or taxed income from trusts or the estate of someone who has died. However, if you get income from trusts that is paid gross, or scrip dividends from a trust, they should be included with any other income of the same type.

Updating your bank or building society

If you are currently receiving interest gross, and you become a taxpayer, let your bank or building society know so that they can start to deduct tax.

Filling in your tax return

Information about UK investments is collected on pages 3 and 4 of the main return. Remember, you do not have to enter tax-free investment income, listed at the beginning of this chapter, and foreign investments go on the Foreign pages (see Chapter 9). You should be able to get the details you need either from your regular statements, or from the certificates of interest paid that are supplied at the end of each tax year by some payers of interest, e.g. banks and building societies.

Question 10 – Did you receive any income from UK savings and investments?

This broad category covers everything listed on page 224, and purchased life annuities. Note that you need to enter the total income you have in each category (there is a working sheet in the Revenue's tax return guide to help you).

Boxes 10.1 to 10.4 Interest from banks and building societies

Remember that you need to enter interest paid with no tax deducted in box 10.1, separately from that paid with tax deducted, which goes in boxes 10.2 to 10.4.

Boxes 10.5 to 10.7 Interest distributions from unit trusts and OEICs

The figures you need should be shown on the tax voucher accompanying the payment.

Boxes 10.8 to 10.11 National Savings & Investments

You should get a statement of interest received towards the end of April each year. If you have income from the Ordinary Account, remember that the first £70 is tax-free; you only enter anything over this amount.

Boxes 10.12 to 10.14 Other income from UK savings and investments

Enter here income from British Government Stock, corporate bonds, other loan stocks and purchased life annuities (see page 225 onwards).

If you bought or sold stocks and the first interest payment after the transaction falls in the 2002–03 tax year, see page 226 to work out whether your tax is affected by accrued interest. If it is:

- *add* together any accrued interest *charges* (amounts of accrued interest on which you are taxed)
- *deduct* any amounts of accrued interest on which you get *reliefs*.

If the result is a positive number (i.e. you have more charges than reliefs), add it to the figure you enter in box 10.14; if it is a negative number, deduct it. Do not change the figure in box 10.13.

Finding the gross or net amount of interest

If you receive interest after tax (net), you will need to show in your tax return the before-tax (gross) figures as well as the tax itself. To find the gross figure if you know the net amount, divide the net figure by 0.8. To find the net figure if you know the gross amount, multiply the gross amount by 0.8. The tax is, of course, the difference between the gross and net figures.

Common mistakes

Double-check your entries if you find that you have figures in both box 10.1 (gross interest) and boxes 10.2 to 10.4 (taxed interest). It suggests either that you could claim to get interest paid gross, or that you have incorrectly been claiming gross interest on one account.

Boxes 10.15 to 10.26 Dividends

Income that is classed as dividends is listed on page 228. A cash payment from a company or unit trust goes in the top two rows, as appropriate. But if you get a non-cash distribution, you need to check which row to enter it in – if in doubt, contact the company.

Boxes 10.15 to 10.23 Dividends, dividend distributions and scrip dividends

The information needed should be shown on the tax voucher that accompanies each payment. Add up the total dividends (or distributions) in each category, and the tax credits, and transfer the totals to the tax return. Then add the total tax credits (or notional tax, as appropriate) to the total dividends or distributions and enter the result in the right-hand column.

There are a few traps you should be aware of:

- If you are affected by the IR35 rules as an employee of your own service company (see Chapter 5), you *may* be able to claim that dividends received from your company are tax-free. (See the Revenue's notes.)
- When entering unit trust or OEIC distributions, include any distributions from 'accumulation' units – these are retained in the trust, rather than paid out to you, but they count as taxable income and you should get a tax voucher. You do not have to enter any figures shown as 'equalisation' – these are relevant only for capital gains tax.
- If you have higher-rate tax to pay on the redemption of bonus shares or securities, you may be able to claim tax relief (in box 15.12 of the tax return) for any higher-rate tax that you paid when the shares were first issued (see the Revenue notes to the tax return and page 77).
- A 'qualifying distribution' catches things like receiving goods at preferential rates. This is most likely to apply to employee shareholders, in which case it would be taxable as earnings. The same applies to a loan written off (see below).

Working out the tax credit

You can work out the tax credit (or notional tax, for scrip dividends paid out as shares, rather than cash) simply by dividing the dividend or distribution by 9.

Hang on to tax vouchers and certificates of tax deducted

You should not send these in with your tax return, but you must keep them in case your tax office asks to see them in future.

Boxes 10.24 to 10.26 Non-qualifying distributions and loans written off

The tax you are treated as having paid is calculated differently for each type:

- For non-qualifying distributions (see page 229), leave box 10.24 blank. Instead, enter the taxable amount of the distribution in the *last* box (10.26). Multiply box 10.26 by 10 per cent – this gives you the amount of notional tax to enter in box 10.25.
- For loans written off, enter the amount of the loan written off in box 10.24. Enter ⅑ of the figure in box 10.24 in box 10.25. Add the two boxes together and enter the result in box 10.26.

Question 12 – Gains on UK life insurance policies etc.

Boxes 12.1 to 12.5 Gains on UK life insurance policies

Complete this section only if you have made a taxable gain on a non-qualifying life insurance policy. If so, the insurance company should send you a 'chargeable event' certificate showing the taxable amount. See Inland Revenue help sheet IR320 *Gains on UK life insurance policies* if it does not.

First check on the certificate whether the policy is treated as having had tax paid on it. This will almost certainly be the case.

Assuming your policy is treated as having paid tax, enter the taxable amount in box 12.5. Multiply this figure by 22 per cent to find the tax treated as paid and enter it in box 12.4. Finally, enter the number of years you have had the policy in box 12.3.

Note that if you have made a taxable gain on the partial surrender of a policy, you should report it in the tax return for the tax year in which the *next* anniversary of taking out your policy falls. A surrender in January 2003, say, should go in your 2003–04 return if you bought the policy in May. This applies only to partial surrenders – other gains are taxable in the tax year they occur.

More than one policy?

You should enter the total gains from all your policies, and the total tax treated as paid. However, if you have more than one policy, do not complete the 'Number of years' box (12.1 or 12.3). Instead, give details of the gain, tax paid and number of years for *each* policy in the 'Additional information' box at the end of the return.

Sometimes, insurance policies are sold in 'clusters' – your money is invested in several identical policies to give flexibility when cashing them in.

If you have identical gains from any such policies you can add all the gains together and enter them as one policy.

Boxes 12.6 to 12.8 Gains on life insurance policies in void ISAs

This will apply only if you have invested in the insurance component of an ISA which is invalid because of a breach of the ISA rules (see page 221). Your ISA manager should tell you what to enter.

Box 12.9 Corresponding deficiency relief

This will apply only if you paid tax on a partial withdrawal from a policy in the past, the policy has now come to an end and the tax you paid earlier proves to have been too high. You can claim tax relief only if you are a higher-rate taxpayer. (See help sheet IR320.)

Boxes 12.10 to 12.12 Refunds of surplus funds from AVCs

If you pay additional voluntary contributions to a free-standing scheme (i.e. run by a pension company rather than your employer) and contribute more than allowed by the Revenue rules (see Chapter 7), the excess contributions are refunded on your retirement or death, minus a 32 per cent deduction. The certificate from the pension company will give you the information you need.

This does not apply if you receive a refund of your contributions to an employer's pension scheme that you left in the first two years.

Example 10.4: **Entering your taxable investment income**

Page 4 of Andy's tax return is shown in Figure 10.2. He received £248 after tax from his two building society accounts: he enters this in box 10.2 and then divides it by 0.80 to find the before tax amount (£310) to enter in box 10.4. The tax (which goes in box 10.3) is £310 − £248 = £62. Andy also received dividends of £153 in total, which go in box 10.15. He divides this by 9 to find the tax credit to enter in box 10.16 (£17), and then adds the dividend and tax credit together. The result (£153 + £17 = £170) goes in box 10.17.

Andy's other investment income (£712 from British Government Stock) is paid out before tax, so he just enters the amount received in the right-hand column.

Figure 10.2: Question 10 (see Example 10.4)

INCOME *for the year ended 5 April 2003*

Q10 Did you receive any income from UK savings and investments? YES ✓

If yes, tick this box and then fill in boxes 10.1 to 10.26 as appropriate. Include only your share from any joint savings and investments. If not applicable, go to Question 11.

■ ***Interest***

- Interest from UK banks, building societies and deposit takers (interest from UK Internet accounts must be included) - *If you have more than one bank or building society etc account enter **totals** in the boxes.*

- enter any bank, building society etc interest that **has not** had tax taken off. (Most interest is taxed by your bank or building society etc. so make sure you should be filling in box 10.1, rather than boxes 10.2 to 10.4)

	Taxable amount
	10.1 £

- enter details of your **taxed** bank or building society etc interest. *The Working Sheet on page 10 of your Tax Return Guide will help you fill in boxes 10.2 to 10.4.*

Amount after tax deducted	Tax deducted	Gross amount **before** tax
10.2 £ 248	10.3 £ 62	10.4 £ 310

- Interest distributions from UK authorised unit trusts and open-ended investment companies (dividend distributions go below)

Amount after tax deducted	Tax deducted	Gross amount **before** tax
10.5 £	10.6 £	10.7 £

- National Savings & Investments (other than First Option Bonds and Fixed Rate Savings Bonds and the first £70 of interest from an Ordinary Account)

Taxable amount
10.8 £

- National Savings & Investments First Option Bonds and Fixed Rate Savings Bonds

Amount after tax deducted	Tax deducted	Gross amount **before** tax
10.9 £	10.10 £	10.11 £

- Other income from UK savings and investments (except dividends)

Amount after tax deducted	Tax deducted	Gross amount **before** tax
10.12 £	10.13 £	10.14 £ 712

■ ***Dividends***

- Dividends and other qualifying distributions from UK companies

Dividend/distribution	Tax credit	Dividend/distribution **plus** credit
10.15 £ 153	10.16 £ 17	10.17 £ 170

- Dividend distributions from UK authorised unit trusts and open-ended investment companies

Dividend/distribution	Tax credit	Dividend/distribution **plus** credit
10.18 £	10.19 £	10.20 £

- Scrip dividends from UK companies

Dividend	Notional tax	Dividend **plus** notional tax
10.21 £	10.22 £	10.23 £

- Non-qualifying distributions and loans written off

Distribution/Loan	Notional tax	Taxable amount
10.24 £	10.25 £	10.26 £

Record-keeping

You must keep your savings income records for at least 22 months from the end of the tax year to which they relate (five years and ten months if you have business or letting income). This is the sort of thing to keep:

- *Shares and unit trusts:* tax vouchers sent with any dividend or distribution (you should get one even if the dividend is paid direct to your bank account).
- *British Government Stocks:* you will get an annual statement of interest if the interest is paid direct to a bank, otherwise a tax voucher is attached to the cheque. Keep any contract notes when you buy or sell.
- *Enterprise Investment Scheme or Venture Capital Trusts:* certificates provided by the company.
- *Interest and annuities:* you may get a 'certificate of tax deducted' (R185) at the end of each year, otherwise the after-tax amount of interest paid will be shown on your statements or passbook.
- *Life insurance:* policy documents; notes of date and amount of any withdrawal; any 'chargeable event' certificates from the insurer.
- *Trusts and estates:* details of any income received and any vouchers or form R185 from the trustees or executors.

Tax-planning hints

1 Always compare the after-tax return from different investments. Higher-rate taxpayers may benefit from tax-free investments even if the headline interest rate is not the best.
2 Non-taxpayers should consider investments that pay out before tax (e.g. most National Savings or British Government Stock) and remember that the tax credit on shares and unit trusts cannot be reclaimed. With a bank or building society, you can register to receive interest gross.
3 If you give your child investments that produce an income of more than £100 a year, you may have to pay tax on it. You can avoid this by choosing a tax-free investment or if a friend or relative, such as a grandparent, makes the gift.

4 Make the most of the ISA rules for tax-free investing (see page 221). If you have a maturing TESSA, you can reinvest it in an ISA on top of the normal ISA limits – but you have only six months to do so.
5 You can choose to have interest from British Government Stock paid gross or net.
6 If you are 65 or over, and have an income of more than £18,300, plan your investments to avoid the income affecting your age-related allowances (see Chapter 4).
7 You do not have to pay tax directly on a taxable life insurance policy unless you are a higher-rate taxpayer. But if you receive the age-related personal allowance, a taxable insurance gain may affect your allowance.
8 Gains on withdrawals from an insurance bond are taxable, but you can put off paying tax until the policy ends if you withdraw no more than 5 per cent per year of the premium value.
9 Couples may be able to save tax by transferring investments to the lower-income partner.
10 If you are a beneficiary of a discretionary trust and not a higher-rate taxpayer, you will be able to reclaim tax on income paid out to you.

11

Capital gains tax

You sell some shares at a profit. You retire and your children take over your business. You sell a property that you've been renting out.

All these transactions, and some others, may have capital gains tax implications. Capital gains tax is simply a tax on the capital sum produced when you 'dispose' of an 'asset'. The most common disposal arises when you sell something, but you also make a taxable disposal if, for example, you give something away (or sell it at an artificially low price) and receive no financial benefit.

If you do have to pay capital gains tax, your gains are taxed as if they were extra investment income you received.

Does this affect you?

You don't need to worry about paying capital gains tax if your total capital gains in a tax year are less than the annual tax-free amount (£7,700 in the 2002–03 tax year, rising to £7,900 in 2003–04). However, you should notify the Revenue if you have made a loss on selling a capital asset, as this can be set against any future taxable gains.

Even if your total gains come to more than £7,700, there are deductions and reliefs which will reduce the tax, or bring the gain below the £7,700 limit. And some gains are completely tax-free – they don't count towards the £7,700 limit, and don't have to be declared to the Revenue.

Tax-free gains

Gains on the following items

- Private cars.
- Foreign currency for your and your family's use.
- Decorations for valour (unless you bought them).
- Personal effects and goods disposed of for £6,000 or less, such as household furniture, paintings and antiques (the Revenue call these 'chattels'). If the disposal proceeds are more than £6,000, you pay tax on either your gain, or five-thirds of the amount over £6,000 if less.
- 'Wasting assets', with a predictable life of 50 years or less, providing they were not eligible for capital allowances for use in a business. Machinery is treated as a wasting asset – including antique clocks and vintage cars – if owned personally and not used in a business.

Gains on the following investments

- Investments held in a Personal Equity Plan (PEP) or Individual Savings Account (ISA).
- National Savings Certificates.
- Tax Exempt Special Savings Accounts (TESSA) or SAYE schemes.
- Shares in a Venture Capital Trust or (with some conditions) an Enterprise Investment Scheme.
- Life insurance policies (unless you bought the policy second-hand).
- Pension plans (assuming the scheme is tax-approved).
- British Government Stock and most types of corporate bond.

Other tax-free gains

- Premium Bond prizes, and betting, lottery or pools winnings.
- Gifts to charity or for 'public benefit' (e.g. art given to the nation).
- Gifts to amateur sports clubs open to the whole community.
- Gains when an estate is disposed of at death (but watch out for inheritance tax instead, see Chapter 12).
- Cashbacks received as an inducement to buy something (e.g. a new car) or take out a loan.
- Compensation for personal injury or pension mis-selling (on policies sold between 28 April 1988 and 30 June 1994).

- Compensation for loss or damage (such as insurance payouts), unless you use all of it to replace or repair the damaged property.

On gains made when selling your main home, and transfers of property between husband and wife, you can claim special reliefs that mean there is usually no tax to pay (see page 257). There are also many business reliefs.

One downside of tax-free assets is that if you make a loss on them, the loss cannot be set against your gains. The exception is shares in the Enterprise Investment Scheme.

How capital gains tax is worked out

Capital gains tax is notorious for being complicated, but the basic principles are quite simple.

1. Work out your gain on each asset you have disposed of in the tax year. This is done by taking the disposal proceeds, deducting the allowable cost of acquiring the asset, and claiming any reliefs that apply.
2. Add together the taxable gains on all the assets you have disposed of in the tax year, deduct any losses, and deduct the annual tax-free amount.
3. Work out the tax on what's left.

These principles apply to all your gains that don't fall within one of the tax-free categories above. However, there are many different tax reliefs and exemptions you can claim.

Working out the gain or loss on each asset

Start with the disposal proceeds. This is the sale price, if you sold the asset. If you didn't sell it (or you sold it for less than its full price) the disposal proceeds are the market value of the asset at the time.

From the disposal proceeds you can deduct the allowable costs of the asset. The main allowable cost is usually the purchase price if you bought the asset, its probate value if you inherited it, or its market value if you acquired it in some other way. You can also deduct other allowable expenses, such as the costs of buying and selling the asset, stamp duty and anything spent improving the asset (but not ordinary maintenance costs).

Selling something acquired by you before April 1982

Only gains made since 31 March 1982 are taken into account. This works by using the market value of the asset on that date as the allowable cost. This can exaggerate your gain or loss and you should use the original cost instead if that produces a smaller gain or loss. If one method produces a gain and the other a loss, you are treated as having made neither a gain nor a loss. You can, instead, opt to use the March 1982 value for all your assets. (See Inland Revenue help sheet IR280 *Rebasing – assets held at 31 March 1982.*)

Indexation allowance

After deducting allowable costs, you end up with either a gain or an allowable loss. If you made a gain and you owned the asset before 1 April 1998, you can also deduct indexation allowance, to compensate for inflation running from April 1982 up until the end of April 1998. You cannot claim it for periods starting after that date – instead, you may be able to claim taper relief, but this is worked out at a later stage.

To work out indexation allowance, multiply your allowable costs by the 'indexation factor' for the month in which each cost occurred (see Example 11.1). Indexation factors are given in the Fact File or you can get them from your tax office. However, you can use indexation only if you made a gain – you cannot use indexation to create or increase a loss. So if the indexed allowable cost is more than the proceeds of the disposal, your gain is zero.

Summing up

Disposal proceeds

Minus

Allowable costs

(multiplied by indexation factor if cost incurred before April 1998)

Gives

Your gain (after indexation) *or* your allowable loss

Example 11.1: **Indexation factors**

Philip bought some shares for £10,000 in July 1990 and sold them in 2003. The indexation factor for assets bought in July 1990 and sold after April 1998 is 1.282. So the indexed cost of Philip's shares is £10,000 × 1.282 = £12,820. If Philip sells his shares for £15,000, he has made a gain of £15,000 – £12,280 = £2,720. But if his shares sell for only £11,000, he cannot use the indexation to claim a loss – he has made no gain and no loss. He can claim a loss only if he sells for less than the unindexed cost, i.e. £10,000.

Working out your overall gains for the year

Once you have worked out your gains or losses on all the disposals you have made in the year, add up all your gains and deduct all your losses:

- If the overall gain for the year is below the level of the annual tax-free amount (£7,700 in 2002–03, £7,900 in 2003–04), you can stop here – there is no tax to pay.
- If your losses are more than your gains, you can carry any unused losses forward to future years, but you must notify your tax office (by letter or through your tax return) within five years and ten months after the end of the tax year (that is, by 31 January 2009 for losses made in 2002–03).
- If the overall gain for the year is above £7,700, look back to see if you have any unused losses from earlier years. If so, you deduct just as much of those losses as you need to reduce your gains (before taper relief) to £7,700.

Taper relief

If your gains are still above £7,700, you can apply taper relief. This was introduced in 1998 as a replacement for indexation allowance. It works by charging tax on only a percentage of your gain. The percentage of the gain that is chargeable (the 'taper rate', shown in Table 11.1) is reduced in line with the number of complete years you owned the asset after 5 April 1998.

You don't get taper relief for periods before April 1998, but any non-business assets that you owned on 17 March 1998 (budget day in that year) qualify for an extra year. Otherwise, taper relief is much more generous for business assets – defined on the next page.

Table 11.1: Taper relief for disposals after 5 April 2002

No. of whole years after 5 April 1998	*Taper rate (% of gain chargeable)*	*Effective rate of tax if you pay 20% tax*	*40% tax*
*Non-business assets**			
Under 3	100	20	40
3	95	19	38
4	90	18	36
5	85	17	34
6	80	16	32
7	75	15	30
8	70	14	28
9	65	13	26
10 or more	60	12	24
Business assets			
Less than 1	100	20	40
1	50	10	20
2 or more	25	5	10

*Add extra year's ownership for non-business asset owned on 17 March 1998

Example 11.2: **Taper relief**

In May 2003 Susie sold some shares she inherited in January 1998, with a gain of £4,000. She has owned the shares for five complete years since 5 April 1998, and can add an extra year because they are non-business assets owned on 17 March 1998. Her six years mean that only 80% of her £4,000 gain is taxable – £3,200.

Business assets are widely defined, and you don't have to own your own business to have them. From 6 April 2000, business assets are:

- shares or securities in an unlisted trading company
- shares or securities in a listed trading company in which you can exercise at least 5 per cent of the voting rights
- shares or securities in a company which employs you (listed or unlisted), unless it is a non-trading company and you have an interest of more than 10 per cent in it
- assets which you use in your own trading business, either as a sole trader or partner, or through a trading company which is unlisted or where you have at least 5 per cent of the voting rights
- assets that you use for your work if you are an employee or director of a trading company.

'Trading' in this context excludes businesses set up purely for investment or property development – though letting furnished holiday accommodation does count as a trade (see Chapter 8). But from April 2004, the definition of a business asset will widen further to include property you let to an unincorporated trader.

Note that the definition of business assets was more restrictive before 6 April 2000 – see Inland Revenue help sheet IR279 *Taper relief*. Also see this help sheet if you own something which you use partly privately; the taper relief has to be split between the private and business use.

Finally, after you have multiplied each remaining gain by the appropriate taper rate, deduct the annual tax-free amount (£7,700 in 2002–03, £7,900 in 2003–04). What's left is your taxable capital gains for the year.

Making the most of your losses

You make the most of your losses by setting them first against the gain that qualifies for the least taper relief. This is because taper relief is worked out after you have deducted your losses: you don't get full benefit from the loss if the taper relief itself would bring your gains down below the annual tax-free amount (£7,700 in 2002–03). You can't get round this by only deducting enough of the loss to bring your tapered gains down to £7,700.

Summing up

Total gains for the year (after any indexation)
Minus
Total losses for the year
Minus
Any unused losses from previous years
(but only enough to reduce your overall gains to £7,700)
Minus
Taper relief on each gain
Minus
Annual tax-free amount (£7,700 in 2003–03)
Gives
Your taxable capital gains

Working out the tax

You pay tax on your taxable capital gains at 10, 20 (the basic rate applied to capital gains) or 40 per cent, depending on how much taxable income you have. Your tax bands are used first by your income, and then by any capital gains. Your capital gains will be taxed at your top rate of income tax, but you may have to pay a higher rate of tax on gains that when added to your income fall within a higher tax band.

Example 11.3: **Which rate of tax?**

Susie's total taxable income in 2002–03 is £27,500. This all falls within the lower- and basic-rate bands. Her unused basic-rate band is £29,900 minus £27,500, that is £2,400. If she has taxable capital gains of £5,000, Susie will pay tax at 20% on the first £2,400 of her gains (£480) and at 40% on the remaining £2,600 (£1,040). This gives a capital gains tax bill of £480 + £1,040 = £1,520.

Which shares or unit trusts are you selling?

Imagine you have ordinary shares in British Utility plc. You first bought some when the company was privatised, and you bought more a couple of years later when prices seemed low. Now you are selling half the holding. To work out which shares you are selling you need to sort them into the following groups. Group 1 shares are sold first, then any Group 2 shares and so on. Example 11.5 on page 256 shows how this works.

- *Group 1:* shares acquired on the same day as the disposal in question.
- *Group 2:* shares acquired in the 30 days *following* the sale. This was devised by the Revenue as a way of discouraging 'bed-and-breakfasting' (see opposite).
- *Group 3:* shares acquired after 5 April 1998, taking the most recent acquisitions first.
- *Group 4:* shares acquired before 6 April 1998 but after 5 April 1982, on a 'pooled' basis (this means that the allowable cost of each share is the average value of all the shares, see below).
- *Group 5:* shares acquired before 6 April 1982 but after 6 April 1965. These are also pooled, but separately from Group 4 shares, usually using the market value of the shares on 31 March 1982.
- *Group 6:* shares acquired before 6 April 1965, using first the shares acquired last, but you will probably need to speak to your tax office about what to use as the allowable cost.
- *Group 7:* (if you get this far) shares acquired more than 30 days after the sale of the shares in question.

The same rules, with added touches, apply to unit trusts and shares in investment trust companies and Open Ended Investment Companies (OEICs). The full rules are given in Inland Revenue help sheet IR284 *Shares and Capital Gains Tax*.

Pooling

The cost of all the shares in a pool is added together. Each share in the pool is treated as if acquired at the same average cost. Indexation allowance is accounted for by adjusting the value of all the shares in the pool each time you change the number of shares in the pool (to do this, you need various indexation factors, see the Fact File.)

Example 11.4: **How pooling works**

Ernie bought 2,000 shares in British Bottles plc in July 1985 for £2,000 and another 2,000 shares in July 1990 for £3,000. These form a Group 4 pool. To work out the indexed cost, he takes the allowable cost of the first group of shares (£2,000) and multiplies it by the indexation factor for the period between July 1985 and his next purchase in July 1990 (1.332). This gives him the indexed value of the first 2,000 shares in his pool at July 1990 (£2,000 × 1.332 = £2,664). He adds the cost of the next 2,000 shares (£2,664 + £3,000 = £5,664).

Finally, he multiplies the cost at July 1990 by the indexation factor for the period between July 1990 and March 1998, when indexation was frozen (£5,664 × 1.282 = £7,261). £7,261 is the allowable cost of all Ernie's shares. But as he is selling only one-quarter of them, the allowable cost of the shares sold is £7,261 × ¼ = £1,815.

Employee share schemes

Special treatment applies when you sell shares you acquired free or cheap in your employer's company. Any gain you make may still count for capital gains tax purposes, but the way the tax is worked out will depend on how the scheme is set up. You may also be eligible for business assets taper relief. (See the Fact File for useful Revenue booklets.)

Bed-and-breakfasting

'Bed-and-breakfasting' means selling shares and buying them back the next day. The advantage of doing this used to be that it allowed you to realise a gain to set against your annual tax-free amount. Under rules introduced in 1998, if you buy back within 30 days, the price of the new purchase is used as the cost of the shares. This sounds odd, but it means that you won't realise a gain unless the share price falls within the 30 days. However, selling and buying back may still be worthwhile if your spouse buys back the shares, or if you wait 30 days.

Example 11.5: Which shares have you sold?

Ernie acquired shares in British Bottles plc on four occasions:

July 1985	2,000 shares bought for £2,000	('pooled' in Group 4,
July 1990	2,000 shares bought for £3,000	see Example 11.4)
January 2000	2,500 shares bought for £6,000 (Group 3)	
July 2002	500 shares bought for £1,000 (Group 3)	

When Ernie sells 4,000 shares in May 2003, he takes the shares from Group 3 first (he has no Group 1 or 2 shares). This gives him 2,500 + 500 = 3,000 shares. He takes the remaining 1,000 shares he is selling from Group 4.

Mergers, takeovers and other reorganisations

If a company in which you have shares has issued extra shares, or has been taken over, merged or otherwise reorganised, the company will usually tell you how the Revenue are treating the reorganisation, in the circular or prospectus sent to shareholders. Also see Inland Revenue help sheet IR285 *Share reorganisations, company take-overs and Capital Gains Tax*.

Scrip or stock dividends

These are extra shares issued instead of a cash dividend. The dividend voucher will tell you the 'appropriate amount' of the dividend on which income tax is liable. For capital gains tax purposes, you are treated as if you paid the appropriate amount in cash for the new shares.

Unit trusts

Unit trusts are treated like shares, but there is some special treatment:

- You might see a figure for 'equalisation' on the tax voucher that accompanies distributions. This is a repayment of the capital you used to buy the units and should be deducted from the allowable cost.
- With 'accumulation' units, any income is reinvested automatically by increasing the value of your existing units. The increase in value is

treated as extra expenditure on your original holding, and taper relief runs from the date of original purchase.

- If you make regular investments in a unit trust, each counts as a new purchase. To simplify the calculations for indexation allowance, you can opt to treat all your investments in one year as having been made as one payment in the seventh month. A guidance sheet on how to work this out is being developed by the Revenue – ask your tax office where you can find this. This is not necessary for taper relief, as this is worked out on an annual basis anyway.

ISA advantages

You can avoid any worries about capital gains tax if you invest in shares, unit trusts or investment trusts through an Individual Savings Account (see Chapter 10).

Tax reliefs you can claim to reduce your capital gains

There is a checklist of reliefs on page CGN18 of the Revenue's notes to the Capital Gains pages, but here are the main ones.

Your only or main home

If you sell your only or main home, 'private residence relief' makes any gain tax-free. However, you may lose part or all of your relief if:

- you have tenants (but not a single lodger) – you may be able to claim lettings relief instead (see page 259)
- part of your home is used exclusively for business (see Chapter 6)
- you sell off part of your property
- the garden is larger than necessary 'for your reasonable enjoyment' (the Revenue uses half a hectare as a guide to what is reasonable)
- the Revenue think you are in the business of property development.

If only part of your home qualifies, the gain will be split between parts of the home which qualify and parts which do not. There are no set rules for how the gain is split: the number of rooms and the relative value of each part will be taken into account.

You may also lose part of your relief if the home was classed as your only or main home for just part of the time. The gain is split depending on how long it was your only or main home – so if you owned the house for 120 months, say, and lost relief for 40 of those months, $\frac{40}{120}$ of the gain is potentially taxable. You can ignore the period before April 1982 provided you use the value at the end of March 1982 to work out the allowable cost; and you do not lose the relief for:

- the first year of ownership (exceptionally two years) if you have not been able to live in the home because you are doing it up or have still to sell your old home
- absences if you are living in job-related accommodation
- the final three years of your ownership.

Other absences that count as periods of residence, providing you lived in the property before and after the absence and had no other main home are:

- absences because you are working outside the UK
- absences of up to four years, if your home is too far from your work or your employer requires you to work away from home
- other absences which add up to less than three years altogether.

Example 11.6: **Is your home tax-free?**

Martin bought a Cotswolds cottage in January 1993 and sold it in December 2003 for a gain of £90,000. It was his main home for the first two years, but then he moved to London, letting out his cottage until he sold it. The first two years qualify for private residence relief and the final three years always do – five years in total. He qualifies for private residence relief on $\frac{5}{10}$ of the gain, i.e. £90,000 × $\frac{5}{10}$ = £45,000.

More than one home

You can choose which home is your main one, but you must do so within two years of the date you had a particular combination of homes. A new two-year period begins on any further change in your combination of homes. If you do not choose, the Revenue will.

Lettings relief

If you let out part or all of your home, you can deduct lettings relief from the taxable gain. This is worth the same as private residence relief, up to a ceiling of £40,000. So if your private residence relief is:

- £40,000 or less, just double the private residence relief
- over £40,000, you add £40,000 to your private residence relief.

The relief is available only if you let out residential accommodation in what is or has been part of your only or main home. It is part of your home if you have made no structural alterations, even if the let part has its own kitchen and bathroom, but you could not claim it for a self-contained flat.

Example 11.7: Tax on a home that you let

Martin made a gain of £90,000 when he sold his Cotswold cottage, £45,000 of which qualifies for private residence relief (see Example 11.6). However, Martin can also claim lettings relief. The relief is either the same amount as his private residence relief, or £40,000 if less. So Martin's taxable gain is:

Gain	£90,000
Minus – private residence relief	–£45,000
– lettings relief	–£40,000
Taxable gain	£5,000

Tax on your home if you have a partner

If you are married, your main home (for private residence relief) must be same for both of you, unless you are separated and living apart. If you make a taxable capital gain on a property you own with someone else, the gain will be split between you. And, whether or not you are married, both partners or spouses can claim lettings relief on their share of a gain – so lettings relief of up to £80,000 on one property may be available.

Reliefs for husbands and wives

Husbands and wives each get their own annual tax-free amount. If you give (or even sell) something to your husband or wife, there is no tax to pay at the time, provided that you are living together, or in the year of separation. Any tax is payable only when your spouse disposes of the asset – but at that stage, the gain is worked out as if your spouse had owned the asset from the moment you acquired it. If you are unmarried, you do not qualify for this special treatment.

Reliefs for your business

As well as the generous taper relief for business assets, there are the following reliefs from capital gains tax:

- *Roll-over relief* allows you to put off paying tax on disposing of business assets if you reinvest the gains in new business assets. (See Inland Revenue help sheet IR290 *Business asset roll-over relief*.)
- *Incorporation relief* allows you to put off paying tax if you transfer your business to a company in exchange for shares.
- *Retirement relief* has been abolished for disposals after 5 April 2003.

Note that if you have unused losses from self-employment, a partnership or furnished holiday lettings, you can choose to set them against your capital gains rather than carry them forward to future years. The capital gains pages call these 'income losses'.

What to tell the Inland Revenue

If you aren't sent a tax return, you should tell the Revenue by 5 October after the end of the tax year in which you make the gain if you have a taxable capital gain above the annual tax-free amount.

If you have losses that you want to set against gains made in past or future years, you should tell the Revenue about them by 31 January in the sixth year after the tax year in which they were incurred. That means by 31 January 2009 for losses made in 2002–03. The only exceptions are losses made before 6 April 1996 (when self-assessment started). Once notified, you can carry forward losses indefinitely – they do not have to be used within the six-year time limit.

Filling in the Capital Gains supplementary pages

To help you decide whether you need to fill in the Capital Gains pages, first go to Question 8 on page 2 of your main tax return. If you have:

- sold your home and, for any of the reasons on page 257, any gain you have made on it is not completely tax-free – tick the top 'Yes' box
- disposed of assets (excluding tax-free ones) worth more than £15,400, tick the middle 'Yes' box
- taxable capital gains of more than £7,700, even if losses and reliefs will bring the gains below £7,700 – tick the bottom 'Yes' box.

Figure 11.1: Question 8 – capital gains

Q8 Capital gains - read the guidance on page 7 of the Tax Return Guide.

- If you have disposed of your only or main residence do you need the Capital Gains Pages? YES
- Did you dispose of other chargeable assets worth more than £15,400 in total? YES ✓
- Were your total chargeable gains more than £7,700 or do you want to make a claim or election for the year? YES

CAPITAL GAINS ✓

If you ticked any box in Question 8, now go to the Capital Gains supplementary pages. Everyone has to complete page 8 of these – it records your overall gains for the tax year and provides a record of your losses (past and present). You also have to complete either pages 2 and 3 or, if your disposals were quite straightforward, just page 1. Pages 4, 5 and 6 apply only if you have disposed of unquoted shares, property or other assets and page 7 is for additional information.

Page 1

This simplified version of pages 2 and 3 is for people with straightforward capital gains that don't qualify for taper relief (i.e. you have owned them for less than three years, or one year if they are classed as a business asset) on UK unit trusts, or quoted stocks and shares. In addition, it cannot be used if you are claiming any reliefs.

Pages 2 and 3

These pages are for details of each disposal, if you cannot use the simplified version on page 1. Enter your disposals in different sections according to whether they are losses or gains.

Enter each transaction on a different row, giving brief details of the asset in column A. If necessary, photocopy the page. In column AA, you need to code each disposal as Q, U, L, T or O, depending on the type of asset. Write Q if the asset is quoted shares. If it consists of unquoted shares (U), you must give further details on page 4; for land or property (L), further details go on page 5; and for other assets (O) use page 6. Code T applies only if a gain of a trust you set up is treated as yours, and you are making a special election (this is covered in Revenue help sheet IR277 *Trusts with settler interest: taper and losses*). Tick column B if you had to estimate any figures or are relying on a valuation.

Tick column C if you owned the asset concerned on 31 March 1982, because only gains arising after that date are taxed. Similarly, in column D you enter either 16 March 1998 or the date of acquisition if later, because taper relief applies only after this date. However, you must enter the date of disposal at E in all cases, and the disposal proceeds (which may be the sale price or the market value, see page 248) in column F.

Column G is for details of any tax reliefs you want to claim, such as private residence relief. Check the Revenue notes in case you also have to complete a claim form.

Gains on assets which are partly business assets and partly non-business assets (e.g. a home you let out) go in rows 9 and 10. Once you have completed columns A to G with the overall information for the asset, split the gain into two parts (business and non-business) when completing the other columns, because different taper rates apply.

Enter the taxable gain after deducting allowable costs and any indexation allowance in column H, showing any loss in brackets. Write 'Bus' in column I if the asset is a business asset (see page 252 for a definition) and write the relevant taper rate (from Table 11.1) in column J.

Deduct any losses in columns K1, K2 and K3. Taper relief is worked out after losses have been deducted, so losses have to be set off against each gain in turn. Losses for the year come from box 8.2 at the bottom of the page; you can only work out what income losses (i.e. trading losses) you have once you have completed your Self-employment, Partnership or Land and Property supplementary pages. Unused losses on disposing of capital gains from earlier years will come from your records (such as page 8 of previous years' Capital Gains pages).

Remember: if you have both gains and losses to enter on pages 2 and 3, enter first the gains with the highest taper rate (i.e. those with a taper rate of 100 per cent at the top, then those at 95 per cent and so on). Then you can work down the rows, taking just as much as you need from each category of loss to reduce each gain to the optimum amount. That way, you'll make the most of your losses.

Attributed gains

There are various tax avoidance rules to stop people using trusts to avoid capital gains tax. If you fall foul of these rules, gains made by the trust may be 'attributed' to you and taxed as yours. See the Revenue notes to the Capital Gains supplementary pages.

Using losses

When entering income losses in column K2 (trading losses which you are claiming to set against gains) and unused losses from earlier years (in column K3), remember there is no point deducting more than you need to reduce your overall gains to the level of the annual tax-free amount (£7,700 in 2002–03). Any other losses can be carried forward. But you have to deduct the whole of any losses for the current year.

Example 11.8: **Filling in pages 2 and 3**

Andrea made overall gains of £12,000 in 2002–03. Because these take her above her annual tax-free amount, she also decides to get rid of some shares that have fallen in value, giving her a £2,000 loss at box 8.2 (see Figure 11.2). She gives details of her gains in all the columns up to column K, listing the gain with the highest taper rate first, and enters the total in box 8.1.

Next Andrea carries her £2,000 loss for the year to column K1. This leaves gains after losses for the year at £12,000 – £2,000 = £10,000. She also has £3,000 unused losses from earlier years, but she needs only £2,300 of these losses to reduce her gains to the tax-free amount of £7,700. She takes £1,000 of the losses from earlier years to reduce her gains in row 1 to zero, and sets another £1,300 against the losses in row 2. She has £3,000 – £2,300 = £700 in losses left to carry forward.

Moving to column L, Andrea's gains are now zero, £3,700 and £4,000. She multiplies the gains by the relevant taper rate in column J and enters the results in row M. Adding up column M, her gains after taper relief (in box 8.3) are now £4,330 – below her annual tax-free amount. She has no tax to pay but some of her losses brought forward are wasted.

The way the tax rules are written mean that Andrea cannot choose to deduct fewer losses to compensate for the taper relief. But she could have chosen to hang on to her under-performing shares, instead of selling them for a £2,000 loss. She would have used up all her £3,000 loss from earlier years against her first gain, but her taper relief would still have reduced her other gains below the level of the tax-free slice.

Figure 11.2: Capital gains (see Example 11.8)

	H Chargeable Gains after reliefs but before losses and taper	I Enter 'Bus' if business asset	J Taper rate	K Losses deducted: K1 Allowable losses of the year	K2 Income losses of 2002-03 set against gains	K3 Unused losses b/f from earlier years	L Gains after losses	M Tapered gains (gains from column L x % in column J)
	£ 3,000		100 %	£ 2,000	£	£ 1,000	£ 0	£ 0
	£ 5,000		90 %	£	£	£ 1,300	£ 3,700	£ 3,330
	£ 4,000	BUS	25 %	£	£	£	£ 4,000	£ 1,000
	£		%	£	£	£	£	£
	£		%	£	£	£	£	£
	£		%	£	£	£	£	£
	£		%	£	£	£	£	£
	£		%	£	£	£	£	£
	£	Bus	%	£	£	£	£	£
	£		%	£	£	£	£	£
	£	Bus	%	£	£	£	£	£
	£		%	£	£	£	£	£
Total	8.1 £ 12,000 *Total column H*				8.5 £ *Total column K2*	8.6 £ 2,300 *Total column K3*		8.3 £ 4,330 *Total column M*

11 **Attributed gains from UK resident trusts where no election has been made for the set off of personal** losses (see page CGN4) *(enter the name of the Trust on Page CG7)* £

12 **Attributed gains from non UK resident trusts where no election has been made for the set off of personal** losses (see page CGN4) *(enter the name of the Trust on Page CG7)* £

Total of attributed gains where no election has been made (total of rows 11 and 12) 8.4 £ 4,330

Total taxable gains **(after allowable losses and taper relief)** box 8.3 + box 8.4 £

Copy to box 8.7 on Page CG8 and complete Pages CG4 to CG6 for all U, L and O transactions

Losses arising
£ 2,000
£
£
£
year 8.2 £ 2,000

Copy to box 8.10 on Page CG8 and, unless you need only complete the totals boxes (see page CGN5), complete column K1

If you don't know the market value

You can estimate an asset's market value if necessary. You should notify the Revenue (on your tax return) if you have used an estimate and their specialist valuers may check it. You can appeal if you do not agree with their valuation. You can also ask your tax office to check a valuation before sending in your return (ask for form CG34).

Connected persons and clogged losses

A 'connected person' is your husband or wife, close family member, business partner or a company or trust you control. There are rules designed to stop you using your connections to avoid tax. In particular, if you give or sell something to a connected person (except your husband or wife, see page 260), the price used when working out the tax is replaced by the market value. Any loss on a transaction with a connected person is a 'clogged loss' that can only be set against a future gain made on a disposal to that person.

Page 8

This gives the Revenue a summary of your capital gains for the year. Everything on the top part of the page (up to box 8.8) summarises information given elsewhere in the Capital Gains pages, whereas the bottom half summarises your losses. There are just a few things to note:

- *Additional liability in respect of non-resident or dual resident trusts* (box 8.9) applies if you received a benefit from an offshore trust which is caught by anti-avoidance rules. See Inland Revenue help sheet IR301 *Capital gains on benefits from non-resident and dual resident trusts.*
- In a very few circumstances, you do not have to set this year's losses against this year's gains (boxes 8.12, 8.13A and 8.13B). If you have made a loss on shares in an unlisted trading company, or an Enterprise Investment Scheme, you can claim to set these against your income. See Inland Revenue help sheets IR286 *Negligible value claims* and IR297 *Enterprise Investment Scheme and capital gains tax.*

- If you have carried forward unused losses made before 6 April 1996, at boxes 8.15 to 8.21, you have to record these separately from losses made on or after that date, because the losses made after 6 April 1996 have to be used up first.

Record-keeping

The tax return doesn't ask you to give details of how you arrive at the taxable value of any gain. But keep the following for at least 22 months or, if you have a business or rental income, for five years and ten months from the end of the tax year to which they relate.

- Contract notes, correspondence or other documentation when you buy, sell, lease or exchange assets such as investments.
- Scrip dividend vouchers.
- Invoices or other evidence of payment records (e.g. bank statements) for costs you claim for the purchase, improvement or sale of assets.
- Documentation describing assets you acquired but did not buy yourself, such as gifts or from an inheritance.
- Details of assets you have given away or put into a trust.
- Copies of valuations taken into account in your calculation of gains and losses (e.g. probate values for inherited assets).
- If you acquired or disposed of quoted shares in any other way than on the open market (e.g. if you gave shares away), a copy of a newspaper showing the share price for that day.
- If you use an asset partly for business, partly privately, records to show what proportion of the use is for each purpose.
- If you start using an asset for a purpose that might change its tax treatment (e.g. you start letting out part of your home, or you start using an asset for work), notes of dates on which the use changes.

Tax-planning hints

1. Keep careful records – not least because any losses can be used to

reduce your capital gains in future years.

2 Remember to notify the Revenue that you have made a loss within five years and ten months of the end of the tax year in which it was made – otherwise you will not be able to use it.

3 If you don't use all your tax-free amount in one tax year, you can't carry it forward. So if you expect to make capital gains, it can be worth spreading your disposals over more than one year.

4 You get a greater rate of taper relief for each full year of ownership. Time your disposals to maximise this – selling just after (rather than just before) the anniversary of purchase.

5 Married? You each have an annual tax-free amount, so consider splitting assets between you so that you can both make full use of it.

6 You don't have to worry about capital gains tax if you invest in British Government Stock or via a tax-free scheme such as an ISA (see Chapter 10).

7 Working from home? You may lose some of your home's exemption from tax if you use part of it exclusively for business, so try to keep some regular residential use of the business part.

8 If you have more than one home, nominate which one you want as your 'main' home within two years of acquiring the second home. Choose whichever you think you will make the biggest gain on.

9 Taper relief is much more generous for business assets, and the definition of a 'business asset' is quite broad and may apply even if you are an employee (see page 252).

10 The rate of capital gains tax depends on your taxable income. So if you have an unavoidable capital gain in a year when you are on the verge of paying higher-rate tax, you may be able to keep your gain below the higher-rate band by reducing your taxable income through, say, a one-off pension contribution.

12

Inheritance tax

Inheritance tax is a tax on gifts. A gift includes whatever you leave when you die (your 'estate'), and lifetime gifts of cash, property or anything else you own, to individuals, trusts or companies.

The tax is payable when the taxable value of your estate is above £250,000 (for deaths in 2002–03, £255,000 in 2003–04), including any property you leave. The rate of tax is 40 per cent of everything above the £250,000 threshold, with reductions for lifetime gifts.

Do you need to worry about inheritance tax?

Inheritance tax may affect you if you are:

- making a gift during your lifetime (a 'lifetime transfer' in tax-speak)
- planning how to pass on your money after your death
- the recipient – or likely recipient – of a lifetime gift or an inheritance
- the executor of somebody's will, or other personal representative sorting out someone's estate.

Lifetime gifts

Some lifetime gifts are tax-free (see page 272) and almost all other lifetime gifts are 'Potentially Exempt Transfers' (PETs). A PET is completely tax-free if you survive for at least seven years after making the gift, and taxable on a reducing scale if you die after three years but within seven years. But beware: a gift in name only – e.g. giving away a house which you continue to live in – will count as part of your estate unless you pay a market rent for your use of it.

Although some lifetime gifts may be taken into account for inheritance tax, tax is only payable on death – unless you transfer money or assets to a company or discretionary trust. Tax is payable on such 'chargeable transfers' immediately if, within a seven-year period, they come to more than the inheritance tax threshold. The rate is only 20 per cent, but on death the tax is recalculated and more may be payable.

Capital gains tax

Even if no inheritance tax is payable on a lifetime gift, capital gains tax may be payable. However, a gift on death is not liable to capital gains tax. See Chapter 11.

Planning to pass on your money

Inheritance tax-planning can get complicated. There is a constant battle between the Inland Revenue, attempting to plug loopholes, and tax advisers, attempting to find new ones. This chapter concentrates on straightforward matters. If a lot of money is at stake, you should get professional advice.

After your death

Tax is payable if everything you own on your death, plus any PETs made in the previous seven years (minus tax-free gifts and debts), comes to more than the inheritance tax threshold.

If you are leaving everything to your husband or wife, there is no immediate tax to pay, because gifts between spouses are tax-free. But you may merely be postponing, or even increasing, the overall bill, because you are wasting one person's tax-free threshold (see Example 12.1).

Example 12.1: **Using the tax-free threshold**

George and Ethel have a £500,000 estate between them – £400,000 in George's name and £100,000 in Ethel's. When George dies in May 2002, leaving his £400,000 to Ethel, there is no tax to pay because they were married. But when she dies in March 2003, there is tax on £500,000 − £250,000 = £250,000 × 40% = £100,000. They have lost 25% of their joint estate in tax.

Had George left £250,000 to someone else, it would have been within his tax-free threshold, leaving Ethel's tax-free threshold to cover the remaining £250,000: no tax to pay. It can be difficult to do this if your money is tied up in property. But even if George had left just £50,000 to someone else, there would be £20,000 less tax to pay on Ethel's estate.

Receiving a gift or inheritance

You need to worry about having to pay inheritance tax on a gift or legacy only if:

- The will says your legacy is before tax ('subject to the payment of taxes'or must 'bear its own tax'). Otherwise, the tax comes out of the estate.
- The estate pays the tax, but there is not enough left after all legacies have been paid. If so, specific bequests may have to be reduced.
- You received a PET within seven years of death. If so, you are liable to pay any inheritance tax on it – though the money may be provided by a further gift from the estate.

If you received a PET

After the donor's death, all PETs must be declared to the Revenue by the executors. The Revenue will contact you if you have tax to pay on a PET, so make sure you keep records of PETs received, and that your records are consistent with the donor's.

An executor or personal representative

You are responsible for sorting out the paperwork and paying at least part of any tax due before the money in the estate can be distributed. (See page 281 and Inland Revenue leaflet IHT14 *Inheritance tax: the personal representative's responsibilities*.)

Tax-free gifts

Tax-free lifetime gifts

- Gifts to someone getting married – up to £5,000 if you are a parent of one of the couple, £2,500 if you are a grandparent, otherwise £1,000.
- Payments to maintain your family or dependant relatives. This includes ex-wives and ex-husbands.
- Gifts that are part of your normal expenditure – e.g. regular payments into an insurance policy for the benefit of your children.
- Small gifts – up to a maximum of £250 per person in any tax year.
- An annual exemption of £3,000 in each tax year, plus any unused balance of £3,000 from the previous tax year. If you give more than £3,000, the amount above £3,000 counts as a PET.

You can combine the tax-free gifts above, with the exception of the small gifts exemption – e.g. you could give a grandchild a £2,500 wedding gift plus £3,000 under your annual exemption, but not a 'small gift' of £250 as well.

Always tax-free

- Gifts to spouses – though if they are 'domiciled' abroad (see Chapter 9), the tax-free amount is only £55,000.
- Gifts to good causes – i.e. UK charities, community amateur sports clubs or housing associations.
- Gifts to some national institutions, such as universities, national museums and the National Trust.
- Gifts to political parties.

- Gifts of decorations for valour or gallant conduct, provided that these have never been sold.
- The estate of someone who dies on active service.

Saving tax as a married couple

If you are married, you each have your own tax threshold and your own set of tax-free gifts, and transfers between you are also tax-free. This means that if one of you has most of the money, you can give some to your husband or wife, so that he or she can make use of the exemptions. (But any gift to your husband and wife must be outright, without strings.) And when making a will leave the maximum tax-free allowance to someone other than your spouse – unless he or she needs the money (see Example 12.1 on page 271).

ISAs and PEPs become taxable on death

Any investments in a Personal Equity Plan (PEP) or Individual Savings Account (ISA) form part of your estate and lose their tax-free status when you die.

How inheritance tax is worked out

If you haven't made any chargeable transfers (i.e. gifts to companies or discretionary trusts, see page 270), the process is as follows.

- *Step 1:* set the tax-free threshold applying at the date of death (i.e. £250,000 for deaths in 2002–03, £255,000 in 2003–04) against any PETs made in the seven years before death, starting with the earliest gift (see Example 12.2).
- *Step 2:* work out the tax on any PETs above the tax-free threshold. This is 40 per cent of the taxable amount, reduced by taper relief if death occurs three or more years after the gift (see Table 12.1). The recipients are liable to pay this tax.

- *Step 3:* work out how much tax-free threshold is left, after deducting any PETs. So if someone dies in 2002–03 with PETs of £120,000, say, the remaining tax-free threshold is £250,000 – £120,000 = £130,000.
- *Step 4:* calculate the taxable value of the estate on death (see page 276).
- *Step 5:* if the taxable value of the estate is below the remaining tax-free threshold (from step 3), there is no tax to pay on it. If it is above, deduct the tax-free threshold. So if someone dies with an estate of £300,000, and has a tax-free threshold after PETs of £130,000, tax is payable on £300,000 – £130,000 = £170,000.
- *Step 6:* work out tax at 40 per cent on everything above the tax-free threshold.
- *Step 7:* share out the tax bill between the beneficiaries of the estate (see page 278).

There are examples and ready reckoners in Inland Revenue leaflet IHT15 *Inheritance tax. How to calculate the liability*. Note that if you have made chargeable transfers, this will affect the calculation and you will probably need professional advice.

Example 12.2: **Tax on PETs**

Mr Kumar gave £100,000 to each of his children when they reached 21. The first child reached 21 in 1996, the second in 1998 and the third in 2000. He died in September 2002. All the gifts are taxable because they were made in the seven years before his death, but the first £3,000 of each gift falls within the annual exemption for each year, and a further £3,000 within the annual exemption unused in the previous year, so the taxable amount of each gift is £94,000.

The first two gifts fall within the £250,000 tax-free threshold, leaving only £250,000 – £94,000 – £94,000 = £62,000 threshold available for the third gift. So his third child must pay tax on £94,000 – £62,000 = £32,000. This amounts to £32,000 × 40% = £12,800, and because the gift was made less than three years before Mr Kumar died, no taper relief is available. Because the tax-free threshold has been used up by his PETs, the whole of Mr Kumar's estate on death is taxable at 40 per cent, apart from any tax-free gifts.

Table 12.1 Taper relief on lifetime gifts

Years between date of gift and death	*Percentage of full tax payable*	*Equivalent to tax rate of*
Less than 3 years	100%	40%
More than 3 but less than 4	80%	32%
More than 4 but less than 5	60%	24%
More than 5 but less than 6	40%	16%
More than 6 but less than 7	20%	8%
7 or more years	No tax	No tax

Example 12.3: **How taper relief works**

If you have to pay tax on a lifetime gift that was made at least three years before death, a reduced rate of tax is payable. So in Example 12.2, Mr Kumar's youngest child received a PET of £32,000 within three years of his father's death, on which £12,800 tax was payable. But if Mr Kumar had died during the fourth year after the gift, only 80 per cent of the full tax bill would have been payable: £12,800 × 80% = £10,240.

Lifetime gifts can increase the tax

The tax-free threshold (£250,000 for deaths in 2002–03, £255,000 in 2003–04) is set first against your lifetime gifts, with anything left over set against your estate on death. So tax is not payable on a PET, even if this was made within seven years of death, unless your total taxable lifetime gifts come to more than the tax-free threshold. But even if your gifts in the seven years before death are not themselves taxable, they can still push your estate on death above the inheritance tax threshold. And do not pin too much hope on taper relief. It reduces the tax payable, not the taxable value of the gift, so it applies only if the PET is taxable – i.e. above the £250,000 threshold for deaths in 2002–03.

The taxable value of an estate

When you die, your 'estate' consists of:

- everything owned in your own name
- your share of any jointly owned property (see below)
- a payout on your death from a life insurance policy that you took out (see below)
- 'gifts with reservation' – a gift from which you or your spouse continue to benefit. This would catch you if you put your home in your children's name but still continued to live there
- assets in a trust from which you have a right to some personal benefit, such as an income (see opposite)
- *minus* any tax-free gifts (see page 272), such as a gift to a spouse
- *minus* reasonable funeral expenses (including a headstone)
- *minus* any money or property owed by you
- *minus* some forms of compensation, e.g. to holocaust survivors or British prisoners of war in Japanese camps.

Saving tax on life insurance

Ask the insurance company about getting your policy 'written in trust' for someone else (your children, say) – the payout will go immediately to them without forming part of your estate. The premiums count as a gift to your beneficiaries, but these are normally tax-free as a gift out of your normal expenditure.

Jointly owned property

The assumption is that joint property is shared equally, in the absence of any documents that say otherwise – e.g. the deeds to a house. But with a joint money account, your share (for inheritance tax purposes) is in line with the money you each contributed to it.

Often, jointly owned assets such as houses and bank accounts are set up so that they pass automatically to the survivor (although the deceased person's share still counts as part of his or her estate). Under English law, this is called a 'joint tenancy'; in Scotland, this is called passing 'by survivorship' (although with a joint bank account, the survivor may operate the account but not necessarily be entitled to the money in it).

Automatic transfer has the advantage of giving the survivor immediate access to the money. However, there can be advantages to owning joint assets as 'tenants in common' (in England) or with no special destination (in Scotland). If this applies, you can leave your share to whomever you wish.

Saving tax on the family home

You might want to leave half your house to someone else, rather than your spouse, in order to use up your own tax threshold (£255,000 in 2003–04). You can do this if you own the house as tenants in common rather than joint tenants. But your widow or widower risks having to move if the other owners want to sell.

There are tax-saving schemes involving trusts or giving your house away and then paying a market rent to live in it, but professional advice is essential. A simpler way to save tax is to move to a smaller home or take out a mortgage, giving away the cash released.

Assets in a trust

Trusts – legal arrangements that hold investments or other assets in the care of trustees for the benefit of one or more 'beneficiaries' – are often used in inheritance tax-planning.

For inheritance tax purposes, there are three main types of trust:

- Trusts with an 'interest in possession' – where someone has a right to use trust property or receive income from it.
- Discretionary trusts – ones without an interest in possession, for example where the trustees have discretion over who receives the income.
- Special trusts – discretionary trusts with special, more favourable, tax rules. They include trusts for the benefit of particular groups of

employees, trusts for disabled people and accumulation and maintenance trusts. To be classed as an accumulation and maintenance trust, at least one beneficiary must be entitled to trust assets or income by the age of 25 (until which time any income must either be used for their maintenance or be accumulated), and the trust must last for a maximum of 25 years unless all the beneficiaries have a common grandparent.

You don't necessarily save tax by setting up a trust: the money going in is a PET or chargeable transfer (see page 270) and the trust itself may be liable to income tax and capital gains tax. Money coming out of a trust may be liable to some inheritance tax, although not when the beneficiaries of some special trusts become entitled to their money.

Trusts can give you flexibility and reduce the risks of an outright gift. And once your money is in a trust any growth in its value falls outside your estate. But up-to-date legal advice is essential and running a trust can be costly.

Sharing out a tax bill

Any inheritance due is paid out of the 'residue' of the estate (what is left after all specific legacies have been paid), unless the will says that a gift should 'bear its own tax' (see Example 12.4). But tax is payable on the loss to the giver, not the benefit to the recipient. So if a gift is intended to be tax-free in the hands of the recipient, it must be 'grossed-up' to find the amount that, after 40 per cent tax, leaves the intended gift. An after-tax legacy of £12,000, say, would actually count as a gift of £20,000 *minus* tax of £20,000 × 40% = £8,000, i.e. £20,000 − £8,000 = £12,000.

Make a will

Think about how any tax will be paid and don't give so much in specific bequests free-of-tax that whoever inherits the residue (e.g. your spouse or partner) has less to live on than you intended. If possible, it is simpler for gifts in a will to bear their own tax.

Example 12.4: **Tax on an estate**

Mr Smith-Jones made no PETs in his lifetime. When he died in May 2002, he left:

- a house worth £300,000 to his wife – this was tax-free as a gift to his wife
- £200,000 to his son – tax-free as it fell within the tax-free threshold
- the residue of his estate (£150,000) split between his son and his wife. His wife's share is tax-free: his son's share is taxable, but there is still £250,000 – £200,000 = £50,000 of the tax-free threshold to set against it.

If the will says the residue should be divided before tax, his son and his wife will both get £150,000 ÷ 2 = £75,000, and his son will have to pay tax at 40% on £75,000 – £50,000 = £25,000. If it is after tax, the gift has to be 'grossed-up' to include the tax, and the calculations can be very complex.

Deeds of variation

However carefully you do your tax-planning, you never know when you will die or what the inheritance tax position will be. Your heirs, however, should bear in mind that they can 're-arrange' your will after your death, by using a 'deed of variation'. It can also be used if someone dies without leaving a will ('intestate'). A variation allows beneficiaries to disclaim gifts and legacies in favour of their children, say. It must be made in writing within two years of death, but you cannot sign for a child – court approval may be needed, so consult a lawyer. (See Inland Revenue leaflet IHT8 *Alterations to an inheritance following a death.*)

Tax reliefs you can claim

Agricultural property relief

Tax relief may be available if you give away agricultural land and property during your lifetime or on your death, provided that you or your spouse used it for agricultural purposes for at least two years. If you did not use it yourself, you must have owned it for at least seven years and it must have been tenanted for agricultural purposes throughout.

If the property is let on a tenancy that commences after 31 August 1995, 100 per cent relief applies. If not, 100 per cent relief still applies if you have the right to vacant possession within 24 months or the property is valued at roughly the vacant possession value, or if the property was dedicated to wildlife habitats. Otherwise, the rate of relief is normally 50 per cent. (See Inland Revenue leaflet IHT17 *Inheritance tax. Businesses, farms and woodlands.*)

Business property relief

If you give away a business or a share in a business, or unquoted shares in a business, 100 per cent relief is available provided that you or your spouse owned it for at least two years. However, if you make a lifetime gift of business land, buildings, plant or machinery, or a controlling shareholding in a quoted company, rather than the whole business, only 50 per cent relief is available.

Relief is not available for pure investment companies, nor is it available for plant or machinery used partly for the business, partly privately. You can claim relief for just part of land or buildings, provided that that part is used exclusively for the business. (See Inland Revenue leaflet IHT17 *Inheritance tax. Businesses, farms and woodlands.)*

Double taxation relief

If you have property or assets abroad, the overseas tax authorities may charge the equivalent of inheritance tax on any gift or bequest. If so, you can claim some relief for it against UK inheritance tax. (See Inland Revenue leaflet IHT18 *Inheritance tax. Foreign aspects.*)

Quick succession relief

This relief (known to the Revenue as 'successive charges' relief) applies where one person has inherited assets on the death of another and the two deaths occur within five years. If inheritance tax was paid when the first person died, the tax payable on the second death is reduced. (See Inland Revenue leaflet IHT15 *Inheritance tax. How to calculate the liability.*)

What to tell the Inland Revenue

You do not have to tell the Revenue about tax-free gifts or PETs made during your lifetime. Nor do you have to notify them about chargeable transfers you have made if they come to £10,000 or less in a tax year, provided that your total chargeable transfers in the previous ten years are £40,000 or less.

When someone dies, whoever is handling their affairs has to get legal authority (such as a grant of probate or, in Scotland, grant of confirmation) before they can distribute the assets of the estate. An account of all the taxable assets of the deceased person has to be sent to the Revenue's Capital Taxes Office, and at least part of any inheritance tax paid, before a grant of probate or confirmation is given. This account also covers lifetime gifts, so that the Revenue can check whether tax is due on those.

Inheritance tax must be paid within six months of the death, or before you get the grant of probate or confirmation. If the deceased person had money in National Savings & Investments or British Government Stock, this can be used to pay the tax (see Inland Revenue leaflet IHT11 *Payment of inheritance tax from National Savings or British Government Stock)*. From April 2003 it is possible to use the money in his or her bank or building society account as well. And if the assets in the estate are not easily saleable, you may be able to pay by instalments. Otherwise, the executor or personal representative may have to take out a loan.

Insuring to pay the tax

You can take out a life insurance policy to ensure that cash is available to pay inheritance tax. If the policy is 'written in trust' for your beneficiaries, it is not part of your estate and can be paid out before probate is granted. Alternatively, your beneficiaries may be able to take out a policy on your life.

Record-keeping

Keep track of the value of your assets in the same way as for capital gains tax (see Chapter 11), and make sure there is documentation to prove the value of any assets at the date you give them away.

You should also keep records of any gifts you have made or received for at least seven years (14 years in the case of chargeable transfers). Even if gifts are not taxable, good records are helpful for winding up your estate on your death. Also keep records of any inheritance tax you have paid.

Filling in the forms

Whoever is handling the legal side of things will normally do all this.

The main form is IHT200 *Inland Revenue Account for Inheritance Tax*, but there is a special short form for an 'excepted' estate (broadly, one valued at less than £220,000, and otherwise straightforward). All the forms are available on the Revenue website, and IHT200 also has a working sheet which tells you how to calculate the tax.

IHT200 consists of a main form and supplementary sheets. Figure 12.1 shows the form listing the supplementary sheets. Use it as a guide to the sorts of things you need to keep records of.

Tax-planning hints

1. Do not jeopardise your or your partner's security for the sake of saving tax, but do plan ahead to ensure that the cash is there to pay any tax, and that your partner has enough ready money to live on until your estate can be distributed.
2. Giving money away in your lifetime may incur capital gains tax. You need to balance this against the potential inheritance tax saving.
3. Make a will – particularly if you are living with someone without being married.
4. Keep good records. It will simplify matters after your death and may mean lower legal bills.

Figure 12.1: Extract from IHT200

D Supplementary pages

You must answer all of the questions in this section. You should read the notes starting at page 10 of form IHT 210 before answering the questions.

If you answer "Yes" to a question you will need to fill in the supplementary page shown. If you do not have all the supplementary pages you need you should telephone our Orderline on 0845 2341000

		No	Yes	Page
• **The Will**	Did the deceased leave a Will?		✔	D1
• **Domicile outside the United Kingdom**	Was the deceased domiciled outside the UK at the date of death?			D2
• **Gifts and other transfers of value**	Did the deceased make any gift or any other transfer of value on or after 18 March 1986?		✔	D3
• **Joint assets**	Did the deceased hold any asset(s) in joint names with another person?		✔	D4
• **Nominated assets**	Did the deceased, at any time during their lifetime, give written instructions (usually called a "nomination") that any asset was to pass to a particular person on their death?			D4
• **Assets held in trust**	Did the deceased have any right to any benefit from any assets held in trust or in a settlement at the date of death?			D5
• **Pensions**	Did the deceased have provision for a pension from employers, a personal pension policy or other provisions made for retirement other than the State Pension?		✔	D6
• **Stocks and shares**	Did the deceased own any stocks or shares?		✔	D7
• **Debts due to the estate**	Did the deceased lend any money, either on mortgage or by personal loan, that had not been repaid by the date of death?			D8
• **Life insurance and annuities**	Did the deceased pay any premiums on any life insurance policies or annuities which are payable to either the estate or to someone else or which continue after death?			D9
• **Household and personal goods**	Did the deceased own any household goods or other personal possessions?		✔	D10
• **Interest in another estate**	Did the deceased have a right to a legacy or a share of an estate of someone who died before them, but which they had not received before they died?			D11
• **Land, buildings and interests in land**	Did the deceased own any land or buildings in the UK?		✔	D12
• **Agricultural relief**	Are you deducting agricultural relief?			D13
• **Business interests**	Did the deceased own all or part of a business or were they a partner in a business?			D14
• **Business relief**	Are you deducting business relief?			D14
• **Foreign assets**	Did the deceased own any assets outside the UK?			D15
• **Debts owed by the estate**	Are you claiming a deduction against the estate for any money that the deceased had borrowed from relatives, close friends, or trustees, or other loans, overdrafts or guarantee debts?			D16

2

5 A gift to charity in your will is tax-free, but it may be worth more to the charity if made during your lifetime under the Gift Aid scheme.
6 You can make significant inroads into a potential tax bill by making the most of tax-free gifts and the tax-free threshold (£255,000 in 2003–04). Share your wealth with your partner so that he or she can do so too.
7 Most lifetime gifts are tax-free if you survive at least seven years after making them – give early, if you can afford to do so.
8 Your share of jointly owned property forms part of your estate. You may want to own things as 'tenants in common' so that you can leave your share to someone apart from the other owner.
9 Beware of 'gifts with reservation' (where you retain the right to benefit from the property). They are still taxed as part of your estate.
10 There are no foolproof ways of passing on the family home for families of modest means. The simplest way is to release cash by taking out a mortgage or trading down, and then give away any surplus.
11 If you take out life insurance, ask the insurance company about writing the policy 'in trust' so that the proceeds do not form part of your estate.
12 Trusts can give flexibility in inheritance tax-planning and reduce the risks of an outright gift, but get professional advice.
13 Think about 'generation skipping' – leaving money to the next generation, rather than all to your husband or wife – to make better use of your £255,000 tax-free band.
14 Remember that your family can vary your will within two years after your death, with a deed of variation. This allows your money to be passed on in the way that best suits family circumstances at the time.

Fact file

Checklist of tax-free income

- Adoption allowances
- Betting winnings, including Premium Bonds and lottery winnings
- Compensation for mis-sold pension products
- Damages and compensation for personal injury
- Employment grants from some government schemes
- Foreign service allowance paid to servants of the Crown
- Some fringe benefits paid by employers (see Chapter 5)
- German and Austrian annuities and pensions for victims of Nazi persecution
- Housing grants
- From April 2003, most income as a foster carer
- Insurance payouts from a family income benefit life insurance policy, and from some permanent health, personal accident, sickness or income protection policies, and some long-term care policies (see Inland Revenue leaflet IR153 *Tax exemption for sickness or unemployment insurance payments*)
- Interest on damages for personal injuries or death
- Interest on a tax refund
- Interest on British Government Stock if you are not ordinarily resident in the UK (see Chapter 9)
- Interest, dividends and other income from savings and investments in special government schemes, i.e. ISAs (Individual Savings Accounts), TESSAs (Tax-Exempt Special Savings Accounts), PEPs (Personal Equity Plans), SAYE (Save As You Earn) schemes and Venture Capital Trusts (see Chapter 10)
- Interest from some National Savings & Investments schemes (see Chapter 10)
- Long-service awards
- Maintenance and alimony
- Overseas income if you are not resident in the UK (see Chapter 9)
- Some payments on leaving a job (see Chapter 5)
- Payouts from some life insurance policies (see Chapter 10)
- Some pensions and pension lump sums (see Chapter 7)
- Rental income under the Rent-a-Room scheme (see Chapter 8)
- Scholarship income and bursaries
- Some social security benefits (see Chapter 7)
- War gratuities and bounties, including the annual bounty to Territorial Army members.

Form finder

If you have received a tax form you are struggling with, use the table below to find more help.

Form reference	*Name/explanation*	*Where to find more information*
BR735	Notification of taxable amount of state benefits received	Chapter 7
575	*Transfer of married couple's allowance*	Chapter 4
CG34	Application for a post transaction valuation check	Chapter 11
DOM1	*Income and chargeable gains – domicile*	Chapter 9
EIS3, EIS5	You should receive one of these if you invest in an Enterprise Investment Scheme or fund	Chapters 4 and 10
Form 17	*Notice of declaration of beneficial interests in joint property and income*	Chapter 10
IHT200	*Inland Revenue Account for Inheritance Tax*	Chapter 12
P9D	*Expenses payments and income from which tax cannot be deducted*	Chapters 2, 3 and 5
P11D	*Expenses and Benefits*	Chapters 2, 3 and 5
P38S	*Student employees*	Chapter 2
P45	Details of employee leaving work	Chapters 2 and 5
P45U, P45(IB)	Provided by your Benefit Office when you stop claiming Jobseeker's Allowance or Incapacity Benefit	Chapter 7
P46	PAYE employer's notice to Inland Revenue office	Chapter 2
P50	*Claim for income tax repayments*	Chapters 2 and 7
P60	*End of year certificate*	Chapters 2, 3, 5 and 7
P60U, P60(IB)	Statements of taxable amount of Jobseeker's Allowance or Incapacity Benefit paid in a tax year	Chapter 7
P85	*Income Tax claim when you have left or are about to leave the UK*	Chapter 9
P86	*Arrival in the United Kingdom*	Chapter 9
P87	*Expenses Claim form*	Chapter 5
P91	Form asking for details of your previous jobs so that your PAYE code can be sorted out	Chapter 2
P161	*Pension enquiry*	Chapters 2 and 7
PP43	*Election to carry back contributions*	Chapter 7
P810	If you do not get a tax return, your tax office may issue this form to check your deductions	Chapter 2
PP120	Used if you want to claim higher-rate tax relief on pension payments and do not get a tax return	Chapter 7
R40	*Claim for repayment*	Chapters 2 and 3

R85	*Savings: application to receive interest without tax taken off*	Chapters 2 and 10
R86 or R89	*Application for an annuity to be paid without tax deducted*	Chapters 7 and 10
R105	*Application for a not ordinarily resident saver to receive interest without tax taken off*	Chapter 9
R185	*Certificate of deduction of income tax*	Chapter 10
SA302	Notice from the Inland Revenue showing how they have worked out your tax	Chapter 3
SA303	*Claim to reduce payments on account*	Chapter 3
SA316	*Notice to complete a tax return*	Chapter 3
TC600	*Tax credits claim form*	Chapter 7

Tax Return questions

If you are trying to complete a tax return, you can use this list to find further information that might help you with a particular question.

Question 1	Employment	Chapter 5
Question 2	Share schemes	Chapter 5
Question 3	Self-employment	Chapter 6
Question 4	Partnership	Chapter 6
Question 5	Land and property	Chapter 8
Question 6	Foreign income	Chapter 9
Question 7	Trusts and estates	Chapter 10
Question 8	Capital gains	Chapter 11
Question 9	Non-residence etc.	Chapter 9
Question 10	UK savings and investments	Chapter 10
Question 11	UK pension or Social Security benefit	Chapter 7
Question 12	UK life insurance policies, refunds of additional voluntary contributions	Chapter 10
Question 13	Other taxable income	Chapter 6
Question 14	Tax relief on pension contributions	Chapters 4 and 7
Question 15	Other reliefs	Chapters 4 and 7
Question 15A	Relief on gifts to charity	Chapter 4
Question 16	Blind person's allowance, married couple's allowance, Children's Tax Credit	Chapters 4 and 7
Question 17	Student Loan Repayments	Chapter 3
Question 18	Calculating your tax	Chapter 3

Summary of tax allowances and rates

Income tax	*2002–03*	*2003–04*
Personal allowance		
Aged under 65 throughout tax year	£ 4,615	£4,615
Maximum allowance if aged 65 or over in tax year	£ 6,100	£6,610
Maximum allowance if aged 75 or over in tax year	£ 6,370	£6,720
Age allowance income limit	£ 17,900	£18,300
Minimum where income exceeds limit	£ 4,615	£4,615
Married couple's allowance (10% relief)		
Either spouse born before 6 April 1935	£ 5,465	£5,565
Either spouse aged 75 or over in tax year	£ 5,535	£5,635
Age allowance income limit	£ 17,900	£18,300
Minimum where income exceeds limit	£ 2,110	£2,150
Blind person's allowance	£ 1,480	£1,510
Children's Tax Credit (10% relief, income related)		
Basic amount	£ 5,290	Replaced by child tax credit of £545
Amount in year of birth	£ 10,490	£1,090
Income tax rates		
Starting rate	10%	10%
On taxable income up to	£ 1,920	£1,960
Basic rate	22%	22%
On taxable income from starting rate limit up to	£ 29,900	£30,500
Higher rate	40%	40%
On taxable income over	£ 29,900	£30,500
Lower rate on savings income and capital gains	20%	20%
Lower dividend rate	10%	10%
Higher dividend rate	32.5%	32.5%

Capital gains tax	*2002–03*	*2003–04*
Rate (depending on your taxable income; may be reduced by taper relief)	10%, 20% or 40%	10%, 20% or 40%
Annual tax-free amount	£ 7,700	£7,900

Inheritance tax	*2002–03*	*2003–04*
Threshold for tax-free gifts	£ 250,000	£255,000
Rate for gifts on death	40%	40%

National Insurance contributions	*2002–03*	*2003–04*
Class 1 contributions		
For employees	10% (8.4%*) on earnings between £89 and £585 p.w.	11% (9.4%*) on earnings between £89 and £595 p.w. 1% on earnings above £595 p.w
Rate for married women who opted for reduced rate before 6 April 1977	3.85%	4.85%
For employers	11.8%* on earnings above £89 p.w.	12.8%*on earnings above £89 p.w.
Class 2 contributions for self-employed	£2 p.w. on earnings above £4,025 p.a.	£2 p.w. on earnings above £4,095 p.a.
Class 3 voluntary contributions to improve benefits	£6.85 p.w.	£6.95 p.w.
Class 4 contributions for self-employed	7% on profits between £4,615 and £30,420	8% on profits between £4,615 and £30,940, 1% on earnings above £30,940

* Lower rate if employer has contracted-out of the State Earnings Related Pension (SERPS)

'Gross' and 'net' figures

When filling in your tax return, you often need to know the gross (before tax) figure of income you receive net (after tax). This is called 'grossing-up'.

For example, the statements from your savings account may show only the net amount of interest received, but the tax return asks for the gross amount and the tax deducted as well. The same applies if you contribute to a personal pension – the amount you hand over is the net amount but the tax return asks for the gross figures.

Ready reckoner for gross and net figures

Rate of tax	*If you know the:*	*Do this:*		*To find the:*
10%	Amount of a share dividend received (i.e. the net amount)	Divide the dividend by 0.9	=	Gross amount before tax
		Divide the dividend by 9	=	Tax credit
20%	After-tax (net) amount of savings interest	Divide the net interest by 0.8	=	Gross amount before tax
		Divide the net interest by 4	=	Amount of tax deducted
22%	After-tax (net) amount of pension contribution or Gift Aid donation	Divide the net payment by 0.78	=	Gross amount before tax
		Multiply the net payment by 22/78 (in practice it is easier to find the gross amount and deduct the net)	=	Amount of basic rate tax relief

If tax rates change, this is how you can work it out for yourself:

- Find the relevant rate of tax – 30%, say.
- To find the amount of tax on income at that rate, multiply the income by that percentage – so income of £200 taxed at 30%, say, is £200 × 0.30 = £60. This leaves you with net income of £200 × (1 – 0.30) = £200 × 0.7 = £140.
- If you already know the after-tax amount but want to find the before-tax amount, you simply do the same in reverse. So the gross

equivalent of £140, before tax at 30%, is £140 ÷ 0.7 = £200.

- The foolproof way to find the amount of tax, if you know the after-tax amount, is to work out the gross equivalent and deduct the after-tax amount: £200 − £140 = £60. For some rates of tax, you can do it by simple division of the after-tax amount – see table on page 290.

Capital gains tax indexation factors

Indexation compensates you for any increase in the value of an asset which occurs purely because of inflation. Indexation was frozen from April 1998 and does not apply to periods before March 1982 because only gains made since then are taxable.

You can find the indexed cost of an asset you disposed of after April 1998 by multiplying the cost of the asset by the relevant indexation factor for the month you acquired it. Indexation factors are shown in the table on page 292. If, for example, you bought your holiday home in June 1990 for £100,000, the relevant indexation factor is 1.283 and the indexed cost is:

$$£100{,}000 \times 1.283 = £128{,}300$$

But watch out for two things:

Warning 1: You can use the table on page 292 *only* if you are working out indexation for periods up to April 1998. If you need to work it out for earlier periods (if, say, you are working out your gain on a parcel of shares and you disposed of part of it before April 1998) you need another set of factors. Ask your tax office for a table of factors for the month of the part disposal.

Warning 2: These factors give you the *indexed cost*, i.e. the cost of the asset plus the indexation allowance. The Revenue's tables give you just the indexation allowance, to be added to the cost – so, in the example above, the Revenue's tables would show a factor of 0.283, giving an indexation allowance of £28,300, which you would then need to add to the cost. Both methods give the same result, but our method saves you a step.

Indexation factors – assets disposed of after 31 March 1998

Year	*Jan*	*Feb*	*March*	*April*	*May*	*June*	*July*	*Aug*	*Sept*	*Oct*	*Nov*	*Dec*
1982	–	–	2.047	2.006	1.992	1.987	1.986	1.985	1.987	1.977	1.967	1.971
1983	1.968	1.960	1.956	1.929	1.921	1.917	1.906	1.898	1.889	1.883	1.876	1.871
1984	1.872	1.865	1.859	1.834	1.828	1.823	1.825	1.808	1.804	1.793	1.788	1.789
1985	1.783	1.769	1.752	1.716	1.708	1.704	1.707	1.703	1.704	1.701	1.695	1.693
1986	1.689	1.683	1.681	1.665	1.662	1.663	1.667	1.662	1.654	1.652	1.638	1.632
1987	1.626	1.620	1.616	1.597	1.596	1.596	1.597	1.593	1.588	1.580	1.573	1.574
1988	1.574	1.568	1.562	1.537	1.531	1.525	1.524	1.507	1.500	1.485	1.478	1.474
1989	1.465	1.454	1.448	1.423	1.414	1.409	1.408	1.404	1.395	1.384	1.372	1.369
1990	1.361	1.353	1.339	1.300	1.288	1.283	1.282	1.269	1.258	1.248	1.251	1.252
1991	1.249	1.242	1.237	1.222	1.218	1.213	1.215	1.213	1.208	1.204	1.199	1.198
1992	1.199	1.193	1.189	1.171	1.167	1.167	1.171	1.171	1.166	1.162	1.164	1.168
1993	1.179	1.171	1.167	1.156	1.152	1.153	1.156	1.151	1.146	1.147	1.148	1.146
1994	1.151	1.144	1.141	1.128	1.124	1.124	1.129	1.124	1.121	1.120	1.119	1.114
1995	1.114	1.107	1.102	1.091	1.087	1.085	1.091	1.085	1.080	1.085	1.085	1.079
1996	1.083	1.078	1.073	1.066	1.063	1.063	1.067	1.062	1.057	1.057	1.057	1.053
1997	1.053	1.049	1.046	1.040	1.036	1.032	1.032	1.026	1.021	1.019	1.019	1.016
1998	1.019	1.014	1.011									

Useful leaflets

These are available from tax offices (look in the phone book under 'Inland Revenue'), from the self-assessment orderline (Tel: 0845 9000 404) or on-line at www.inlandrevenue.gov.uk/leaflets or www.inlandrevenue.gov.uk/sa/forms/content.htm.

General

A01 *How to complain about the Inland Revenue and the Valuation Office Agency*
CA01 *National Insurance contributions for employees*
CA08 *Voluntary National Insurance contributions*
CA13 *National Insurance contributions for women with reduced elections*
CA25 *Agencies and people working through agencies*

CA72 *National Insurance contributions: deferring payment*
Code of Practice (COP) 1 *Putting things right when we make mistakes*
COP10 *Information and Advice*
COP11 *Self assessment. Local office enquiries*
COP20 *National Minimum Wage – information for workers*
IR33 *Income tax and school leavers*
IR37 *Appeals*
IR41 *Income tax and job seekers*
IR60 *Students and the Inland Revenue*
IR120 *You and the Inland Revenue National Insurance Contributions Office*
IR235 *Calculation of Student Loan Repayments on an Income Contingent Student Loan*

Self-assessment

SA/BK4 *Self-Assessment. A general guide to keeping records*
SA/BK6 *Self Assessment. Penalties for late tax returns*
SA/BK7 *Self Assessment. Surcharges for late payment of tax*
SA/BK8 *Self Assessment. Your guide*

Allowances and reliefs

IR65 *Giving to charity by individuals*
IR121 *Income tax and pensioners*
IR170 *Blind person's allowance*
IR178 *Giving shares and securities to charity*
IR340 *Interest eligible for relief on qualifying loans*
IR341 *Enterprise Investment Scheme – income tax relief*
IR342 *Charitable giving*
IR343 *Claiming Children's Tax Credit when your circumstances change*

Employment

490 *Employee travel, a tax and NICs guide for employers*
IR16 *Share acquisitions by directors and employees*
IR95 *Approved profit-sharing schemes*
IR97 *Approved Save As You Earn share option schemes*
IR101 *Approved company share option plans*
IR124 *Using your own vehicle for work*

IR134 *Income Tax and relocation packages*
IR136 *Income Tax and company vans*
IR145 *Low interest loans provided by employers*
IR172 *Income tax and company cars*
IR175 *Supplying services through a limited company or partnership*
IR201 *Vouchers, credit cards and tokens*
IR202 *Living accommodation*
IR203 *Car benefits and car fuel benefits*
IR204 *Lump sums and compensation payments*
IR205 *Foreign earnings deductions: seafarers*
IR206 *Capital allowances for employees and office holders*
IR207 *Non-taxable payments or benefits for employees*
IR208 *Payslips and coding notices*
IR210 *Assets provided for private use*
IR211 *Employment – residence and domicile issues*
IR213 *Payments in kind – assets transferred*
IR216 *Shares as benefits*
IR217 *Shares acquired: post acquisition charges*
IR218 *Shares acquired: operation of PAYE*
IR219 *Shares acquired: from your employment*
IR287 *Employee share schemes and capital gains tax*
IR2002 *Share incentive plans*
IR2003 *Supplying services. How to calculate the deemed payment*
IR2006 *Enterprise Management Incentives. A guide*

Self-employment

CA02 *National Insurance contributions for self-employed people with small earnings*
CA11 *National Insurance for share fishermen*
CWL2 *National Insurance contributions for self-employed people*
HMCE (MISC5) *Help for your business in the construction industry*
IR14/15 *Construction industry tax deduction scheme*
IR56 *Employed or self-employed?*
IR220 *More than one business*
IR222 *How to calculate your taxable profits*
IR223 *Rent a Room for traders*
IR224 *Farmers and market gardeners*
IR227 *Losses*
IR229 *Information from your accounts*
IR231 *Doctors' expenses*
IR232 *Farm stock valuation*

IR233 *The 'true and fair view' for professions*
IR234 *Averaging for creators of literary or artistic works*
P/SE/1 *Thinking of working for yourself?*
SA/BK3 *Self Assessment. A guide to keeping records for the self-employed*
URN 03/609 *The no-nonsense guide to government rules and regulations for setting up your business* (from DTI Publications Orderline, 0870 150 2500)

Pensions and benefits

IR41 *Income tax and job seekers*
IR78 *Looking to the future. Tax reliefs to help you save for retirement*
IR121 *Income tax and pensioners*
IR144 *Income tax and Incapacity Benefit*
IR310 *War Widow's and dependant's pensions*
IR330 *Pension payments*
WTC1 *Child Tax Credit and Working Tax Credit. An introduction*

Land and property

IR87 *Letting and your home*
IR140 *Non-resident landlords, their agents and tenants*
IR150 *Taxation of rents. A guide to property income*
IR223 *Rent a Room for traders*
IR250 *Capital allowances and balancing charges in a rental business*
IR2007 *Capital allowances for flats over shops*

Income from abroad

IR20 *Residents and non-residents*
IR140 *Non-resident landlords, their agents and tenants*
IR261 *Foreign tax credit relief: capital gains*
IR278 *Temporary non-residents and capital gains tax*
IR300 *Non-residents and investment income*
IR301 *Capital gains on benefits from non-resident and dual resident trusts*
IR302 *Dual residents*
IR303 *Non-resident entertainers and sports persons*
IR304 *Non-residents – relief under Double Taxation Agreements*

IR321 *Gains on foreign life insurance policies*
NI38 *Social Security Abroad*
DWP leaflet SA29 *Your social security insurance, benefits and health care rights in the European Community* (see address on page 298)

Savings and investments

IR68 *Accrued income scheme. Taxing securities on transfer*
IR110 *Bank and building society interest. A guide for savers*
IR137 *The Enterprise Investment Scheme*
IR169 *Venture Capital Trusts (VCTs). A brief guide*
IR320 *Gains on UK life insurance policies*
IR2008 *ISAs, PEPs and TESSAs*

Capital gains tax

IR279 *Taper relief*
IR280 *Rebasing – assets held at 31 March 1982*
IR281 *Husband and wife, divorce and separation*
IR282 *Death, personal representatives and legatees*
IR283 *Private residence relief*
IR284 *Shares and capital gains tax*
IR285 *Share reorganisations, company take-overs and capital gains tax*
IR286 *Negligible value claims and income tax losses for shares you have subscribed for in unlisted trading companies*
IR287 *Employee share schemes and capital gains tax*
IR288 *Partnerships and capital gains tax*
IR289 *Retirement relief and capital gains tax*
IR290 *Business asset roll-over relief*
IR292 *Land and leases, the valuation of land and capital gains tax*
IR293 *Chattels and capital gains tax*
IR294 *Trusts and capital gains tax*
IR295 *Relief for gifts and similar transactions*
IR296 *Debts and capital gains tax*
IR297 *Enterprise Investment Scheme and capital gains tax*
IR298 *Venture Capital Trusts and capital gains tax*
IR301 *Capital gains on benefits from non-resident and dual resident trusts*

Inheritance tax

IHT3 *Inheritance tax: an introduction*
IHT8 *Alterations to an inheritance following a death*
IHT11 *Payment of inheritance tax from National Savings or British Government Stock*
IHT14 *Inheritance tax. The personal representatives' responsibilities*
IHT15 *Inheritance tax. How to calculate the liability*
IHT16 *Inheritance tax. Settled property*
IHT17 *Inheritance tax. Businesses, farms and woodlands*
IHT18 *Inheritance tax. Foreign aspects*

Useful addresses

Adjudicator's Office
Haymarket House, 28 Haymarket
London SW1Y 4SP
Tel: 020 7930 2292
Fax: 020 7930 2298
www.adjudicatorsoffice.gov.uk

Age Concern England
Astral House
1268 London Road
London SW16 4ER
Information Line: 0800 009966
(24 hours)
www.ace.org.uk

Age Concern Scotland
113 Rose Street
Edinburgh EH2 3DT
Tel: 0131 220 3345

Age Concern Northern Ireland
3 Lower Crescent
Belfast BT7 1NR
Tel: 028 9024 5729

Age Concern Cymru (Wales)
4th Floor, 1 Cathedral Road
Cardiff CF11 9SD
Tel: 029 2037 1566

Association of Chartered Certified Accountants
29 Lincoln's Inn Fields
London WC2A 3EE
Tel: 020 7396 7000
Fax: 020 7396 5750
www.acca.org.uk

The Association of Taxation Technicians
12 Upper Belgrave Street
London SW1X 8BB
Tel: 020 7235 2544
Fax: 020 7235 4571
www.att.org.uk

Bank Of England Registrar's Department
Southgate House
Southgate Street
Gloucester GL1 1UW
Tel: 01452 398080
Fax: 01452 398098
www.bankofengland.co.uk

The Chartered Institute of Taxation
12 Upper Belgrave Street
London SW1X 8BB
Tel: 020 7235 9381
Fax: 020 7235 2562
www.tax.org.uk

Department for Work and Pensions
Correspondence Unit
Room 540, The Adelphi
1–11 John Adam Street
London WC2N 6HT
Tel: 020 7712 2171
(9.00am–5.00pm Monday–Friday)
Fax: 020 7712 2386
www.dwp.gov.uk

Financial Services Authority
25 The North Colonnade
Canary Wharf
London E14 5HS
Tel: 0845 606 1234
Fax: 020 7676 1099
fsa.gov.uk/consumer

Inland Revenue
If you are not sure which tax office deals with your affairs, contact your nearest Enquiry Centre (in the phone book, under 'Inland Revenue'). See page 299 for useful phone numbers.

HM Customs and Excise
National Advice Service
Tel: 0845 010 9000
www.hmce.gov.uk

The Institute of Chartered Accountants in England & Wales
Chartered Accountants' Hall
PO Box 433
London EC2P 2BJ
Tel: 020 7920 8100
Fax: 020 7920 8547
www.icaew.co.uk

Institute of Chartered Accountants of Scotland
CA House,
21 Haymarket Yards
Edinburgh EH12 5BH
Tel: 0131 347 0100
Fax: 0131 347 0105
www.icas.org.uk

The Parliamentary Commissioner for Administration
Millbank Tower
Millbank
London SW1P 4QP
Tel: 0845 015 4033
Fax: 020 7217 4160
www.ombudsman.org.uk

The Society of Motor Manufacturers and Traders
Forbes House
Halkin Street
London SW1X 7DS
Tel: 020 7235 7000
Fax: 020 7235 7112
www.smmt.co.uk

TaxAid
Room 304, Linton House
164–180 Union Street
London SE1 0LH
Tel: 020 7803 4959
(10.00am–12.00 midday, Monday–Thursday)
www.taxaid.org.uk

Inland Revenue helplines and websites

The Inland Revenue's website is at www.inlandrevenue.gov.uk. The website for the enhanced capital allowances scheme (listing Revenue-approved energy-saving equipment) is at www.eca.gov.uk. If you need to convert from a foreign currency into sterling, you can use the average exchange rates at www.inlandrevenue.gov.uk/exrate.

You can find a full index of helplines on the Revenue's website at: www.inlandrevenue.gov.uk/menus/helpline.htm. Below is a selection.

General enquiries	020 7667 4001
Centre for Non-Residents helplines	
Non-resident individuals	0151 472 6196
Non-resident landlords	0151 472 6208/6209
Residence status (individuals)	0151 472 6137
Charity helplines	
IR Charities (Bootle)	0151 472 6036/7

IR Charities (Scotland)	0131 777 4040
Gift Aid	0151 472 6038
Construction Industry Scheme (CIS)	
Contractors	0845 733 5588
Sub-contractors	0845 300 0581
Employers' helplines (guidance on PAYE, National Insurance and basic VAT registration)	
New employers	0845 607 0143
Established employers	0845 714 3143
Foot and Mouth helpline (for farmers and others affected by foot and mouth disease)	0845 300 0157
Individual Savings Accounts helpline (general queries about the tax rules for ISAs)	0845 604 1701
Inheritance Tax and Probate	0845 302 0900
IR35 (if you are supplying services through a limited company or partnership)	0845 303 3535
National Insurance	
Registrations	0845 915 7006/5670
Self Employed helpline	0845 915 4655
Other queries	0191 213 5000
National Minimum Wage	
Great Britain	0845 600 0678
Northern Ireland	0845 650 0207
Newly self-employed	0845 915 4515
Self-assessment	
General helpline	0845 900 0444
Orderline for form/leaflet requests	0845 900 0404
Internet services	0845 605 5999
Minicom	0845 900 0404
Stamp duty	0845 603 0135
Tax and benefits confidential (offers people operating in the hidden economy confidential help and information to help them put their affairs in order)	0845 608 6000
Taxback if you think you might be able to claim tax back	0845 077 6543
Tax credits (Child Tax Credit, Working Tax Credit)	
Great Britain	0845 300 3900
Northern Ireland	0845 603 2000
Welsh speakers contact centre	0845 302 1489

Index

Numbers in bold indicate Tables; those in italics indicate Figures.

Q

R

S